Leonardo da Vinci as a Musician

Leonardo da Vinci
as a
Musician

Emanuel Winternitz

YALE UNIVERSITY PRESS
NEW HAVEN AND LONDON

Published with assistance from the foundation established in memory of Philip Hamilton McMillan of the Class of 1894, Yale College.

"The Viola Organista" (chap. 8), "Melodic and Chordal Drums; Other Membranophones; Tunable Bells" (chap. 9), and "Wind Instruments: The Glissando Flute, Key Mechanisms for Wind Instruments, New Bellows" (chap. 11) are adapted, respectively, from "Leonardo's Invention of the Viola Organista," "Melodic, Chordal, and Other Drums Invented by Leonardo da Vinci," and "Leonardo's Invention of Key Mechanisms for Wind Instruments," which were published as number 20 of *Estratto da Raccolta Vinciana* (Milan, 1964). "The Role of Music in Leonardo's *Paragone*" (chap. 12) is adapted from an article of the same title published as a contribution to a Festschrift for Alfred Schutz in *Phenomenology and Social Reality*, edited by Maurice Natanson (The Hague: Martinus Nijhoff, 1971).

Designed by James J. Johnson and set in Palatino Roman by the Composing Room of Michigan. Printed in the United States of America by The Murray Printing Co., Westford, Mass.

Library of Congress Cataloging in Publication Data

Winternitz, Emanuel.
    Leonardo da Vinci as a musician.

    Includes index.
    1. Leonardo, da Vinci, 1452–1519. 2. Music—Italy—History and criticism—Medieval, 400–1500.
    3. Musical instruments. I. Title.
ML429.L46W5   780'.92'4   81–16475
ISBN 0–300–02631–5   AACR2

10 9 8 7 6 5 4 3 2 1

IN GRATITUDE TO MISS MARY McCLANE

Her sense of style and her gift for organizing ideas,
her unfailing memory, her learned love of early music,
and her strict pruning of my effusive Viennese English
contributed no end to the completion of this book.

Die ungeheuren Umrisse von Leonardos Wesen wird man ewig nur von ferne ahnen können.

The colossal contours of Leonardo's being will always be divined only from afar.

—Jakob Burckhardt, *Die Kultur der*
Renaissance in Italien

Contents

List of Illustrations

Preface

In the translations of Leonardo da Vinci's language, smoothness would often not be appropriate, particularly if it damages or diminishes or blurs the originality of his message or the novelty of his observations. Here I have aimed at the maximum clarity of his own language, even at the cost of style. Therefore I do not necessarily feel bound to the translations by Richter and MacCurdy.* In some cases Leonardo's original Italian is reprinted to enable the reader to evaluate the English translation.

In his notebooks Leonardo several times mentions books and scripts of his, including some on music, which have not come down to us; it is probable that he only planned to write them or did not finish them. On the other hand, the recent discovery of seven hundred pages of his writings, known as the Madrid Codices, warns us against premature assumptions that they are lost forever. At any rate, in the present volume devoted to Leonardo and music it seems appropriate to list treatises on musical subjects written or planned by him but not known to exist.†

Windsor AN. B 19037 (B 20 v), Brizio p. 153, Esche p. 117, Richter paragraph 797, O'Malley 71, contain Leonardo's plans for a comprehensive book on anatomy, listing an elaborate program ranging from the conception and birth of human beings to detailed descriptions of bones, muscles, vessels, and nerves. He called upon himself to explore "perspective through the function of sight, and ... *hearing*. You will speak of *music* and treat of other senses. Then describe the nature of the five senses." This was probably written in 1489.

Quaderni d'Anatomia IV 10 r: Confusion has arisen about whether Leonardo wrote a book on musical instruments or whether he just quoted from such a book by another author. The divergence stems from Quaderni d'Anatomia IV 10 r, where Leonardo interrupts his discussion about the noise produced by cannons and the influence of their length upon pitch by referring to the fact that this matter has been

---

*Jean-Paul Richter, *The Literary Works of Leonardo da Vinci* (London: Oxford University Press, 1939) and Edward MacCurdy, *The Notebooks of Leonardo da Vinci* (London: Jonathan Cape, 1938).

†The most comprehensive recent discussion of the problem of lost and planned but not written treatises of Leonardo is found in Augusto Marinoni's contribution to *The Unknown Leonardo* (New York: McGraw-Hill, 1974): "The Writer, Leonardo's Literary Legacy."

fully treated in the book on musical instruments. The paragraph with this passage is rather pale in Leonardo's original script, yet it clearly says:

E in questo più non mi stenterò perchè nel libro delli strumenti armonici ne ho trattato assai copiosamente.

I shall not go into this at greater length because I have fully treated it in the book on musical instruments.

It is not clear from the translation by MacCurdy whether Leonardo refers to a book by another author or one written by himself. Richter (p. 70) says *ne ho trattato* ("I have treated"); Brizio (*Scritti Scelti,* [Turin, 1952], p. 502) reads *n'è trattato* ("has been treated"), which does not correspond to the original text. Therefore, it is probable that here, as in many other cases, Leonardo refers to a book already planned in his mind but not written for lack of time.

ACKNOWLEDGMENTS

For generous support of my research, I am grateful to the American Philosophical Society, the American Council of Learned Societies, and the Heinemann Foundation.

My sincere thanks go to the late Professor Ladislao Reti, who, after his rediscovery of the two Leonardo Codices in the Biblioteca Nacional in Madrid, kindly helped me to obtain the rich organological material therein that was relevant to my book; to Professors Augusto Marinoni and Carlo Pedretti for valuable information and exchanges of opinion leading to correct interpretations of sketches for new and fantastic musical instruments; also to Professor Marinoni for his kind permission to reproduce some of his interpretations of Leonardo's picture rebuses.

As so often before, I owe special thanks to my colleague at the Metropolitan Museum of Art, Dr. Olga Raggio, who, in innumerable discussions, helped me to clarify tricky problems in Leonardo's peculiar Latin and capricious Italian.

May I thank the Biblioteca Comunale of Lodi and its staff for kind help in my research on the relations between Franchino Gaffurius and Leonardo, and the late Monsignore Angelo Ciceri of the Venerabile Fabbrica del Duomo di Milano for enthusiastic support of my examination of works by Gaspar van Weerbecke and other composers contemporary with Leonardo. With Bo Lawergren, professor of physics at Hunter College, I had many interesting and helpful conversations about Leonardo's inventions of musical instruments, and on the chapter on acoustical experiments. He also helped considerably in shaping the index.

May I express my gratitude to the Metropolitan Museum of Art, my working place for no less than forty-two years, and for the use of its magnificent library and, for illustrations, its photographic collection and slide library; to Miss Janet Byrne, of the Museum's Print Department, for her kind help with illustrations; and also to the Gabinetto Fotografico, Florence, for photographs.

Many thanks are due to the Yale University Press, above all to Edward Tripp for his constructive optimism and helpful conversations about the form of the script, and to Maura Tantillo for her speedy and exact editing of a difficult text.

LEONARDO'S MANUSCRIPTS
REFERRED TO IN THIS BOOK

Abbreviation	*Description and/or location*
MSS A through M	Institut de France, Paris
Arundel 263 (BM)	British Museum
CA	Codice Atlantico, Ambrosiana, Milan
Forster I, II, III	Forster Codices, Victoria and Albert Museum, London
Madrid MS I, II	Biblioteca Nacional, Madrid
Metropolitan Museum	Drawing at Metropolitan Museum of Art, New York
Quaderni d'Anatomia I–VI	6 volumes of anatomical drawings in Royal Library, Windsor (sometimes referred to as Anatomical MS. C)
TP	Trattato della Pittura, Codex Urbinas, Vatican Library
Triv.	Codex Trivulzio, Castello Sforzesco, Milan
Windsor	Folios in Royal Library, Windsor
Windsor AN. A, B	2 manuscripts of anatomical drawings in Royal Library, Windsor (Fogli dell' Anatomia A and B)
MS 2037 Bib. Nat.	Institut de France
MS 2038 Bib. Nat.	Institut de France

Introduction

"Musica, la Figurazione delle cose Invisibili"
—LEONARDO, *Paragone*

Was Leonardo also a musician? If he was, how can we explain that this important facet of his genius has been neglected? In fact the towering and ever-growing mountain of Leonardo literature does not contain a systematic analysis of Leonardo's musical interests but only some occasional, superficial attempts by art historians not versed in musical history and the environment of Leonardo. Yet Leonardo's manuscripts contain a large body of musical thoughts, ideas, experiments, and inventions, a cosmos indeed, for these are not isolated but interrelated and integrated in many ways.

There are also a great number of testimonials from Leonardo's contemporaries and from the following generation extolling him as a supreme musician. Could all this be legend?

One major obstacle in the rediscovery of Leonardo as a musician is the fact that no written composition of his has come down to us and, in all probability, never existed. He was an improviser, and it was not customary for improvisers of Leonardo's time to confide their music to paper. Thus it is not surprising that modern musical historians have little interest in the rich and subtle culture of improvisation of the late quattrocento and early cinquecento. Still, had they patiently gone through the thousands of pages in Leonardo's notebooks, they might have been astonished by the wealth of musical material, sketches, inventions, and suggestions.

As for the art historians, why should they spend much time on Leonardo's musical interests if they were not of sufficient importance to the historians of music?

Leonardo was, in fact, profoundly occupied with music. He was a performer and teacher of music; he was deeply interested in acoustics and made many experiments in this field that had immediate bearing on music; he wrestled with the concept of musical time, and he invented a considerable number of ingenious musical instruments and made improvements on existing ones. He also had some highly original ideas about the philosophy of music that were intimately connected with his philosophy of painting. It is characteristic that in his *Paragone*, which forms an introduction to his *Treatise on Painting*, he accorded music the highest place among the arts after painting. If we knew nothing of his classification of music other than his remark calling it "figurazione delle cose invisibili" (the shaping of the invisible), we would have a clear indication of the depth and originality of his musical thought.

Leonardo's involvement with music was not one facet, one particle among many others, of his creative power but an essential, indispensable, integral, organic part of the whole structure of his scientific-artistic energy, interrelated with the many other aspects that the universe had for him. Music—as an activity as well as the subject of meditation—is an element of his *forma mentis* or, as he might have said, *figurazione della mente.* The interpenetration of this element, music, with many of his other activities and studies is the theme of this book.

May I illustrate this by a few examples?

Ingredients of music, that is, acoustical phenomena (such as echo) are explored, often in analogy to the behavior of light, as contributions to theoretical physics.

Proportion theory is enriched by the concept of a perspective of sound in analogy to proportion in the visual realm.

Anatomy, the study of the living organism as a machine, provides him with an opportunity for creating new or better musical instruments, for instance, in the image of the larynx and its cartilage rings; or by the imitation of hand and finger tendons for the construction of keys for wind and other instruments.

In the colorful masks, processions, and stage plays in which Leonardo participated as organizer, designer, and stage engineer, he must have enthusiastically welcomed the opportunity to adapt himself to the music that permeated the visual phantasmagories and even did construct fantastic instruments for the occasion.

Finally, esthetics: in his *Paragone* Leonardo found another opportunity to relate music to the other spatial and temporal arts. The *Paragone* was the customary more or less learned discussion of the comparative rank of painting, sculpture, poetry, and music held in summer gardens by circles of courtiers with philosophical pretensions.

Renaissance painting, despite the development of linear perspective on exact mathematical foundations, was not yet considered one of the liberal arts. Why not elevate it to the rank of music, which since antiquity, by virtue of its mathematical basis, was one of the sisters of the quadrivium, together with arithmetic, geometry, and astronomy?

Leonardo's musical talent was attested to by contemporaries or near contemporaries: Luca Pacioli, the Anonimo Gaddiano, Paolo Giovio, Benvenuto Cellini, and, soon after, Vasari and Lomazzo.

The great mathematician Luca Pacioli, whose relation with Leonardo is described in chapter 2, calls Leonardo "degnissimo pictore, prospectivo, architecto, musico."

The *Codice del Anonimo Gaddiano* (Cod. Magliabecchiano 17), a book owned by Antonio Billi, written between 1506 and 1532 (published by Carl V. Fabriczy in Arch Stor. Ital. in 1893) says:

Fu eloquente nel parlare, et raro sonatore di lira et fu maestro di quella d'Atalante Migliorotti.

Leonardo was an eloquent speaker and an outstanding player of the lira [da braccio] and also the teacher in lira playing of Atalante Migliorotti.

Dal detto Magnifico Lorenzo fu mandato al duca di Milano a presentarli insieme con Atalante Migliorotti una lira, che unico era in sonare tale extrumento.

From Lorenzo the Magnificent [Medici], he was sent to the Duke of Milan [Lodovico il Moro, of the Sforza family] to present to him, together with Atalante Migliorotti, a *lira*, since he was unique in playing this instrument.

Paolo Giovio (1483–1552), who wrote Leonardo's vita twenty years after the master's death, says:

Fuit ingenio valde, comi nitido, liberali, vultu autem longe venustissimo; et cum elegantiae omnis delitiarumque maxime theatralium mirificus inventor ac arbiter esset, ad liramque scyte caneret, cunctis per omnem aetatem principibus mire placuit.

He had an extraordinary power of mind [he was of extraordinary genius]; he was gracious [friendly], precise, and generous, with a radiant, graceful appearance [expression]; and since he was a magic inventor and connoisseur of all subtleties and delights for the stage, and played the *lira* [lira da braccio] with the bow [scythe] he miraculously pleased all the princes through his whole life.

Benvenuto Cellini, who owned a manuscript copy of Leonardo's *Treatise on Painting*, refers in his autobiography, begun in Florence in 1558, to Leonardo as "painter, sculptor, architect, philosopher, musician; a veritable angel incarnate."

Giorgio Vasari in his *Vite* refers twice to Leonardo's musical activities. The *Vite* appeared in two editions, the first in 1550, the second, revised and enlarged, in 1568. I quote from the second edition (Vasari, ed. Milanesi [Sansoni, 1906], vol. 4, p. 18):

Dette alquanto d'opera alla musica; ma tosto si risolvè a imparare a suonare la lira, come quello che dalla natura aveva spirito elevatissimo e pieno di leggiadria, onde sopra quella cantò divinamente all improvviso.

[He] devoted much effort to music; above all, he determined to learn playing the lira, since by nature he possessed a lofty and graceful spirit; he sang divinely, improvising his own accompaniment on the lira.

Vasari (vol. 4, p. 28) also relates:

Avvenne che morto Giovan Galeazzo duca di Milano, e creato Lodovico Sforza nel grado medesimo l'anno 1494, fu condotto a Milano con gran riputazione Lionardo al duca, il quale molto si dilettava del suono della lira,[1] perche sonasse; e Lionardo porto quello strumento ch'egli aveva di suo mano fabbricato d'argento gran parte in forma d'un teschio di cavallo, cosa bizzarra e nuova, acciocche l'armonia fosse con maggior tuba e piu sonora di voce; laonde superò tutti i musici che quivi erano concorsi a sonare. Oltra cio, fu il migliore dicitore di rime all 'improvviso del tempo suo.

1. Ludwig Goldscheider, in *Leonardo da Vinci* (Vienna: Phaidon, 1954), p. 9, uses an English translation of Vasari which reads, "to play the lute [*sic!*], in which the prince greatly delighted" (a frequent mistake in translations because the translators did not know what to do with *lira*).

It came about that the Duke of Milan, Giovan Galeazzo, died and that Lodovico Sforza was established as his successor in the year 1494. At that time Leonardo, with great fanfare, was brought to the duke to play for him, since the duke had a great liking for the sound of the lira; and Leonardo brought there the instrument which he had built with his own hands, made largely of silver, in the shape of a horse skull—a bizarre, new thing—so that the sound [*l'armonia*] would have greater loudness and sonority; with this, he surpassed all the musicians who came there to play. In addition, he was the best improviser of rhymes of his time.

Apart from the detailed description of the lyre, the most interesting statement here is the accent on the fact that Leonardo went to Milan for musical reasons, to play the lira for the duke. Could it be that Leonardo—who, in his application for a position at the Milan court, referred so strongly to the duke's plan for the giant bronze equestrian monument for his (the duke's) father—thought it a good idea to remind the duke, by a new and bizarre idea of a horse-skull instrument, of his familiarity with horse anatomy?[2]

We should also mention the treatises of the Milanese painter Giovanni Paolo Lomazzo (1538–1600), especially his *Trattato dell'arte della pittura* (1584) and *Idea del tempio della pittura* (1590). But they repeat largely secondhand information and I will quote here only one interesting suggestion contained in the sixth book of his *Trattato dell'arte della pittura* because it is symptomatic of the sixteenth-century tradition regarding Leonardo as an outstanding master of the art of music. Lomazzo suggests to painters various allegorical subjects appropriate for the decoration of musical instruments, for instance, the nine choirs of music, each devoted to another kind of instrument and each represented by three outstanding masters of these instruments. Now the fourth choir, devoted to the lira, is reserved to "*Leonardo Vinci pittore*" and to two other virtuosi "certainly not unknown to you: Alfonso da Ferrara and Alessandro Striggio mantovano."

In his *Idea del tempio della pittura* Lomazzo describes in great detail a noble edifice to be erected to honor Italy as well as the art of painting, and to exhibit inside the statues of seven *Governatori dell'Arte*, each made of a different metal symbolic of their character and their art. The artists chosen were to be Michelangelo (lead), Gaudenzio Ferrari (tin), Caravaggio (iron), Raphael (brass), Mantegna (quicksilver), Titian (silver), and Leonardo (gold, to reveal his splendor).

Contrary to the enthusiastic admiration of Leonardo's musicianship by his contemporaries and the generation following, the Leonardo scholars in our century do not mention music at all or content themselves at best with quoting remarks by Vasari.[3] Thus an example is Ludwig Heydenreich, *Leonardo da Vinci* (Berlin, 1943),

---

2. The application, of which only a draft survives, states, after an enumeration of Leonardo's many talents, "... again the bronze horse may be taken in hand, which is to be to the immortal glory and eternal honor of the prince, your father of happy memory, and of the illustrious house of Sforza."

3. In the mid-nineteenth century, Jacob Burckhardt, who in several of his writings (for instance, his *Cicerone* [Basel, 1855], p. 866) devotes some of his most clairvoyant and monumental language to drawing a profile of Leonardo's personality, does not fail to mention in the *Cicerone* (p. 859) that Leonardo "als Musiker und Improvisator berühmt war [was famous as a musician and improviser]," evidently on the testimony of Giovio and Vasari. Burckhardt was himself a well-trained musician,

one of the classical treatises on Leonardo's life and work. Sir Kenneth Clark's
Leonardo da Vinci, An Account of his Development as an Artist (Cambridge, 1939; rev. ed.
1958), one of the most perceptive books written about Leonardo the artist, is an
exception. Clark repeats Vasari's report of Leonardo's first visit to the Milanese court
and speaks of a "silver lyre [*sic*] in the form of a horse's head (*testa*) [*sic*]." There are
two inaccuracies: the silver lyre was a lira da braccio, and it was not shaped like a
horse's head but a horse's skull (*cranio*). But this is followed by a very imaginative
sentence: "Since we can no longer hear the music which Leonardo produced from
the lyre, we are inclined to assume that it was less important than his drawings and
pictures, but to his contemporaries it may have seemed the reverse." Certainly his
contemporaries—and among them good musicians—could not have given him
higher acclaim than they did. Benvenuto Cellini and Lomazzo still sounded a strong
echo of it.

The excellent book by Roberto Marcolongo, *Leonardo da Vinci, artista, scienziato*
(Milan, 1950), contains an interesting analysis of Leonardo's scientific achievements
but has nothing to say about Leonardo's musical thoughts and activities, beyond
mentioning that Leonardo was an excellent player of the "cetra" (a term meaning
either the ancient Greek kithara or the Renaissance cittern) and that he constructed
various musical instruments and the monochord—an obvious misunderstanding
because the monochord goes back to antiquity.

The admirable survey of publications about Leonardo by Anna Maria Brizio,
"Rassegna" (in *L'Arte*, 1968, pt. I), includes the statement: "Properly speaking, the
studies on Leonardo and music do not belong in the category of his scientific studies.
..." Would, then, music, and Leonardo's concern with this art and its acoustical
foundations, have no place among his multifarious interests and activities?

J. P. Richter, in *The Literary Works of Leonardo da Vinci* (London, 2d ed., 1939, pp.
69–81), a formidable contribution when it appeared and still indispensable, includes
remarks about Leonardo's "lyra," his other instruments, his statements on sound
and voice, and his comparison of painting and music. Inevitably, the practice of
improvisation was not fully understood in Richter's time, and most of the instruments mentioned, such as the viola organista and the zither, were not recognized for
what they actually were.

---

pianist, and singer (see the epilogue to his *Weltgeschichtliche Betrachtungen*, ed. Rudolf Marx (Kröner,
1935).

During one of my visits to Basel between the two world wars, I visited the house of Burckhardt.
An elderly caretaker who had been employed there during Burckhardt's last years showed me around.
His remarks about Burckhardt's musical inclinations are unforgettable: "When Herr Professor was
tired or wanted to be alone, he withdrew into the 'piano corner' and played *Welsche Weisen*." What
sounded like "Welsche Weisen" to the caretaker was in all probability Mozart, Burckhardt's idol. It is
characteristic that in the section "Greatness in History" in *Weltgeschichtliche Betrachtungen* he repeatedly cites Mozart as an example. We know from students of Burckhardt that he used to improvise
and to sing songs by Schubert to his own accompaniment.

PART I

ROOTS AND GROWTH

Musical environment, traditions and
trends, musical friends, exchange of ideas

CHAPTER ONE

Musical Life in
Florence and Milan

Before we consider Leonardo's many musical achievements and interests, it may be
appropriate to envisage him not as an isolated individual but in the midst of the
musical circles and atmospheres in which he lived, in order to understand the
impact that his musical environment had upon him. This will best be done by
reminding the reader of the musical life in Florence and Milan and showing Leonardo's relation to four friends who had an intimate affinity with music, each in a
different way: one a composer and teacher of music, Gaffurius; one a mathematician
and philosopher, Pacioli; one a famous builder of musical instruments, Lorenzo
Gusnasco da Pavia; and one a disciple of Leonardo in the art of improvisation on the
lira da braccio, Atalante Migliorotti.

Of the musical education of Leonardo during his early years in Florence, few
facts are known, but it is beyond all doubt that the intense musical life there at his
time, at court, at church, and among artisans and peasants, must have influenced
him deeply and lastingly.

There exists such a wealth of sacred and secular music and musical treatises,
biographical material, and reports of festivities, processions, and theatrical performances at the Medici court that a musical panorama of Florence in the second half of
the quattrocento is not needed here.

One important fact related to Leonardo's early musical instruction is found in
Vasari. Vasari's biography of Andrea del Verrocchio begins with a list of his gifts and
activities: "Andrea del Verrocchio, fiorentino, fu ne' tempi suoi orefice, prospettivo,
scultore, intagliatore, pittore e musico [. . . was goldsmith, connoisseur of perspective, sculptor, engraver, painter, and musician]."

Leonardo worked as an apprentice in Verrocchio's workshop from about 1467
to 1476. In 1472 he was accepted into the *compania de San Luca,* the artists' guild in
Florence. There he absorbed his earliest instruction in many arts, and Vasari's inclusion of music among Verrocchio's talents answers a question never asked by art
historians or music historians: where and when the young Leonardo became familiar with the craft of music.[1]

In 1482, when Leonardo decided, at the age of thirty, to leave Florence to enter
the service of Lodovico Sforza, Il Moro, Duke of Milan, his musical abilities must
have played a significant role if we believe the report of Vasari. However, the

---

1. True, Vasari was often maligned for adding complimentary material freely into *The Life of
Artists.* At least as far as music was concerned, I do not think that he deserved this criticism. Going

preserved draft of Leonardo's letter to the duke applying for employment and offering his gifts as a military engineer, and incidentally as an architect, sculptor, and painter, does not mention music. But it alludes significantly to Il Moro's plan for the equestrian monument for his father.

When Leonardo left the town of the Medicis to begin a new life in Milan, he must have found a totally different environment in the rich, aggressive, and politically ambitious city. It attracted him chiefly as a military engineer and for the opportunity to participate in the planning of novel military projects, new types of fortifications, waterworks such as canals and irrigation, new types of artillery, and also another enormous project in the field of bronze casting—the giant equestrian monument in honor of Francesco Sforza.

The Capella del Duomo, which reached back to 1402, assumed an international character under Galeazzo Maria Sforza, who between 1460 and 1470 employed French musicians, of whom the greatest was Josquin Des Prez.

In 1473 Galeazzo established his private chapel at the court and employed all foreign musicians of the Capella del Duomo. Its leader was Antonio Guinati, and his assistant, Gasparo van Weerbecke. Gaffurius tried to strengthen the Capella del Duomo and substantially increased the body of the singers.

He inevitably must have compared the spiritual level of the court of the Sforzas with that of the Medicis. There was no Marsilio Ficino here, little Neoplatonic tradition, and no Politian. Did Leonardo miss the unparalleled intensity of the Florentine humanist tradition and resent the lesser emphasis in Milan on the renascence of the culture of the ancients? We may never know. The artistic ideals and guides inherent in classical antiquity were probably less important to him than to most of his great artist-contemporaries. Leonardo was not an archaeologist, as were Raphael, Gulio Romano, and Filippino Lippi. On the other hand Milan was an international center for music and other arts. Famous German architects collaborated in the colossal task of the building of the Duomo.

Music in Milan, in the last third of the quattrocento, was intensely alive and full of radical innovations that certainly must have affected Leonardo. Nearer than Florence to the sources of transalpine polyphony, Milan had become a melting pot in more than one regard. There was the antagonism and also fusion between local Italian homophonic tradition and the new Flemish and French polyphonic style; there were new compromises and mutual stimuli. A similar process of osmosis went on between sacred and secular music, specifically between the Capella del Duomo favoring the national Italian style, and the private chapel of the Duke, favoring the foreigners such as Josquin, Agricola, Jaquotin, Cordier, and Compère.

---

through the *Vite* again and again for years, I found that he was completely reliable; if he called Raphael, Giorgione, Titian, and many others musicians, we have no right to doubt it. Whoever visits his house in Arezzo can convince himself of Vasari's interest in music by looking at his frescoes on the walls. And most important, in his description of musical scores in paintings of the masters he will not restrict himself to enumerating the instruments of the angels but often explains a detail that only a musical connoisseur could observe—for instance, that in a *sacra conversazione*, one angel plays, another tunes, and a third one waits for this entry.

CHAPTER TWO

Gaffurius and Pacioli

GAFFURIUS

Gaffurius, or as his friends called him, Franchino, was an almost exact contemporary of Leonardo. He was born in 1451, one year before Leonardo, in Lodi, an old and beautiful town southeast of Milan, with a hospitable library at the Chiesa dell' Incoronata, still proudly preserving his books.[1] He died six years after Leonardo, in 1522. Educated in the Benedictine Cloister of Lodivecchio and destined to become a priest, he returned to secular life for several years before being ordained in 1473 or 1474. He studied musical theory with the Carmelite monk of Flemish origin, Johannes Goodendag (Bonadies), and, after a short time as a singer at the Cathedral of Lodi, he began to teach musical theory in Mantua at the court of the Gonzagas and was called as a teacher and composer to Genoa by the Doge Adorno. For political reasons he left for Naples, where, under the influence of Flemish musicians, above all the famous Johannes Tinctoris, he continued his theoretical studies. In 1480 Gaffurius completed his first great treatise, *Theoricum Opus Musicae Disciplinae*, famous, among other things, for its beautiful woodcuts. Probably because of the black plague, he left Naples and returned to Lodi, where the bishop employed him as a teacher of young singers of sacred music; there he began his second great treatise, the *Practica Musicae*. In 1483 he was called to Bergamo as Maestro della Capella del Duomo and completed there his *Practica*, which, however, was published only much later, in 1496 in Milan.

In 1484 he was elected to the prestigious position of Maestro della Capella del Duomo di Milano and stayed there, interrupted only by small journeys, for the rest of his life, thirty-eight years. In 1492 he became Professor Musicae at the Milanese Gymnasium, established shortly before by the Duke Lodovico Moro. Among other famous teachers at the gymnasium was Luca Pacioli, the great mathematician (see p. 10). Gaffurius' third great treatise, *De Harmonia Musicorum Instrumentorum*, com-

---

1. Ten years ago, when I visited Lodi, the staff of the library and of the Museo Civico helped me with greatest courtesy in my research on Gaffurius.

pleting the *Trilogia Gaffuriana,* was written later, in 1500, and published in 1518, after Leonardo's death, in France. Gaffurius was elected to teach music at the venerable University of Pavia, which at the time had the only chair of music at any Italian university, then lauded as a remarkable innovation.

If one is eager to trace Gaffurius' personal relations with Leonardo, one is amply rewarded. Gaffurius worked in Milan from 1484 until his death in 1522. Leonardo lived in Milan from 1483 to 1499,[2] and again from 1506 until his departure for Rome and other cities in 1513; thus they were together in Milan for no fewer than twenty-two years. The fact that Gaffurius' duties were at the cathedral, while Leonardo was closely integrated into the rich social and artistic life of the court with its stage performances, feasts, concerts, and other divertissements, did not prevent an exchange of musical ideas and opinions. Gaffurius did not disdain to write secular music in the new style for the court.

In these twenty-two years there were beyond doubt close friendly relations between Leonardo and Gaffurius. A musical pioneer of the wide and profound knowledge of Gaffurius, who combined the local Italian tradition with the subtleties of Netherlandish counterpoint as a former disciple of Goodendag and Tinctoris, must have been of great interest to Leonardo. They lent each other books. Gaffurius could not have failed to be impressed by Leonardo's mastery of improvisation on the lira da braccio, and he must have admired Leonardo's activity as organizer of feasts, theatrical spectacles, and concerts at the ducal court. Leonardo may also have been curious to acquaint himself with Gaffurius' specific attitude toward the theory of proportions and numerical ratios. At the time that he wrote the *Practica,* Gaffurius worked also on a treatise *Proportioni Practicabili,* which was never published. The title alone evokes relations with Pacioli's *Divina Proportione* and the wide space given in Leonardo's *Paragone* to the role of proportions in the structure of works of art including the art "in time," music.[3]

One is tempted, of course, to scan Gaffurius' *Trilogia* for technical information about the practice of improvisation. In the *Practica,* the most down-to-earth of Gaffurius' treatises, we observe a repudiation of orthodox modal writing and also a certain simplification of rigorous contrapuntal rules in favor of vertical elements of texture, that is, of chordal style, all in line with the easier, less complicated, informal Italian tradition of the Capella del Duomo. In short, the style must have been identical with, or close to, what was practiced by Leonardo as an improviser and by other improvisers. Incidentally, Gaffurius, apart from his outstanding role as a theorist of music, was a fruitful composer of sacred and secular music. The extant works fill three codices preserved in the library of the Milan Cathedral. It would be beyond the scope of this book to analyze the variety of his compromises between the Italian and Flemish styles, and it may be a pity that the theorist has so overshadowed the composer.

2. After the French captured Milan in 1499, Leonardo, who was of course identified with the Sforza court, soon left for Mantua, Venice, and Florence.
    3. See chap. 12.

And if all this suggests, by way of inference, Gaffurius' approval of certain improvisation practices, we find an even stronger argument at the end of the third book of his *Practica,* in which the lira da braccio as an improvisation instrument is directly quoted as an example:

Moreover, a cithara or lyre player should use the tones of the lyre to express the concord which arises from harmonious strings, and from these tones produce consonant melodies in several ways, either by playing a tenor part on the strings and singing the cantus, or vice versa; also by relating the thinness of one tone to the denseness of the other, the rapidity of one to the slowness of the other, and the highness of one to the lowness of the other, so that together they will establish one entirely unified consonance, just as it has been done in the practice of the art and was established in Book 7 of Laws by Plato. For he says that all variations of rhythm are adapted to the tones of the lyre.[4]

The use of *lyra* and *cithara* in this passage of Gaffurius requires a clarification. The terminology of musical instruments in the quattrocento appears confused and confusing to later times. Different instruments are often given the same name; some instruments have several names; contemporary instruments are projected back into Greek antiquity, and Greek names are directly appended to quattrocento instruments. We find the terms *lyra, lira,* and *cythara;* each of these terms has more than one meaning. They may connote the plectrum-plucked famous stringed instrument of classical Greek antiquity, familiar to Leonardo's learned contemporaries from Greek literature, that is, from poets, philosophers, or writers on music; but they may also indicate modern instruments of Leonardo's time.

The present-day reader cannot hope to discover the meaning from dictionaries but only from the historic context and environment. When Gaffurius speaks of contemporary usage in his *Practica,* he often means by "lyra" and "cythara" the bowed lira da braccio (later called by Vincenzo Galilei "lira moderna"). The situation becomes even more confusing to the modern reader because the lira da braccio of the quattrocento was often identified with the κιθαρα or λυρα of the Greeks, chiefly because of its two open, unstoppable strings. Greek poet-musicians were credited with the invention of the bow, evidently because Sappho was believed to have played something like the quattrocento lira da braccio. Similarly in mythological stage plays of the quattrocento (or in paintings), when the author of the play instructed gods or heroes to perform on the "lira," he meant its Renaissance equivalent, the lira da braccio. Poliziano, in his *Favola,* directs Orpheus to enter Hades with his "lira," and the protagonist used the lira da braccio as a matter of course. When Atalante Migliorotti, a disciple of Leonardo who had studied improvisation on the lira da braccio with him, played Orpheus in the famous repeat performance of

4. "Oportet insuper & Cytharistam Lyricumve concentus exprimendi gratia qui ex canoris fidibus provenit Lyrae vocibus uti: ac vocibus ipsis voces suas alterna diversitate reddere consonas: puta vel fidibus ipsis modulando tenorem: ac voce propria cantum: vel econverso: sive etiam unius spissitudinem dinem raritati alterius conferendo sive velocitatem tarditati sive acumen gravitati: ita ut unum omnino simul consonum servent: quod & artis ratione & septimo legum Divi Platonis institutō noscitur observādum. Is enim inquit universam rythmorum varietatem esse Lyrae vocibus accommodandam."

Poliziano's *legenda* at the court of Mantua in 1492, he used, of course, "his instrument," the lira da braccio.[5]

One male portrait, in the Ambrosiana in Milan, has been considered by art historians to be a portrait of Gaffurius, but this seems to be extremely doubtful. Evidently a portrait of a musician from the time when Leonardo and Gaffurius were together in Milan, it shows a young man of great character, serious expression, and appealing beauty (illus. 2.1). If it was painted by Leonardo at all, it would be his only male portrait on canvas. Angela Ottino della Chiesa, in *Leonardo da Vinci* (New York: Rizzoli, 1967; Abrams, 1969) gives a long list of past suggestions as to authorship. Suida, Berenson, Kenneth Clark, and Heydenreich consider Leonardo to be the artist. Morelli suggests Ambrogio de Predis. A. Venturi, Malaguzzi-Valeri, and others are undecided.

The "musician" has stirred up many controversies among modern art historians. There is no agreement about the painter, the possible cooperation of painters, or the identity of the sitter.[6]

Looking for authentic likenesses of Gaffurius, we find, above all, the famous woodcut showing Gaffurius teaching ex cathedra, surrounded by the Pythagorean proportion figures and the symbols of measuring time and space (the hourglass and dividers) (illus. 2.2). It was used in several of his publications. The long face gives the impression of a realistic portrait.

The Museo Civico of Lodi possesses a profile portrait with the title *Francus. Gafurus. Laudensis. Musicae. Moderator.* against a background of large organ pipes (illus. 2.3). In spite of the inscription it seems difficult to reconcile the features with those in the woodcut.

However, a miniature portrait used as the frontispiece of the Codice Laudense XXVIII.A.9 shows a somewhat older man teaching (illus. 2.4 and 2.5). It could be reconciled with the face in the woodcut. Two students listening are portrayed on the opposite rim of the frontispiece.

None of the three representations just discussed could easily be reconciled with the features of the Ambrosiana portrait. However, this would not exclude Leonardo as its painter. The design of the eyes, nose, and mouth, and their relation to the contour of the cheek, are comparable to the features in the angel in the *Virgin of the Rocks*. Kenneth Clark has convincingly pointed to the similarity of the modeling of both faces. Also, the treatment of the curls is characteristic of Leonardo's technique. If the painting is not by Leonardo himself, one could think of one of his closest disciples, Ambrogio de Predis.[7]

5. See p. 84.

6. The notes and catalogue by Angela Ottino della Chiesa in *The Complete Paintings of Leonardo da Vinci* (New York: Harry N. Abrams, 1967), p. 100, give lists of the various opinions about authorship and the identity of the sitter.

7. Waldemar von Seidlitz, in *Leonardo da Vinci* (Vienna: Phaidon-Verlag, 1935), p. 128, believes that everything points to Giovanni Ambrogio Preda as the painter and he quotes Morelli, who has attributed the London Madonna to the artist who painted not only both flanking angel musicians but also the musician's portrait in the Ambrosiana.

2.1. Portrait of a musician, probably by Leonardo da Vinci. Ambrosiana, Milan.

PACIOLI

Another ingenious friend of Leonardo in his Milanese years and even later was not a musician but a mathematician of international fame, Luca Pacioli. Pacioli was born about 1445 at Borgo San Sepolcro and studied mathematics as a boy in Venice, where he later was employed as a tutor for children, teaching mathematics from a treatise that he himself wrote. He entered the Franciscan order and, after studying theology and philosophy, concentrated on the mathematical sciences, writing and teaching in many cities: Perugia, Venice, Zara, Florence, Rome, and Naples.

In Venice he published in 1494 the first of his famous works, the *Summa de Arithmetica Geometria Proportione et Proportionalita*. Two years later Lodovico il Moro called him to Milan and appointed him professor of mathematics. He became a friend of Leonardo, who had already been at the court of the Sforzas since 1483.

It is easy to see how they must have attracted each other as scholars and how much their interests in the exact sciences complemented one another. Leonardo profited from Pacioli's familiarity with the history of mathematics from Greek antiquity, and Pacioli, on the other hand, must have been astonished by the wide use Leonardo made of mathematics, applying it to mechanics, linear perspective, optics, acoustics, anatomy, and to countless experiments in all these fields.

In 1499, after the occupation of Milan by the French army, Leonardo and Pacioli left Milan together by way of Mantua for Venice, where both stayed together.

The *Summa* is an encyclopedic synthesis of mathematical thought from Euclid to Regimontanus, with many original contributions such as the calculus on probability. Besides theoretical sections it contains many practical suggestions and information, for instance, on double-entry bookkeeping and calculation of interests and rates of exchange.[8]

Not being a mathematician,[9] I can say here only a few words about the impulse this work may have given to Leonardo and about some of the similarities and divergences between the ideas of the friends about the nature and usefulness of mathematical thought. Leonardo himself, in the opinion of many mathematicians familiar with his writings and experiments, was a mathematician of genius, although some of the laundry and grocery bills interspersed in his learned diaries show mistakes. His planned book on the science of machines (or what we today would call "theoretical mechanics," or more generally, "theoretical physics") would not have been possible without the constant application of mathematics.[10]

Often quoted are Leonardo's words, "Mechanics is the paradise of the mathematical sciences because by means of it one comes to the fruit of mathematics"

8. For an imaginative and concentrated account of the content and substance of Pacioli's three great treatises and their influence upon his time and the history of mathematics, see Giuseppina Masotti Biggiogero, in *De Divina Proportione de Luca Pacioli* Fontes Ambrosiani, 31 (Milan, 1956), pp. 219–33.

9. See the interesting remarks by V. P. Zubov, *Leonardo da Vinci* (Cambridge: Harvard University Press, 1968), p. 169.

10. See Arturo Uccelli, *Leonardo da Vinci, I Libri di Meccanica* (Milan: Hoepli, 1940).

2.2. Woodcut showing Gaffurius teaching, used as an illustration in his *Angelicum Opus Musice* (Milan, 1508) and other of his publications.

2.3. Portrait of Gaffurius. Museo Civico, Lodi.

2.4. Miniature portrait of a teacher, possibly Gaffurius. *Codice Laudense* XXVIII.A.9.

2.5. Detail of the portrait. *Codice Laudense* XXVIII.A.9.

(E 8 v, Institute de France). Or, to quote one of the most striking examples of this application, "A bird is an instrument working according to mathematical law" (CA 161 ra). All Leonardo's mechanisms, from his anatomical interpretations of living organisms of humans, animals, and plants to his countless freely invented machines including new musical instruments, are governed by mathematical laws and can be conceived in their operation only through the laws of mathematics. This is true to the extent that even the most fantastic creatures designed by Leonardo, his dragons and other monsters, are constructed with respect to mathematical laws, with their legs and wings designed and proportioned as parts of a workable machine—that is, of the "logical" organism. For the same reason, Leonardo the painter, already when serving as an apprentice in Verrocchio's workshop in Florence, developed a disgust for angel wings, evidently because a given set of back and shoulder muscles cannot operate arms and wings at the same time.

The second of the printed works of Pacioli is his Latin edition of the *Elements* of Euclid, published in 1509 and considered to be by far the best edition since the first medieval edition in the thirteenth century.

In the same year (1509) appeared in Venice the third of his main printed works, the famous *De Divina Proportione*,[11] which includes in its formidable compass the role of proportions in sciences and arts, that is, in the language of that time, the seven liberal arts. It is divided into three parts: the *Compendium de Divina Proportione*, the treatise on architecture, and an Italian translation of Piero della Francesca's *De corporibus regularibus*.

Leonardo contributed to Pacioli's *Divina Proportione* sixty drawings of polyhedra. Among them were the platonic "regular bodies," that is, the pyramid symbolizing fire, the cube symbolizing earth, the octahedron symbolizing air, the dodecahedron symbolizing heaven, and the icosahedron symbolizing water.

Leonardo drew the polyhedra in linear perspective by geometric projection, each polyhedron in two parallel versions: as a solid body (called "solido" by Pacioli) and as a frame or skeleton (called "vacuum" by Pacioli) (illus. 2.6 and 2.7). This pedagogical device of replacing the planes of the solid body by frames or skeletons is an exact parallel to Leonardo's didactic technique for drawing illustrations for his anatomical research, for instance, when he replaces muscles by thin cords or wires to obtain a transparent and an intelligible picture of the whole configuration[12] (illus. 2.8).

Pacioli thanked Leonardo repeatedly and profusely for his contribution. In an appendix of twenty chapters added to the seventy-one chapters of *De Divina Proportione* presented to Lodovico il Moro in 1497, Pacioli writes of "the most excellent painter of perspective, architect, *m u s i c i a n*, and man learned in all virtues, Leonardo da Vinci, who deduced and elaborated a series of diagrams of regular solids at the time of his sojourn in Milan [italics mine]." This homage to Leonardo by

11. See Biggiogero, *Divina Proportione*, pp. 219–33.
12. See Emanuel Winternitz, "Anatomy the Teacher—On the Impact of Leonardo's Anatomical Research on his Musical and Other Machines," *Proceedings of the American Philosophical Society* 3 (Aug. 1967).

a learned friend and humanist is significant for several reasons: it is one of the earliest testimonials to Leonardo's musicianship; it is also interesting because Pacioli selected as merits of Leonardo three of his achievements that imply a mastery of the science of proportions in art: painting, using linear perspective, architecture, and music.

In his *De Viribus Quantitatis,* written between 1497 and 1508 (no. 250, University Library, Bologna), Pacioli refers to his *De Divina Proportione* and again pays enthusiastic and tender homage not only to Leonardo the scientist but also to the painter for his

supreme and very graceful figures of all the Platonic and mathematical regular bodies and derivatives, which it would not be possible to make better in perspectival drawing, even if Apelles, Myron, or Polycletus and the others were to return among us, made and shaped by that ineffable left hand, most fitted for all the mathematical disciplines, of the prince among the mortals of today, that first of Florentines, our Leonardo da Vinci, in that happy time when we were together in the most admirable city of Milan, working for the same patron. [13]

Several of Leonardo's drawings of the regular bodies made for Pacioli are found in CA 263 r (illus. 2.9).

It is of great interest to see both Pacioli and Leonardo wrestling with the same new and fashionable problems of their time, for instance, the doctrine of the liberal arts, although with slightly different results. The time-honored canon throughout the Middle Ages and ever since was the bipartition of the seven liberal arts into two groups, a mathematical one, the quadrivium (arithmetic, geometry, astronomy, and music), and the trivium (rhetoric, grammar, and dialectics), that is, disciplines of less exact nature.

In the second half of the fifteenth century this sharp classification was gradually eroded and other disciplines were added. In his preface to *De Divina Proportione* (p. 15), Pacioli explains to the duke that he recognizes as *discipline:* mathematica, arithmetica, geometria, astrologia, musica, prospectiva, architectura, and cosmographia, thus doubling the number of disciplines contained in the old canon. It was Leonardo who had forcefully pleaded for the recognition of linear perspective as a liberal art; for him, the painter was a scientist, and one of his tools, linear perspective, partook of mathematical exactness and therefore belonged with music in the quadrivium. Although music, as a science of proportion, had gradually lost its cosmological importance and thereby its central position in philosophical speculation, it was the doctrine of proportions that became the preoccupation of the draftsmen of the quattrocento and their ideal of the rationally, mathematically "correct" portrayal of nature. Linear perspective became one of the new science-arts,

13. "supreme et legiadrissime figure de tutti i platonici et mathematici regulari et dependenti, ch'in prospectivo disegno non è possibile al mondo farli meglio, quando bene Apelle, Mirone, Policleto et gli altri fra noi tornassero, facte et formate per quella ineffabile senistra mano a tutte discipline mathematici acomodatissima del prencipe oggi fra mortali, pro prima fiorentino, Lionardo nostro da Venci, in quel felici tempo ch'insiemi a medesimi stipendii nella mirabilissima citta di Milano ci trovammo."

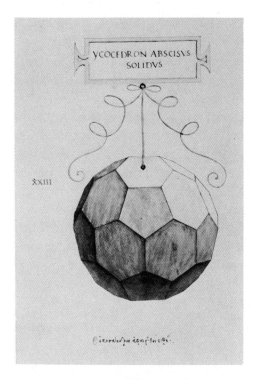

2.6. Drawing of an *"icosahedron solidus"* by Leonardo for Pacioli's *Divina Proportione.*

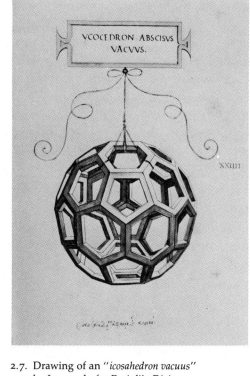

2.7. Drawing of an *"icosahedron vacuus"* by Leonardo for Pacioli's *Divina Proportione.*

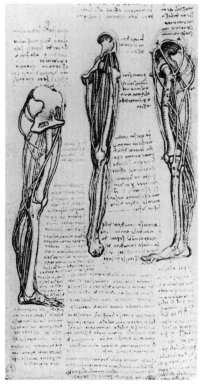

2.8. Sketches by Leonardo of a leg representing the muscles by wires. Quaderni d'Anatomia V 4 r.

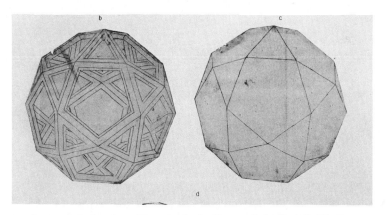

2.9. Leonardo's drawing of two regular bodies, made for Pacioli. CA 263 r.

and Leonardo's plea for its reception among the quadrivium helped the painter to ascend from the social level of an artisan to the rank of a scholar, which the musician had always enjoyed.

There is a bifurcation of the principal directions of Pacioli and Leonardo. Pacioli remains above all a mathematician, believing in mathematical rigor without compromise, although he admits in *De Divina Proportione* (p. 9): "Mathematicae enim scientiae sunt in primo grado certitudinis et naturales sequuntur eas [Mathematics are sciences possessing the first degree of certainty, and the natural sciences follow them]." Leonardo is above all a natural scientist and philosopher of nature, and although he admits mathematical thought is indispensable to mechanics, he continuously relies on experiment as the prime method of research and must often be satisfied with approximate solutions. He searches and thinks in terms of proportions of sound, weights, time and its sections, and also of proportions of shapes and dimensions of living organisms.[14]

14. Giorgio Santillana once called Leonardo's mathematics "not contemplation of the pretersensual world, but a search for the geometric skeleton of reality" (["Léonard et ceux qu'il n'a pas lus"] in *Léonard de Vinci et l'expérience scientifique au XVIe siècle*, Colloques Internationaux [Paris: Presses Universitaires, 1953], pp. 343 ff.).

CHAPTER THREE

Gusnasco aud Migliorotti

GUSNASCO

Another musical friend of Leonardo's was Lorenzo Gusnasco, called Lorenzo da Pavia from his native town Pavia, just a few miles south of Milan. He was a man of many talents and several trades.

He became an outstanding maker of musical instruments of such beauty and such tone that his fame spread all over Lombardy and Venice. Among his instruments were organs, organetti, harpsichords, spinette, clavichords, lutes, viole, citterns, and in all probability lire da braccio.

Many letters reveal his service to the great Lombard courts, Milan, Ferrara, and especially Mantua, whose court was dominated by the art- and music-minded duchess, La Marchesa Isabella d'Este.[1] Gusnasco's correspondence with her began in the 1490s. Among other things, a lute was commissioned by her with a sound-hole rose of ebony and ivory, "perché l'ebano e l'avorio sono due belle compagne insieme [because ebony and ivory make beautiful companions]." But Lorenzo must have known her personally. We know of his visits to Mantua to deliver directly into her hands the delicate instruments commissioned by her with individual instructions.

In 1495 Isabella reminds him of a beautiful clavichord he had made for her sister, Beatrice, duchess of Milan, and wants one of equal beauty for herself, adding, however, the special wish:

> We want only to request that it should be played easily (that is, with a light touch), for we have such a light hand that we cannot play well if we have to strain our hand because of the resistance of the keys. Please understand our wish and what we need: make it in the same shape as you are accustomed. The faster you serve us, the more we will be pleased.

Isabella was kept informed of the progress of the work. From other letters we learn more about the intense, sometimes even fierce musical rivalry between the two sisters. At Christmas 1496 Gusnasco delivers the clavichord personally to Isabella in

---

1. See especially A. Luzio, "Isabella d'Este e la corte Sforza," *Archivio Storico Lombardo* (1901); A. Luzio and R. Renier, "Delle Relazioni di Isabella d'Este Gonzaga con Lodovico e Beatrice Sforza," *Archivio Storico Lombardo* (1890), pp. 74 ff., 364 ff., 614 ff.; A. Luzio and R. Renier, "La cultura e le relazioni letterarie di Isabella d'Este Gonzaga," *Giornale storico della letteratura Italiana,* passim.

Mantua. Incidentally, after Beatrice's death in Milan, Isabella managed to acquire her clavichord also.

In July 1497 Isabella requests a lute "adapted to my voice," but Lorenzo regrets not being able to oblige her because he cannot find ebony black and beautiful enough. He adds, in his somewhat stilted and subservient style, that he was very disconsolate because he had wanted badly to make the lute, that he was certain that he would have made the most beautiful object in Italy or anywhere else, and that he had been most anxious to please the only person who would have understood the value of those objects—a fact that would have inspired him to produce something excellent.

In 1494 Lorenzo had moved to Venice, evidently because the larger town was a more practical residence for his growing occupation as the trusted, knowledgeable, and shrewd agent of Isabella for procuring works of art and curiosities for her collection in the castello of Mantua. Among these objects were pictures, rare books,[2] antiques, gems and cameos, tapestries, Murano glass, amber rosaries, ivory crucifixes, enamels, crystal mirrors, inlaid cabinets, perfume boxes of crystal and ebony, and all kinds of curiosities. But there is good reason to assume that Lorenzo also continued his workshop for musical instruments in Venice; deliveries after 1494 are mentioned in the documents after that time.

It was in Venice that Leonardo in 1499 stayed with Lorenzo and heard that Lodovico had defeated the French army—good news that was soon replaced by the sad tidings that the French had reentered Milan, sacked the city, and imprisoned Lodovico il Moro.

An instrument builder of the rank and originality of Gusnasco must have been of great interest to Leonardo, who was an admired performer and had constructed a great number of new and complex musical instruments. In Milan, Pavia, Mantua, and later in Venice there must have been numerous occasions for meetings between the two. Significant is a letter written by the duke of Mantua to his treasurer in December 1498. The duke writes from one of his country villas in Goïto, instructing his treasurer to pay "Leonardo the Florentine" eleven ducats for certain strings of lute and viol which Leonardo had brought from Milan, and begs him to do this at once that the master may be able to continue his journey.[3] But there were occasions for meetings apart from music. Isabella d'Este used Gusnasco as a shrewd and persuasive intermediary to elicit from Leonardo a promise to paint her portrait.[4] Because it was known that Leonardo was deeply involved in scientific projects, she would, to save time, even content herself with a portrait not after life but after a drawing that Leonardo had done of her some years before, probably the delicate chalk and pastel profile now in the Louvre.[5] Alas for us, Leonardo resisted and could not be persuaded.

2. The workshop of the famous printer of beautiful books, Aldus Manutius, the founder of the Aldine Press, opened in Venice in 1540.

3. Luzio, *Emporium* (1900), p. 352.

4. See letters in Luzio and Renier, "La cultura."

5. From Venice Gusnasco wrote to Isabella d'Este: "Leonardo is in Venice and has shown me a portrait of Your Highness which is exactly like you, and is so well done that it is not possible to be better!" (A. Baschet, *Aldo Manuzio*, [Venice, 1867], pp. 70–75).

A letter of Gusnasco to Isabella in April 1515, preserved in the Gonzaga archives, reports the shipping of musical instruments to the marchesa, especially "di liuti, viole, corone, buccettine, teste di morto ed altri soggetti di ebano e di avorio, oltre un bellissimo gravicembalo" (of lutes, viols, crowns, little horns, skulls and other objects made out of ebony and ivory, and in addition a most beautiful harpsichord).[6] We do not know whether these instruments were made by Gusnasco or only procured for the marchesa. In any case it is significant that keyboard instruments were ordered from Venice. *Gravicembalo* does not mean a heavy or especially large harpsichord. The word is rather equivalent, according to the usage of the time, to *clavicembalo*, that is, "harpsichord."

The date of Gusnasco's death is not known. Carlo dell'Acqua suggested 1517,[7] but later years have been mentioned by other writers. As late as 1539 the famous orientalist Theseo Ambrogio Albonesi in his *Introductio in chaldaicam linguam, syriacam atque armenicam et decem alias linguas* (Pavia, 1809), p. 183, addresses Gusnasco as follows:

And what should I say of you, Lorenzo Gusnasco? Who in the field of artistic woodwork have invented what to few if any people [artists] was given. For how could I overlook that you have made an organ of such musical capacity that no musician could have invented anything so clever and beautiful.[8]

Today Gusnasco is forgotten. Hardly any dictionary of music or art mentions his name and importance as a creative artist. Were it not for the indefatigable archive searches by Alessandro Luzio and Rodolfo Renier, who studied Lombard archives, and for historians such as Julia Cartwright[9] and Jan Lauts,[10] we would know very little about him.

But there may be a living testimony to the subtle artistry of Gusnasco and even to his mastery of creating instruments of noble, silvery sound.

In 1967, by incredibly good luck, I found in New York, of all places, an Italian spinettina (illus. 3.1) so beautiful, so subtly ornamented, and so perfectly preserved that I bought it immediately for the Metropolitan Museum of Art as the curator of its musical instrument collection.

The elegant decoration is carefully planned and executed in different media: intarsia, painting, certosina work, carving, and so on, each applied to a different and precisely limited area. The sound-hole rose, that place par excellence for exquisite ornamentation, is made of several layers of parchment in flamboyant Gothic tracery (illus. 3.2). The wall above the keyboard is divided into nine squares of alternating decoration: four squares have a simple geometric design executed in inlay of

6. Quoted in Antonio Bertolotti, *Artisti in relazione coi Gonzaga Signori di Mantova* (Modena, 1855), p. 108.

7. "Lorenzo Gusnasco e i Lingiardi da Pavia," extract from *Perseveranza* (Milan, 1886).

8. Et de te, Laurenti Gusnache qui dicam? Qui in lignario artificio quod paucis aut forsitan nullis antehac datum fuit, invenisti. Nam ut omittam, quod ligneum quodcumque voluisti musicae facultatis organum ita adfabre fecisti, ut nihil concinuis musici omnes inveniri posse haberentur."

9. *Isabella d'Este, Marchioness of Mantua, 1474–1539* (London, 1903), vols. 1–2; *Beatrice d'Este, Duchess of Milan, 1475–1497* (London, 1928).

10. *Isabella d'Este* (Hamburg: Marion V. Schröder, 1952).

3.1. Spinettina made for the Duchess of Urbino, 1540. Venice. Metropolitan Museum of Art, 53.6. Pulitzer Bequest Fund, 1953.

3.3. Intarsia decoration in double symmetry; detail of spinettina (illus. 3.1).

3.2. Sound-hole rose of spinettina in illus. 3.1.

3.4. Detail of spinettina (illus. 3.1) showing several styles of decoration: sculpture, various forms of intarsia, and certosina work with stars in gothic tracery.

mother-of-pearl; the remaining five squares show elaborate stars also done in Gothic tracery. Even the jackrail is subtly decorated; it is made of gumwood with inlaid strips of walnut and ebony and buttons of black and white segments of ebony and ivory.

The stylistically most revealing decorations are the intarsia panels at the left and right of the projecting keyboard; they show slightly different patterns with stylized dolphins and plant forms. Both patterns are designed in double symmetry, left–right as well as top–bottom (illus. 3.3). Any modern psychologist will be reminded of the Rorschach inkblot test figures in which bilateral symmetry is automatically produced by folding a paper with the inkblot still wet; but the spinettina is immeasurably more sophisticated.[11]

A strip of wood over the keyboard has a motto painted in large gold letters on a blue ground (illus. 3.4):

Riccho son d'oro—et riccho son di suono
Non mi sonar si tu non ha del buono.

I am rich in gold and rich in sound,
O play me not, if no good tune is found.

But the wooden strip is removable, being attached to the instrument by three small pegs. Its back harbors a surprise. There is a long inscription in ink, in Italian chancery of the time: "Ordinata e Fatta per Sua Eccelenza la Sig.ra Duchesa D'Urbino L'anno di Nostra Salute 1540 e pagata 250 Scudi Romani [Commissioned by and made for Her Excellency, the [Lady] Duchess of Urbino in the year of our Redemption 1540 and paid for with 250 Roman scudi]."

This information is more than we usually glean from old keyboard instruments but unfortunately the name of the maker is not mentioned. This is an exceptionally beautiful instrument, and the price mentioned was a large one at the time of manufacture. As we know, Venice then had a substantial number of good instrument makers, but there is no instrument extant that would give us a clue or a basis for comparing shape and decoration.

The outstanding workmanship, tone, shape, and decoration suggest a supreme craftsman, and it may not be farfetched to credit Gusnasco or his artistic tradition with this instrument. As mentioned above, we do not know the exact date of his death, but it is reasonable to assume that even after his death his admired Venetian workshop continued to flourish for a while. No better memorial could be imagined for the subtle craftsmanship of Lorenzo da Pavia than this Venetian spinettina "made of golden sound."

11. See Emanuel Winternitz, "A Spinettina for the Duchess of Urbino," *Metropolitan Museum Journal* 1 (1968): 101 ff.

MIGLIOROTTI

Of Atalante Migliorotti's life only a few facts are known, but they are so significant that they contribute greatly to our knowledge of Leonardo's musical life. Migliorotti, the only musical disciple of Leonardo of whom we know, learned from him in Florence the art of improvisation on the lira da braccio. The date of his birth has been given as 1466.[12] According to the earliest musical reference to Leonardo, the Codice del Anonimo Gaddiano, written between 1506 and 1532, "Leonardo fu raro sonatore di lira et fu maestro di quella d'Atalante Migliorotti [Leonardo was an outstanding performer of the lira da braccio and a teacher of Atalante Migliorotti in this art]." According to the same source, Atalante was with Leonardo when Lorenzo Magnifico sent Leonardo to Lodovico il Moro in Milan in 1483 to present to the duke a lira da braccio, in whose mastery he was unique ("a presentarli insieme con Atalante Migliorotti una lira, che unico era in sonare tale exstrumento").[13]

Migliorotti's name is linked with a famous performance of Poliziano's *Favola d'Orfeo* at the court of Mantua. According to various contradictory sources the first performance of this celebrated pastoral in Mantua has been dated 1471, 1472, and 1480. The role of Orfeo at the first performance was sung by the celebrated improviser Baccio Ugolino. The second performance took place in 1491 with Atalante as protagonist, a sure testimony to his fame as improviser on the lira da braccio. Poliziano's text shows clearly that the whole *Favola* was permeated by music. The obvious interest of Leonardo in Poliziano's *Orfeo* as a musical drama, and Migliorotti's performance will be discussed in chapter 6.

For the year 1513 and the following three years Migliorotti worked as an inspector of constructions ("soprastante alle fabbriche") for Pope Leo. Leonardo was repeatedly in Rome between 1513 and 1516. The last (existing) information about Atalante mentions him as an architect.[14]

This meager evidence gives a rather incoherent picture of Atalante's life but is still colorful enough for us to imagine him as an interesting and versatile musician, echoing the magic personality of Leonardo.

12. In Gaetano Milanesi, *Documenti inediti risguardanti Lionardo da Vinci* (Florence, 1872).

13. The word *lira* was constantly mistaken and erroneously translated in the literature on Leonardo and the object was usually considered a plucked, not a bowed, instrument, until my articles "Lira da braccio," in *Die Musik in Geschichte und Gegenwart* 8 (1960): 935–54, and "Engelskonzert," in *Die Musik in Geschichte und Gegenwart* 16 (suppl.) (1979): 89–95.

14. See Milanesi, *Documenti inediti.*

PART II

THE PERFORMER

Improviser, teacher of music,
organizer of stage plays and entertainments

CHAPTER FOUR

The Lira da Braccio

As mentioned above, Leonardo's instrument for his improvisations was, according to Vasari, the lira. There is no doubt that the word *lira* meant the lira da braccio. True enough, for a long time the Italians used the word *lira* for two instruments, the ancient Greek lyre and the bowed Renaissance instrument equipped with stoppable gut strings and additional open strings that ran outside the fingerboard and could not be stopped.

In fact the lira da braccio was one of the most important stringed instruments of the Italian Renaissance, the instrument used by the performers to improvise a polyphonic accompaniment to their own recitation. As such, the lira da braccio became one of the characteristic tools for the intended revival of the ancient tradition of rhapsodes. The use of the lira da braccio remained limited to Italy with very few exceptions, all of which involved late and larger forms of the instrument.

The instrument in its fully developed form had a flat body, rounded shoulders, and a unique arrangement of strings different from the contemporary viola da gamba, which had a deep body and sloping shoulders. In addition to five melody strings that could be stopped against the fingerboard, the lira da braccio had two "open strings" (often mistakenly called "drones" or "bourdons") that ran freely through the air outside the fingerboard toward the head, to which they were attached by a little protruding wooden stick; they could sound only their full length or one tone when touched by the bow or plucked by the player's fingers. It was just the existence of these open strings that reminded the musicians of the High Renaissance, devoted to the revival of classical antiquity in many fields including music, of the ancient lira and kithara. As late as 1581 Vincenzo Galilei, the father of Galileo Galilei, in his *Dialogo della musica antica e della moderna*, tried to establish an order in this and other terminological confusions and suggested, justifiably, calling the lyre of the Greeks "lira antiqua" and the improvisation instrument of the Renaissance "lira moderna."

For a long time the lira da braccio was also called "viola." In the second half of the sixteenth century the usage still varied: Vasari, for example, speaks of the lira da braccio played by one of the angels in Carpaccio's *Presentation in the Temple* (Ac-

4.1. Lira da braccio by Giovanni d'Andrea, Venice, 1511.

4.2. *Orpheus in Hades,* after a bronze plaque by Moderno.

cademia, Venice) as "una lira ovvero viola" but calls the same instrument, in Fra Bartolommeo's *sacra conversazione* for San Marco in Florence, simply a "lira." Galilei, in his *Dialogo*, maintains that only recently had the viola da braccio been called "lira," and, in another passage, that it had been called "lira" only in his own time ("modernamente"). The fact that earlier sources generally refer to the lira da braccio by the name "viola" is not without importance in view of the many musicians with the nickname "della viola." As we know, during the reign of Alfonso II the court of Ferrara employed Francesco di Viola, a pupil of Willaert, as chapelmaster, and also the madrigal composer Alfonso della Viola. Further evidence for the use of the name "viola" for the lira can be seen in the terminology of the period, which frequently uses "viols with frets" when referring to members of the viol family, obviously to distinguish them from the fretless lira da braccio. Thus, Ganassi's *Regola Rubertina* speaks expressly of the "viola d'arco tastada" in the title of its first part and of the "violone d'arco da tasti" in its second part, while Lanfranco's *Scintille* mentions "violoni da tasti & da Arco."

The most characteristic part of the lira da braccio is its head, sometimes a wooden board shaped like a leaf or a heart, but sometimes in more richly decorated specimens a whole box with a cover on its rear. Whatever the shape of the head, the method of attaching the strings is the same: the seven pegs are inserted from the front rather than from the side as in viols or in the later violins; and the strings are fastened to the small ends of the pegs, which protrude from the rear of the pegboard or from inside the pegbox. In order to be fastened this way, the five melody strings are made to pass from the nut through little holes to the back of the pegboard.

Only very few specimens are preserved from Leonardo's time in their original state. The oldest and at the same time the most beautiful specimen is the lira da braccio made in Verona in 1511 by Giovanni d'Andrea (illus. 4.1). It is today one of the most valuable possessions of the collection of musical instruments in the Kunsthistorisches Museum, Vienna. The fingerboard and the string holder are decorated in typical North Italian style, alla certosina, that is, by a colorful combination of ebony, ivory, bone that has been stained green, and brown wood. The most striking feature, however, is the carving of belly and back, which give the impression of human forms. The belly is shaped like a male torso and, correspondingly, the front of the pegbox shows a grotesque male face. The back shows, in stronger relief, the form of a female torso, with breasts and nipples strongly marked, and, accordingly, the back of the pegbox shows a woman's face. But this is not the end of the sculptural fantasy: acanthus leaves encroach upon the female torso, and on its middle region is a large moustachioed mascherone that overlays the curves of the female form. The sound holes in the belly are unusually large and of tendril shape. The pegbox can be closed, and it is remarkable how cleverly the pegs are inserted so as to disturb as little as possible the grimace of the grotesque face. A little ivory plaque inserted into the back bears the somewhat misspelled Greek inscription,

ΛΥΠΗΣΙΑΤΡΟΣ ΕΣΤΙΝ
ΑΝΘΡΩΠΟΙΣ ΩΑΗ

actually an ancient monostichon: "Men have song as the physician of pain," thus paying respect to humanist learning, so important in the North Italian culture of the time.

How far this masterpiece of applied ornamental sculpture is from the standardized forms of string instruments of later ages! And how much it helps us to visualize other bizarre and fantastic musical instruments such as the lira da braccio that Leonardo built in the shape of a horse skull.

Because so few instruments have been preserved, pictorial sources are indispensable. The number of contemporary depictions of the lira da braccio is enormous, especially in Venetian, Lombard, and Tuscan art (frescoes, paintings on canvas and wood, woodcuts and engravings, sculptures, reliefs and plaquettes, wood intarsias, book vignettes, decorations of frames, and so forth). The greater part of these pictorial representations occurs in mythological and allegorical scenes and in angel concerts. Apollo and Orpheus, as a rule, play the lira da braccio, Apollo in his combat with Marsyas or Pan (the earliest example probably being the woodcut illustration in the *Ovidio Metamorphoseos Volgare* [Venice, 1501]) or as the leader of the Muses (the most famous representation in Raphael's fresco of the Parnassus in the Stanza della Segnatura in the Vatican, innumerable times copied and varied). Orpheus appears as a musician teaching the beasts (for instance, in the engraving by Benedetto Montagna); as the victor over the demons of hell (in Signorelli's fresco cycle in the Chapel of St. Brizio in the dome of Orvieto; in a bronze plaque by Moderno [illus. 4.2]; and in Peruzzi's frieze in the Villa Farnesina in Rome); or as the guide of Euridice (in Marcantonio Raimondi's engraving). Similarly Homer and the royal psalmist David are represented with the lira da braccio.

Thus it is characteristically the famous improvisers of the ancient world and the Old Testament who accompany their songs with the lira da braccio. In the angel concerts of the Renaissance, the lira da braccio appears either in the large ensembles of the Coronation of the Virgin or in small angel groups, usually two or three, sometimes only one, in front of the throne of the Madonna in the *sacre conversazioni*, chiefly in Venetian painting. Portraits of musicians with the lira da braccio are rare. An early one attributed to Raffaellino del Garbo is in the National Gallery, Dublin. The most reliable representations are in the nearly life-size Venetian altarpieces of the Enthroned Virgin, in the numerous still lifes, neglected alike by art historians and music historians, in wood intarsias such as those in the ducal palaces of Urbino, Gubbio, and Mantua, in the choir stalls in Monte Oliveto, Verona, and in other places. Very often in pictures and reliefs there are richly decorated lire da braccio, as in Cima da Conegliano's tondo with the contest between Apollo and Pan in the Uffizi; in the Sforza Book of Hours with the Madonna and two angels playing instruments; in the Enthroned Virgin by Gaudenzio Ferrari in the Pinacoteca, Turin; and in many others. The borderline between the fantasy of the painter and the love of the builder for fanciful decoration is not easy to draw, especially since the building of instruments was by no means standardized, often because of the application of the vocabulary of ornaments from classical antiquity to the instruments.

4.3. Lira da braccio in wood intarsia.
Choir stall in Santa Maria in
Organo, Venice.

4.4. Giovanni Bellini, detail from altarpiece. San Zaccaria, Venice.

THE BOW

Because no bow has been preserved that can be accepted with certainty as a bow for a lira da braccio, we have to rely on pictorial sources. The length of the bow is so different in the pictorial representations that one can hardly establish a norm. The North Italian lira da braccio of Leonardo's time in Milan usually had a very long bow, often longer than sound box and neck together (illus. 4.3 and 4.4). Here we can draw reliable conclusions because the altarpieces (the Venetian ones by Montagna, Carpaccio, Giovanni Bellini, and farther south, by Perugino and Raphael) excel in perspective precision, and the instruments represented at the same time in wood intarsias are usually nearly life-size. Extremely long bows are found in *The Assumption of the Virgin* by Fra Antonio da Bologna in Monte Oliveto, in the reliefs of the Orpheus myth by the Paduan Andrea Riccio, and in the extremely precise engraving of Orpheus by Benedetto Montagna (illus. 4.5). Surprisingly short bows, even allowing for strong perspectival foreshortening, appear in the rendering of the angel playing a lira da braccio painted to flank Leonardo's *Madonna of the Rocks*, by Ambrogio de Predis, and in Carpaccio's *The Presentation in the Temple*, today in the Accademia, Venice (illus. 4.6).

SOCIAL STATUS AND USE BY VIRTUOSI

The musical treatises of the Renaissance that mention the lira da braccio are more concerned with technical problems, such as its accordatura, than with its central place in Renaissance culture, which is taken for granted. But occasional hints in nonmusical writings provide a sufficiently clear picture. In his discussions of Leonardo's musical interests Vasari emphasizes Leonardo's preference for the lira da braccio as that of a man who by nature had a high-flowing spirit, full of gracefulness, and who sang divinely, as an improviser, over its accompaniment.[1] Castiglione in the second book of his Cortegiano distinguishes among several forms of performance: "Beautiful music seems to be singing precisely and with good taste from the score, but much more even the singing to the viola."[2] Here he means the lira da braccio, which we find depicted in various rooms of the ducal palace of Urbino, whose social gatherings he so vividly described (illus. 4.7).

Baccio Ugolino, the famous protagonist in the first performance of Poliziano's *Orfeo* in Mantua, who was rewarded for his musicianship with the Bishop's See of Gaëta, earned the applause of Lorenzo de Medici through his singing "ad lyram." From this and many other passages appears the importance of the lira da braccio as the instrument of virtuosi and also of dilettantes. Masters of the lira da braccio performed regularly at the courts of Ferrara and Milan. According to Vasari, whom

---

1. "... che della natura aveva spirito elevatissimo a pieno di leggiadria, onde sopra quella canto divinamente all' improvviso." (*Vite*, ed. Milanesi, vol. 4, p. 18).

2. "Bella musica ... parmi il cantar bene a libro sicuramente, et con bella maniera: ma anchor molto più il cantare alla viola."

4.5. Benedetto Montagna, *Orpheus*. Engraving, Metropolitan Museum of Art
collection of photographs.

4.6. Vittore Carpaccio, *Presentation in the
Temple*, detail. Accademia, Venice.

4.7. Intarsia of lute and lira da braccio. Studiolo, Palazzo ducale, Urbino.

we quoted on p. xxiii, Leonardo was introduced to the court of Milan in 1494 and presented to the duke, who was himself a player of the lira. As a rule, reports speak of "cantare sopra" or "su la lira." This corresponds precisely to the opinion of the musical archaeologists of the Renaissance about the practice in antiquity. Zarlino, for instance, devoted a whole chapter in the fifth book of his *Istitutioni* to the ancient poets and rhapsodes and their recitation to the "lira" and "cetra."

The use of the lira da braccio without singing or recitation occurs chiefly in the pictures of angel concerts. There our instrument appears within larger instrumental groups but always as the only representative of its kind. Often it is combined with the lute and the rebec, occasionally also with recorder or cromorne. But it also appears as the only instrument in the painting, for instance, in the *sacra conversazione* of Palma Vecchio in S. Zaccaria in Venice (illus. 4.8), where one angel, sitting alone in front of the throne of the Madonna and between the flanking groups of saints, plays the lira da braccio. Nothing could be more eloquent testimony to the elevated rank of this instrument. In the *sacra conversazioni*, so prominent a subject in Venetian painting, the conversation between the saints flanking the Madonna and Child is a silent meditation. No human voice is to break the stillness—only the unearthly sound of the lira da braccio.

4.8. Palma Vecchio, *Sacra conversazione*. San Zaccaria, Venice.

4·9. Allegorical figure of *Musica* in the funeral monument for Sixtus IV, by Pollaiuolo, including a lira da braccio at the lower left.

MYTHOLOGY AND ALLEGORIES

As no other instrument of the Italian Renaissance the lira da braccio is intimately connected with the tendency to revive ancient traditions and, above all, ancient musical practice. Its name and presumed origin in antiquity, the number (seven) of its strings corresponding to the ancient lyre, the use of some open strings, and last but not least, its actual importance as an improvisation instrument in the hands of Renaissance improvisers accompanying themselves—all these facts have given it an allegorical significance that is reflected in the visual arts and in the allegorical and emblematic literature of the time. Already in the quattrocento it appears as the symbolic attribute of the great mythological poets and musicians of antiquity and of the Old Testament. In numerous paintings and sculptures it is depicted in the hands of improvisers and rhapsodes of the remote or mythical past: Apollo, Orpheus, Homer, and King David.

Also in the allegorical representations of the liberal arts, the lira da braccio is often depicted as a symbol of music, as in Pinturicchio's fresco in the appartimenti Borgia of the Vatican and in the bronze funeral monument for Sixtus IV by Pollaiuolo (illus. 4.9). In countless renderings of the contest of Apollo with Marsyas and with Pan, Apollo usually plays the lira da braccio as a symbol of the noble "mathematical" music of strings, as distinguished from the guttural and rustic sound of the various reed instruments in the hands of his musical rivals,[3] the first probably being the famous woodcuts in the first edition of the *Ovidio Metamorphoseos volgare* (Venice, 1501) (illus. 4.10). Later examples are found in paintings by Schiavone and in the

4.10. Contest between Apollo and Pan. Woodcut from *Ovidio metamorphoseos volgare*, 1501, fol. 143 r.

3. See Emanuel Winternitz, "The Curse of Pallas Athena," in *Musical Instruments and Their Symbolism in Western Art,* 2d ed. (New Haven: Yale University Press, 1979).

painting decorating a harpsichord lid in the Hermitage, attributed to Schiavone and to Correggio.[4]

In miniatures and woodcuts of the later quattrocento the royal psalmist David began to replace his harp or psaltery with the lira da braccio. Paintings and prints of the fifteenth century show him consistently with the lira da braccio (illus. 4.11).

Often the number of strings is interpreted as symbolic: the number seven alluding to the seven planets, as by Zarlino in his *Istitutioni Harmoniche* and in Lanfranco's *Scintille di Musica*. Nine strings are used in the lira da braccio played by Apollo in Raphael's fresco of the Parnassus in the Segnatura in the Vatican. This is apparently an allusion to the nine Muses, whose leader Apollo is; we may think also of the nine modes of the Greeks, mentioned by Gaudentios after 200 A.D. and in Leonardo's time by Zarlino.

Finally, as a symbol or an attribute of humanists, the lira da braccio appears in numerous book illustrations and frontispieces. The Plutarch edition (Ferrara, 1501) shows a poet or philosopher with a laurel wreath, absorbed in his writing, a lira da

4.11. King David with a large lira da braccio (lirone), 1497.

4. As for the allegorical importance of the lira da braccio in Giovanni Bellini's famous *Feast of the Gods* in the National Gallery, Washington, see Emanuel Winternitz, "A Lira da Braccio in Giovanni Bellini's 'Feast of the Gods,'" *Art Bulletin* 28 (1946).

4.12. Laureate poet with lira da braccio and bow. From *Epithome Plutarchi,* 1501.

4.14. Lute player, with lira da braccio in background. Title page of Lorenzo de' Medici, *Selve d'amore.*

4.13. Humanist with lira da braccio.

4.15. Lira da braccio player improvising.

braccio and bow suspended from a branch of a tree (illus. 4.12). Notwithstanding the small dimensions of the print, the strings and pegs are marked with the greatest precision. The treatise *De Syllabarum quantitate* of Quintianus Stoa (Pavia, 1511) includes a laurel-crowned humanist writing at his desk, flanked by his lira da braccio and bow (illus. 4.13), the strongly curved bow substantially longer than the instrument. Two instruments for improvisation are available to the musician in the frontispiece of the *Selve d'amore* by Lorenzo de' Medici, the lute and the lira da braccio with its bow (illus. 4.14). An anonymous woodcut of Leonardo's time shows a recital by a young improviser (illus. 4.15).

The fashion of the lira da braccio as an improvisation instrument declined during the second half of the sixteenth century. It was succeeded by the rise of the violin, which inherited several characteristics of the lira da braccio, such as the elegantly curved profile, some peculiarities of tuning, and the absence of frets. An oddly late illustration of the lira da braccio appears in a German musical treatise, the famous *Syntagma Musicum* by Michael Praetorius, especially in its supplement of illustrations, the *Theatrum Instrumentorum*, published after the beginning of the Thirty Years' War in Germany. While all woodcuts showing instruments are of unsurpassed exactness, the picture of the lira da braccio is inaccurate. Evidently the draftsman did not have a specimen at hand.

It was in 1892, after a long period of oblivion, that the musical world in Germany was reminded of the lira da braccio by the first publication devoted exclusively to the description and importance of this instrument. This book appeared in the southernmost corner of the Austrian monarchy, in the Balkans. It was written by an ingenious musical amateur, Alexander Hajdecki: *Die italienische Lira da Braccio. Eine kunst-historische Studie zur Geschichte der Violine* (Mostar (Herzogovina), 1892). Hajdecki was a major in the Austrian army stationed in Bosnia and evidently was inspired by his knowledge of Balkan instruments, especially the use of drone and other open strings in the folk instruments there.[5]

5. See the bibliography on the lira da braccio in my article on this instrument in *Die Musik in Geschichte und Gegenwart* 8 (1960): 935–54.

CHAPTER FIVE

The Mystery of the Skull Lyre

We have mentioned at the beginning of this book (p. xxiii) Vasari's enthusiastic report of Leonardo's arrival in Milan to improvise, that is, to sing with his own accompaniment on the "lyre," and how he with this performance was found to excel all the other musicians at the court. The instrument itself is simply described as a "*lyra,* made largely of silver, in the shape of a horse skull," certainly an unusual, bizarre instrument which could not fail to astonish the Duke and the courtiers.

A reconstruction of this silver lyre requires familiarity with substantial facts of technical and artistic importance in the culture of which Leonardo was a part, among them the fantastic as an element in Renaissance art in general. Leonardo had a penchant for fantastic shapes, from machines to magic tricks, and gave rein to this penchant during his employment at the Milanese court, where he served as an entertainer and organizer of spectacles, feasts, and other amusements. Not fantastic, but related to pictorial allegories and symbolism, was the Renaissance tradition of using human and animal skulls and bones as subjects of aesthetic appreciation and meditation. Leonardo is well known as a master in drawing skulls, apparently being attracted by their structure and complex curvature of surface with its interplay of light and shadow. His extensive anatomical research included studies in comparative anatomy, for example, the legs of different animals. He made a great number of sketches of the anatomy of the horse, including proportion studies of horse heads as a preparation for the gigantic equestrian monument planned for the court of the Castello in Milan.

Another strand in the artistic traditions leading toward Leonardo's silver lyre is the status and nature of musical performance and the unparalleled inventive freedom and individuality of the great instrument builders, who often were painters, sculptors, and musicians at the same time. Their use of strange shapes and decorations often seems confused or blurred in retrospect if we are not familiar with their esteem—sometimes archaeologically sound, sometimes naive or mistaken— for the ancient classical Greek lyre. They frequently identified the Renaissance lira da braccio, a bowed fiddle with some stopped and some open strings, with what they knew of the ancient lyre of the Greeks. Only against this complex background of heterogeneous aesthetic elements, visual and musical traditions, fashions, and stylistic tendencies can a fantastic tool such as Leonardo's horse-skull lyre be envisaged. We will try to do this by analyzing a number of examples from the visual arts, particularly because they bear more precise and reliable testimony than verbal explanations.

We may begin with one drawing by Leonardo himself. In Leonardo's notebook is a curious page (Paris, Bibliothèque Nationale MS 2037 Bib. Nat. C r)[1] showing on one half some Italian folk instruments, on the other half a bizarre composite of animal parts (illus. 5.1). Here Leonardo, for fun or to let his playful pen move freely, drew a bizarre goat skull or, rather, a composite of elements of goat anatomy and a bird beak with hair or remnants of feathers. But it is clearly a musical instrument. Three strings are fastened to the teeth at one end and to the upper projections of the jaw at the other end. The strings are not drawn with a ruler, but with a free yet miraculously sure hand; if the eye focuses closely on either end of the strings, they appear tremulous, as if they still preserved some vibration. To strengthen the illusion of a musical instrument, a great number of slightly curved frets are drawn under the strings.

This bizarre string instrument is only one burlesque form of the amusing composite contraptions, exceeding or improving nature, which abounded in Leonardo's fertile imagination. In his *Trattato della Pittura* (TP27 and TP31) he states explicitly that "painting deals with forms that can be found and such that cannot be found in nature" and that "nature is full of innumerable principles that were not translated into actual reality." In fact his unceasing observation of nature and his experiments showed Leonardo how to supplement nature with free imitations and even to improve on it by new inventions adapted to its principles.[2]

The "improvement" of nature by combining parts of various animals into monsters must have started in Leonardo's early years in Florence. If we can believe Vasari, Leonardo invented such a monster as the fitting background for a painting of his showing the head of Medusa. Vasari reports in his *Vite* that "Leonardo took lizards, newts, maggots, snakes, butterflies, locusts, bats, and other animals of that kind, out of which he composed a horrible and terrible monster of poisonous breath, issuing from a dark and broken rock, belching poison from its open throat, fire from its eyes, and smoke from its nostrils, of truly terrible and horrible aspect."

In greatest possible contrast to these monsters are Leonardo's studies of animals based on exact observations of nature, such as his proportion studies of horses and especially horse heads.

1. One of the many Leonardo notebooks, including the Codice Atlantico of the Ambrosiana, seized by Napoleon in the course of his Italian campaign and shipped to Paris, the intellectual center of the modern world. At the Vienna Congress of 1815 Canova was appointed by an art commission to supervise the restitution, but a number of Leonardo's notebooks, including Bib. Nat. 2037, were forgotten and have remained in Paris until this day.

2. See chap. 11 on musical instruments (the glissando flutes and the new key system for wind instruments) and my essay "Anatomy the Teacher," *Proceedings of the American Philosophical Society* 3, no. 4 (Aug.) 1967: 234-37. V. P. Zubov, *Leonardo da Vinci* (Cambridge: Harvard University Press, 1968), pp. 264 ff., in his perceptive chapter on *homo faber* mentions some sources of these notions of Leonardo, above all Pliny's *Natural History* published in Italian translation (Venice, 1476).

5.1. Bizarre musical instrument. Drawing by Leonardo. Bibliothèque Nationale, Paris, MS 2037 Bib. Nat. C r.

The noble form of the horse was doubly dignified for its beauty and as a status symbol for the nobleman (cavaliere). It goes without saying that Leonardo, as a horseman, draftsman, painter, sculptor, anatomist, and physiologist, was interested in the configuration and proportions of horses all his life.

What a hunting ground Florence and, later, Milan must have been for Leonardo when he was engaged in his grandiose project for the equestrian monument for Francesco Sforza. Of course he must have made comparisons among horses of different physiognomies, such as the classical horses of San Marco in Venice, the calm and dignified horse of the *Gattamelata*, and the powerful, agitated, high-stepping, almost dancing horse of the *Colleoni*. He must have been happy to examine the gait and temperament of living horses, Turkish, Arabian, Spanish, Sicilian, and Florentine, in the various stables.[3] The Sforza court was famous for the variety and quality of its horses. In Leonardo's years there, the most celebrated *giostra* (tournament) was held on January 26, 1491, in the palace of Galeazzo da Sanseverino.[4] In C 15 v, Leonardo mentions that "on this day he went to the house of Messer Galeazzo da Sanseverino to arrange the pageant for his tournament." In Windsor 12294 he refers to "the Sicilian of Messer Galeazzo"; in Windsor 12319 to "the big jennet" ("giannetto grosso"—swift horse of North African or Hispanic breed); in Forster III 88 r, Leonardo notes the locations of the stables of other horses exceptional for their necks or heads or haunches, or for their size. Leonardo's projects for large stables are found in CA 96 va and B 39 r.

Which of his many extant sketches of horses, especially of horse heads, can be related to the creation of his silver lyre in the shape of a horse skull?

There were three great works of Leonardo in which the study of the horse was essential: the *Adoration of the Magi*, the *Anghiari Battle*, and the equestrian monument for Francesco Sforza.

The *Adoration of the Magi* kept Leonardo occupied during the years 1480–82, and studies of horse heads have been reliably dated in those years.

The studies of the *Anghiari Battle* must be attributed to the later years (1503–04), that is, after his return to Florence in 1500, seven years after he had appeared for the first time in Milan with his silver lyre and created great attention by his improvisations.

More complex is the chronology of Leonardo's occupation with the grandiose plan for the colossal equestrian monument for Francesco Sforza, the father of Galeazzo Maria and Lodovico il Moro.[5] A large number of sketches can be attributed to this work, especially the many drawings for the technical feat of casting, rediscovered only recently in Madrid.

3. On the choice of horses for the equestrian monument, see the remarks by Kenneth Clark, *Leonardo da Vinci* (New York: Penguin Books, 1958), p. 88.

4. See G. B. de Toni, "Feste e Giostre in Milano ai Tempi di Leonardo," in *Per il IV Centenario della Morte di Leonardo da Vinci* (Bergamo, 1919), p. 109.

5. For the history of the equestrian monument for Frencesco Sforza, see especially the chapter "Il Cavallo" by Maria Vittoria Brugnoli in *The Unknown Leonardo* (New York: McGraw-Hill, 1974), pp. 80–108.

5.2. Horses in Leonardo's *Adoration of the Magi*. Uffizi, Florence.

But the project for the big horse goes back much earlier to Leonardo's years in Florence, when he was still connected with Verrocchio and probably when Verrocchio worked on his Colleoni monument for Venice. There is some evidence that Galeazzo Maria decided as early as 1473 to erect a bronze equestrian monument to his father, who had died in 1466, and to look in Florence, Rome, and elsewhere for a master who could do it.[6]

The famous draft of Leonardo's letter offering his services to the Duke of Milan, Lodovico Sforza, is from 1482. It includes nine detailed paragraphs describing Leonardo's experience in architecture, machinery, and offensive and defensive weapons for sea and land war; then Leonardo mentions briefly architecture in peacetime and guiding water from one place to another; then sculpture and painting are briefly referred to: "I can carry out sculpture in marble, bronze, or clay, and also I can do any painting, whatever may be done, as well as any other, be he who he may." Finally—and this is significant—he proceeds to extol with fanfare one specific project: "Again the bronze horse may be taken in hand, which is to be to the immortal glory and eternal honor of the prince, your father of happy memory and of the illustrious house of Sforza." It is hard to resist the assumption that the silver lyre in the shape of a horse skull, brought by Leonardo to the Duke of Milan, according to Vasari's report, was taken there by Leonardo to remind his future patron of how familiar he was with horse anatomy.

On this basis, then, we have to examine two groups of horse-head studies, those related to the *Adoration of the Magi* and those possibly related to the Francesco Sforza monument, with an eye to similarities with some contemporary forms of the lira da braccio.

As early as 1481 a great number of animated horses appear in the middle ground and background of Leonardo's *Adoration of the Magi*, one of them near the left border in strict frontal aspect (illus. 5.2). Perhaps related to it may be a sketch of the head of a horse, also in strictly frontal view, Windsor 12285 (illus. 5.3).[7] Another sketch, Windsor 12286, includes also proportion studies of a horse head in profile and in frontal view, with proportion marks (illus. 5.4);[8] this is similar to 12285 but is probably later. A few lines of text near the drawing relate the proportion marks and numbers to each other.

A sketch in the Institute de France (illus. 5.5) (A 62 v) shows again a horse head in profile and in frontal view, with proportion lines and letters added. On top of the page Leonardo's explanation points out that the distance from one ear to the other corresponds to the length of the ear, and that the ear should be one-fourth the length of the whole face.

6. In 1493 the model for the casting had progressed so far that it could be celebrated by the Milanese court poets as a miracle of art. See Waldemar von Seidlitz, *Leonardo da Vinci* (Vienna: Phaidon, 1935), pp. 130, 131, 460.

7. These studies are associated by Kenneth Clark with the *Adoration of the Kings* in the Uffizi, begun in March 1481. A tracing of this drawing is on p. 75, plate 39, of the Codex Huygens, Pierpont Morgan Library Codex MA1139, published by Erwin Panofsky, *The Codex Huygens and Leonardo's Art Theory* (London, 1940), p. 55, fig. 39.

8. This drawing is also freely copied on the same page of the Codex Huygens quoted above.

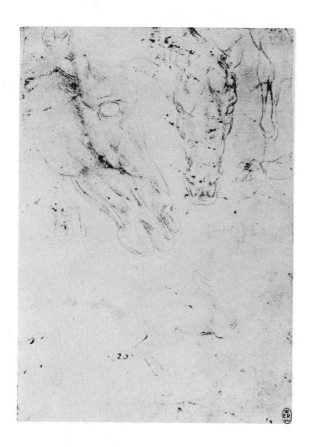

5.3. Horse heads in front view and profile. Windsor 12285.

5.4. Horse head in front and profile views, with proportion numbers. Windsor 12286.

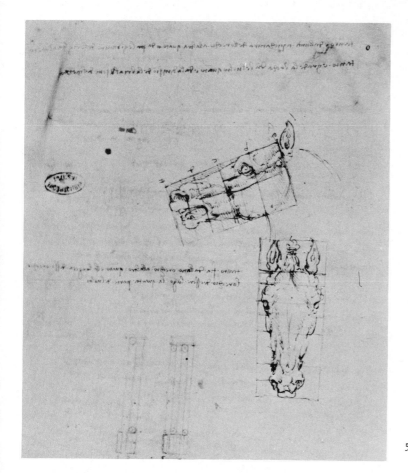

5.5. Horse head in front and profile views. Institut de France, A 62 v.

5.6. Detail from Verrocchio's Colleoni monument, Venice.

Here we must at least mention the probability that Leonardo, long before his departure for Milan in 1483, assisted Verrocchio in some way with the preparation for the Colleoni horse in Venice. The competition was announced in 1479, and in 1481 a full-sized model in wood was completed to be sent to Venice.[9] It is hard to assume that Leonardo would not have been familiar with it. For our purposes it suffices to note the almost flat plane descending from the forehead of the horse down to its nostrils, precisely the space where Leonardo could have stretched the strings over the front of the horse skull, chosen as the basic form for his silver lira da braccio (illus. 5.6).

Trying to discern patterns of historic fascination with the grotesque and fantastic as reflected in Leonardo's oeuvre, including the beauty of bones and their allegorical significance, we may distinguish: (a) the survival of medieval drolleries, especially showing animals using bones, and jawbones in particular, as musical instruments; (b) grotesque or fantastic elements in the structure, function, and ornamentation of musical instruments; and (c) archaeological fantasies with mythological or allegorical purpose, such as the Roman bucrania and the military or heraldic shields (*scudi*) in the stylized shape of horse skulls.

5.7. Page from *The Book of Hours of Jeanne d'Évreux* illustrated by Jean Pucelle. Metropolitan Museum of Art, New York.

Animal jaws made into musical instruments have a long history in burlesque and satirical art. "Musical jawbones" abound in drolleries. For instance, in the Books of Hours of the thirteenth and fourteenth centuries, composite monsters combining

9. See Günter Passavant, *Verrocchio* (London, 1969).

animal and human shapes fill the lacunae where the text leaves part of the line empty. One of the countless examples is the *Hours of Jeanne d'Évreux,* illustrated by Jean Pucelle, circa 1325, whose illustrations admit a crowd of whimsical and jocular creatures among which are fantastic compound animals such as lion-reptiles and snake-goats, dragons with monks' heads, and friars with the hind legs of beasts of prey. Illustration 5.7 shows a typical page with comical pictures. A dog watched by an astonished hare fingers a vertical flute consisting of a bone. A billy goat is disturbed by an aggressive weasel while bowing with human hands a large animal jaw; as a bow he uses a rake. It is not without irony that profane, if not devilish, creatures are permitted to invade the sacred text.[10]

Gaudenzio Ferrari's magnificent fresco of an angel concert in the flat Lombard cupola of the Santuario in Saronno contains many instruments of his time (actually a complete catalogue of existing instruments) but in addition instruments created by the painter's brush, fantastic but nevertheless acoustically feasible, and also instruments that are grotesque inventions with little basis in reality (illus. 5.8).[11] Among the latter is an instrument bowed and blown at the same time (illus. 5.9). The body is that of an elegant cittern; the strings are not marked, but in the whole fresco no strings are painted since the ceiling is too high to have them visible. The bridge is clearly depicted, and the bow with a grotesque spiral handle strikes the imaginary strings. The cittern is penetrated by a recorder whose mouthpiece is held between the angel's lips and its lower end by the left hand, which at the same time opens and closes the finger holes that are, however, too near the lower end of the tube to achieve anything like a normal scale. But in heaven much is possible, for instance, the combination of bowing and blowing in one single instrument.

Illustration 5.10 shows another of Gaudenzio's grotesque instruments, a combination of two bagpipes, or rather a double bagpipe with one blowpipe, two chanters, and two drones—a stunning contraption, grotesque in appearance but not at all fantastic in the sense of being nonfunctional; there is no violation of functional or acoustical laws.

Another bowed–blown instrument appears in Piero di Cosimo's famous cassone painting of *The Liberation of Andromeda* in the Uffizi (illus. 5.11). This painting shows two successive phases of the liberation, with Perseus appearing in both. On the right he is shown descending from the sky, in precisely the same manner as did many angels and deities on the Renaissance stage with the help of special machines, of which perhaps the most famous example is Brunelleschi's *macchina* devised for the descent of the Archangel Gabriel and eight other angels in the spectacles for the *Festa dell' Annunziata.*[12] In the center of our picture Perseus appears again, standing on the sea monster's shoulders and reaching out to deliver the mortal blow. At the left Andromeda is fainting, while the crowd averts its glance. At the right, however, we find the same crowd jubilant over her delivery and, in addition, there are two

10. See Emanuel Winternitz, "Bagpipes for the Lord," in *Metropolitan Museum Bulletin,* June 1958.

11. God the Father, in the center, welcomes the Blessed Virgin into heaven, which is filled with a magnificent profusion of angels, dancing, jubilating, praying, singing, and playing instruments.

12. See Vasari, *Vite,* ed. Milanesi, vol. 2, pp. 375 ff.

5.8. Cupola fresco in the Santuario of Saronno, by Gaudenzio Ferrari.

5.9. Angel bowing and blowing; detail of illus. 5.8.

5.10. Angel blowing a double bagpipe; detail of illus. 5.8.

exotic musicians with strange instruments (illus. 5.12). The instrument at the left, held by a kneeling youth who tunes it, looks fantastic only insofar as the sound box grotesquely imitates a swan or other bird with a long neck but is otherwise completely functional. The other instrument, played by a dark-skinned musician in exotic garb, is much more complex: it has a large sound box, with seven strings running over two bridges. The upper end of the sound box continues in what seem to be two tubes, one short and the other long, bent back to run parallel to the side of the sound box. After this bend the tube develops a bulbous extension in the shape of an animal head. Farther down, we notice five side-holes and then a round bulb like that of a platerspiel (a simple form of bagpipe well known in the Renaissance; through its bulb the tube receives air from the player's mouth by means of a short blowpipe). While the left hand of the player plucks the strings, the right hand stops the finger holes of the long tube. Curiously, the finger holes are not between the blowpipe and the mouth of the tube; thus the entire wind attachment is functional nonsense. However, as a combination of string sound with wind sound it is only one example of a whole line of such instruments that seem to fulfill an old dream of musicians: the one-man orchestra.

This painting is of special significance in the context of this book. There is strong evidence that Leonardo participated in some way in the creation of Piero's painting. The inventory of the Uffizi of 1580 mentions the painting as drawn by Leonardo and colored by Piero di Cosimo. Vasari, in his life of Piero di Cosimo, states: "Piero used to color in oil, after he had seen certain things shaded ["fiumeggiate"] and finished with that extreme care which Leonardo used when he wanted to display his art."[13] Among modern art historians Suida goes even further; he believes that Piero's painting was taken completely from a drawing by Leonardo or was even executed with his help. But there is also some indirect evidence: in my article "Musical Instruments for the Stage," I considered the Perseus–Andromeda painting as a foremost example of those paintings which are designs for scenery of planned stage plays, records for posterity of successful scenery, or at least directly inspired by such scenery.[14] There cannot be any doubt that the whole design reflects a stage design: the dragon in the center, the mountains, coulisses left and right; Perseus, represented twice, as he appears in the sky and then standing on the dragon's back; the same people shown twice, as the frightened and later the jubilant chorus.

That Piero's inventiveness was employed in stage scenery is also attested to by Vasari: "In his youth, since he had a capricious and extravagant imagination ["invenzione"] he was much employed in mascherate." Even his help with music is mentioned there. But there is also another unquestionable trace, never mentioned before, of Leonardo's hand itself in the design of the dragon. As Leonardo's countless anatomical drawings show, he was convinced that the set of shoulder muscles can operate only one set of extremities—arms or wings, but not both, as appears so

13. Ibid., vol. 4, p. 134.

14. "Musical Instruments for the Stage," in *Les Fêtes de la Renaissance*, I (Paris: Editions du Centre National de la Recherche Scientifique, 1956; reprinted as chap. 16 of *Musical Instruments and Their Symbolism in Western Art* [Norton and Faber & Faber, 1967; 2d ed., Yale University Press, 1979]).

5.11. *The Liberation of Andromeda* by Piero di Cosimo. Uffizi, Florence.

5.12. Detail of illus. 5.11.

5.13. Gaudenzio Ferrari, altarpiece. Pinacoteca, Turin.

5.14. Detail from a cassone by Bartolommeo di Giovanni. Louvre, Paris.

often in the wings of angels. This logic of anatomy, as I would briefly call it, is strictly observed by him even for fantastic creatures such as dragons. The present dragon has two pairs of fins, frontal and rear, instead of front wings and rear legs as in many drawings of other dragons. Never did he draw dragons such as Raphael did, with wings added to the two pairs of legs.

Grotesque appearance is often bestowed upon Renaissance instruments not so much through their shape but by their ornamentation. In Gaudenzio Ferrari's altarpiece in the Pinacoteca of Turin showing Mary with the Infant, one of the two accompanying angels plays a lira da braccio of very long and somewhat eccentric shape (illus. 5.13). Its front is decorated with an imaginative network of spirals, leaves, and tendrils.[15] Some of the tendrils spiral out from the side walls of the instrument into open space, a device more graceful than practical, if one considers how easily the bowing could be hampered and the angel wings hurt. The vegetal ornaments on the soundboard could also be seen by an impressionable eye as the face of a singing or shouting male, the two kidney-shaped sound holes as eyes, and the round one as the mouth.

As we mentioned before, *lira* in Leonardo's time meant not only the lira da braccio but also the ancient Greek and Roman *lyra*, familiar to artists from numerous sarcophagi and frescoes; thus, the lyra and its heavier, more complex version, the *kithara*, were often depicted by Renaissance sculptors and painters.[16]

They also occur in fantastic allegorizing shape, usually employing not animal skulls but heads, usually stag heads. Here, the antlers themselves form the lyre arms that carry the yoke to which the upper ends of the strings are attached. Moreover, the stag was the proverbial allegory of speed, including that of sound and music, in Renaissance art. One of our examples (illus. 5.14) shows a detail from a cassone by Bartolommeo di Giovanni in the Louvre, "The Wedding of Thetis and Peleus" (R. F. 1346).[17] A centaur (probably Chiron) crowned with vine leaves competes with Apollo. Apollo plays the customary guitar of the time. The centaur swings a large plectrum to strike the classical seven strings of the stag-head lyre.

Another more complex stag-head lyre is found in Filippino Lippi's *Allegory of Music* (illus. 5.15). This is a combination of utmost realism in the stag head with a pedantic and an archaeologically correct depiction of the shape of the yoke of ancient kitharas (illus. 5.16). Because Filippino could not find an appropriate spot on the stag head to attach the lower ends of the seven strings, he duplicated the yoke to form another similar crossbar. Allegorical instruments such as these two stag-head lyres

15. The widely curving-out spiral tendrils may be taken as evidence that they were thought of as being made of metal, not wood, perhaps of silver. On the use of silver in musical instruments, see also p. 72.

16. For instance, the beautiful kithara in the hands of Erato in Raphael's *Parnassus* in the Stanza della Segnatura in the Vatican. See Emanuel Winternitz, "Musical Archaeology of the Renaissance in Raphael's *Parnassus*," in *Rendiconti della Pontificia Accademia Romana di Archeologia*, XXVII, 1952–54, reprinted in *Musical Instruments*, chap. 14.

17. I want to express my thanks to Laurence Marceillac of the Louvre for the information that the painter is Bartolommeo di Giovanni, changing the earlier attribution to Piero di Cosimo.

5.15. Detail from Filippino Lippi's *Allegory of Music*. Kaiser Friedrich Museum, Berlin.

5.16. Detail of illus. 5.15.

were frequently used in stage performances and feste in the fifteenth and sixteenth centuries.[18]

So much about fantastic and allegorical instruments made of animal heads. Let us remind ourselves of Vasari's statement, which called Leonardo's instrument a "teschio" (skull), not a *testa* (head). Skulls in many forms, animal and human, pervade Renaissance art. They play a role in many religious and mythological paintings; the beauty of the shape of some skulls is admired for its own sake, and it is hardly an exaggeration if we speak of a "craniomania."

In Windsor AN. B 19058v (B41v) we find probably the most delicately shaded human skull among a number of related drawings in the Fogli d'Anatomia. The left and right halves of the skull show different aspects to the student of anatomy (illus. 5.17).

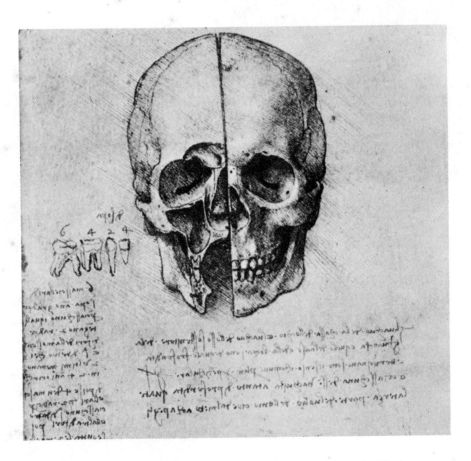

5.17. Leonardo, sketch of the two halves of a skull. Windsor AN. B 19058 v (B41v).

18. See Winternitz, "Musical Instruments for the Stage."

5.18. *Preparation for the Entombment of Christ*, Carpaccio. Dahlem Museum, Berlin.

Not intended for anatomical studies but for allegorical purposes is another skull painted as a memento mori on the back of a panel with a portrait of a youth, now in the collection of the Duke of Devonshire, Chatsworth. The skull stands in a dark niche of a wall; beneath it is the inscription "Insigne sum Ieronymi Casii." The modeling of the skull is masterly, in a sfumato comparable to that of the skull in Windsor 19058 v. The portrait of the youth is generally attributed to Boltraffio, who was mentioned as Leonardo's favorite collaborator.[19]

One of the most striking examples of skulls and bones used as symbols of the decomposition of the mortal body is found in Carpaccio's great picture in the Staatliche Gemälde-Sammlungen, Berlin-Dahlem, which I may call, differently from its customary title, *Preparations for the Entombment of Christ* (illus. 5.18).

The scenario follows precisely the words in the Bible but adds a profound comment, the contrast between the supernatural beauty of the body of Christ, sleeping, as it were, and the reign of decay around it: the new grave cut into the rock, the new door being fitted, Joseph of Arimathea, the clean linen prepared in the background, the figures of Mary, St. John, and Magdalene.[20]

The accent, however, is on the foreground: the marble table bearing the body of Christ and surrounded by a profusion of skulls and bones and other symbols of decay and putrescence. The earthquake, which rent the veil in the Temple, has also shaken the rocks and opened the graves (Matthew 28:51,52). A headless remnant of a decaying body tries with a withered hand to clutch a corner of Christ's loincloth. This profound and poetic symbolism is underlined by the fact that this cadaver has to strain itself beyond all physical possibility to reach the cloth because it is actually lying far behind the marble table (illus. 5.19).[21]

A description of the various bones would require a monograph. There are clusters and several single human skulls. Among the animal skulls we see that of a pig and, to the right of the pedestal of the table, the skull of a dog;[22] finally, in front of the stone door leading to the tomb, is a horse skull (illus. 5.20).[23]

---

19. In his chapter "The School of Leonardo da Vinci" in *Leonardo da Vinci* (Reynal & Co. [New York: 1956], pp. 315–36) Wilhelm Suida refers to the Bolognese poet Girolamo Casio, who, in an epigraph, calls Boltraffio "the only pupil of Leonardo da Vinci" and suggests that this would indicate that Boltraffio had a position of exceptional distinction among the many students of Leonardo.

20. Compare the half-naked man in deep meditation leaning against the tree with one of the protagonists in the *Meditation on the Passion* (signed by Carpaccio) in the Metropolitan Museum of Art, *Catalogue of Italian Paintings*, Venetian School.

21. This painting was the first work of art acquired by Wilhelm Bode for the Kaiser Friedrich Museum in Berlin. With justifiable pride he announced the purchase and described it with a perception not yet rivaled in more recent literature on Carpaccio. Strangely enough, he does not emphasize the allegorical significance of the skulls and bones surrounding the incorruptible flesh. However, he finds some irregularities of linear perspective in the way the dark green cloth is depicted behind Christ's body, and the unreality of the large distance between the mummified body behind the table and the edge of the cloth that the withered hand is trying to clutch, an error that, far from a blunder of the artist, underlines the victory of immortality over decay.

22. I am indebted to Marie A. Lawrence of the American Museum of Natural History for these identifications.

23. Carpaccio, who is familiar enough with the Bible to characterize Joseph as "a rich man" (Matthew 27:57) by his elegant clothing, would be at a loss to explain the presence of animal bones. The tombs shaken by the earthquake yielded only human relics (Matthew 27:51–53).

5.19. Detail of illus. 5.18.

5.20. Detail of illus. 5.18, including a horse skull.

5.21. Juxtaposition of human and animal skulls. Engraving by Battista Franco.

The fascination with skulls, human as well as animal, continued after Leonardo's time. An extreme example can be found in the engraving by Battista Franco (illus. 5.21), a Venetian painter and engraver born in 1498. It compares a large heap of animal bones, of dogs and cats to be specific,[24] with human skulls in all possible positions—intriguing to a master of perspective.

While discussing skulls in Renaissance art, we should at least mention the ancient Roman bucranio. It was customary to decorate temple friezes, especially of the Doric order, with bovine skulls, often crowned with flowers or carrying garlands. In friezes of the Ionic and the Corinthian order these skulls carry festoons of fruit and flowers attached to the horns.[25] The custom of *bucrania* was revived in Renaissance Italy with ram skulls often replacing those of the sacrificial bulls. Michelangelo adapted the ram skull to his particular decorative vocabulary.

In Donatello's time the shape was utilized for the form of shields, or scudi. A characteristic variety of scudi appears in his own works in a more or less stylized way

24. Again I credit Marie A. Lawrence of the American Museum of Natural History for the identification.

25. Illustrations of bucrania of this type can be seen in the *Encyclopedia Italiana*, vol. 8, pp. 21, 22.

5.22. St. George with a *scudo*, Donatello. Museo Nazionale, Florence.

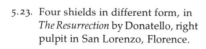

5.23. Four shields in different form, in *The Resurrection* by Donatello, right pulpit in San Lorenzo, Florence.

5.24. Donatello, *Marzocco,* with heraldic shield. Museo Nazionale, Florence.

5.25. Emblematic shields attached to the *Tree of Life,* Giorgione. Louvre, Paris.

approximating the shape of the *teschio di cavallo,* or horse skull. His statue of St. George in the Museo Nazionale, Florence (illus. 5.22) holds a long, slender shield vaguely echoing the teschio. His low relief of the Resurrection in the right pulpit in San Lorenzo, Florence, depicts four different shields near the legionnaires sleeping in front of the tomb (illus. 5.23). Two of the shields are broad and exquisitely decorated in relief and are standing on the tomb, one of them with incurving, the other with straight, outlines. The third slender *scudo,* close in outline to the teschio, is on the extreme right supporting the left elbow of one of the sleeping soldiers. The fourth large and asymmetrical one shows the heraldic sign of the scorpion. Another scudo, likewise in the Museo Nazionale, is held by the paws of a *Marzocco,* [26] the heraldic Florentine lion. It carries the traditional crest of Florence, the lily (illus. 5.24). Two emblematic shields attached to the tree of life are found in a painting by Giorgione (illus. 5.25).

In the school of Mantegna several traditional forms merge. In his *Battle of the Sea Gods* a large animal skull serves as a shield (illus. 5.26). Legionnaires carry the typical shields of horse-skull shape in triumph, as in the *Triumph of Caesar* (Hampton Court), as do Roman soldiers guarding the tomb of Christ (from the predella of the triptych in San Zeno in Verona, now in the Tours Museum). In the *Trial of St. James* (in the fresco in the Eremitani Chapel), a page leaning against the throne of the judge carries a highly decorated scudo (illus. 5.27), whose profile approximates that of a horse skull (in the Chapel of St. Andrea, Mantua), and there, where Mantegna is buried, a *putto* exhibits "Mantegna's shield" (illus. 5.28).

The many examples shown above certainly reveal the infatuation of Leonardo's time with the beauty and decorative value of the skull, human as well as animal, and its employment in many phases of the evolution of forms. Significant as these examples are, one single drawing of a teschio di cavallo from the hand of Leonardo himself would bring the problem into direct focus. And indeed, there is one such design: CA 279 va shows, on a large page together with many *lunulae,* the design for a monumental portal; two teschi, precisely outlining horse skulls, are seen decoratively suspended left and right from its entablature (illus. 5.29).

How can we reconcile the shape of a horse skull with that of a lira da braccio? Not easily, as long as we think of the lira da braccio played with fingerboard and peg disk pointing upward. But it so happens that in Lombardy and Emilia we find representations of the lira da braccio played with its head down, and in this position the shape of the instrument, diminishing in width and depth and ending in a long, thin fingerboard and with a round pegbox or peg leaf to accommodate the pegs, matches the shape of the horse skull.

In the frontal view of a horse skull (illus. 5.30)[27] we note the rather flat plane of the forehead continuing toward the mouth (a region over which the melody strings would be strung on the lira da braccio); marked projections some distance beneath

---

26. From Mars, the legendary protector of ancient Florence.

27. I would like to express my gratitude to the American Museum of Natural History, which made this photograph for me.

5.26. Animal skull used as shield in the *Battle of the Sea Gods,* School of Mantegna.

5.27. Mantegna, page with shield, in the
Trial of St. James fresco in the
Eremitani Chapel, Padua.

5.28. *Putto* with shield, Mantegna St.
Andrea, Mantua.

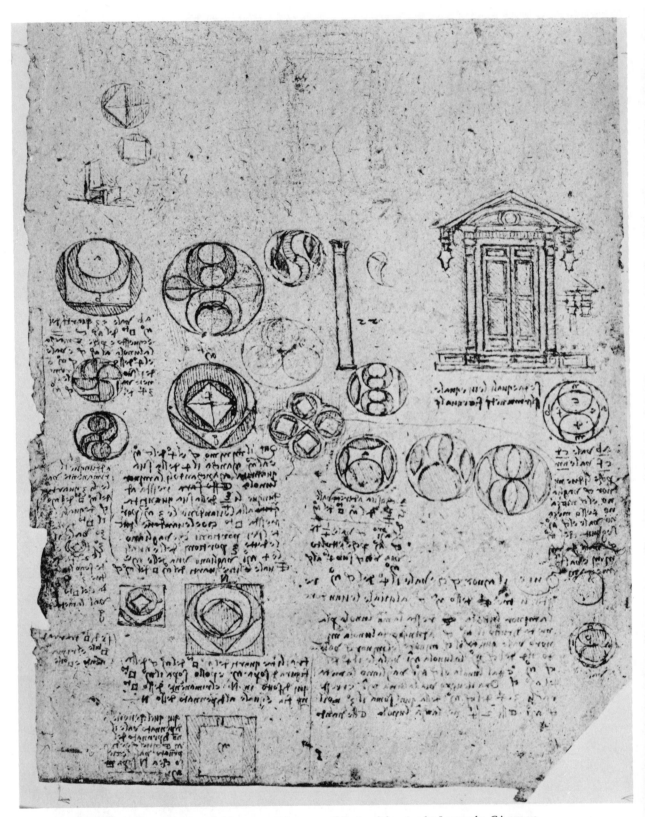

5.29. Ornamental *teschi di cavallo* suspended from a portal, in an architectural drawing by Leonardo. CA 279 va.

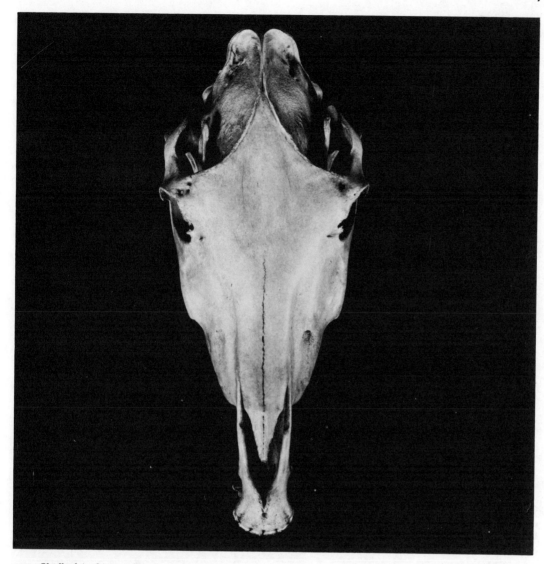

5.30. Skull of Arabian stallion in dorsal view. American Museum of Natural History, New York.

the eyes (found in the lira da braccio as the projecting corners of the side walls dividing the broad section of the soundboard from the narrower section); and the rounded termination of the jaws with the teeth (comparable to the peg boxes or peg leaves in many lire da braccio).

Ambrogio de Predis's instrument (illus. 5.31 and 5.32) is very elegant, with a round contour, smoothly incurved and without a sharp division between the broader and narrower parts of the soundboard. Also, the side walls are incurved, with the front and back of the corpus widely projecting over the side walls. The head, carrying five pegs, consists of a leaf-shaped pegbox. There are four melody strings and one open string.

The origin of this simple but elegant lira da braccio is closely interwoven with the history of Leonardo's famous *Virgin of the Rocks*, and it is not at all unlikely that

5.31. Ambrogio de Predis, angel playing a lira da braccio; to the right of Leonardo's *Virgin of the Rocks*. National Gallery, London.

5.32. Detail of illus. 5.31.

5.33. Lorenzo Costa, *Musician playing Lira da Braccio*. Louvre, Paris.

5.34. Detail of illus. 5.33.

he himself took a hand in its design.[28] It is played by the left of two musical angels, painted by Ambrogio de Predis for a sumptuous gilded wooden altarpiece, which was to accommodate Leonardo's *Virgin of the Rocks,* some carvings and reliefs, and flanking Leonardo's painting, the playing angels. The angel opposite the lira da braccio player plays a lute.[29]

The other lira da braccio of interest to us here is found in one of two mysterious paintings by Lorenzo Costa, painted for the studiolo of Isabella d'Este in the Palazzo Ducale in Mantua and now in the Louvre. Both resemble actual stage sets.[30] In one of these paintings, frequently referred to as *The Court of the Muses of Isabella d'Este,* four musicians encircle a central scene, one probably representing Orpheus enraptured and looking toward heaven; he plays a lira da braccio (illus. 5.33 and 5.34). The instrument has four melody strings and one open string. It is simpler in workmanship than the one by Ambrogio de Predis. The side walls meet the soundboard and the back without any projections. There is no gradual tapering from the wide section of the soundboard toward the fingerboard but a sudden narrowing of the wide part with the sound holes toward a narrower part, which then narrows down even more toward the neck. Thus, the outline of the body is marked by two projecting corners, exactly in the manner of a horse skull.

Finally, it may be pointed out that the horse-skull shape was occasionally given to other instruments. One is an unusual fiddle (illus. 5.35) played by one of two angels in front of the throne of the Blessed Virgin, in a *sacra conversazione* by Francia, now in the Hermitage. Here the resemblance to a horse skull appears only if we disregard the long, thin neck attached to the instrument. The other instrument is a ghironda (hurdy-gurdy) played by a boy in a group of musicians in a pastoral setting by Giulio and Domenico Campagnola (illus. 5.36 and 5.37).[31]

I have tried to put together the facts about the artistic and musical currents to which Leonardo's silver lyre owed its invention. We have, alas, no drawing or any other visual statement from Leonardo's hand to suggest its shape.[32] But because we know that it was a lira da braccio, one of the most subtle bowed instruments ever known, and served the improvisations enthusiastically acclaimed at the Sforza court, we may safely assume that it was not a jocular, fantastic, or grotesque instrument but rather the very opposite of the goat-jaw, bird-beak composite with which we introduced this chapter.

Vasari says that it is "partially of silver"; no doubt the other material used was

28. The work was commissioned by the Confraternity of the Immaculate Conception in a contract of 1483 to three painters, Leonardo and two brothers, Ambrogio and Evangelista de Predis. Its history is complicated by a dispute between the confraternity and the painters that lasted no less than 25 years and was settled only in 1508. Evangelista had died in 1491.

29. Angela Ottino della Chiesa, *The Complete Paintings of Leonardo da Vinci* (New York: Harry N. Abrams, 1967), p. 93 ff.

30. See Winternitz, "Musical Instruments for the Stage."

31. Metropolitan Museum of Art, Print Department 1925.1; Hind H.499.11.

32. Von Seidlitz (*Leonardo da Vinci,* p. 445, n. 160) mentions numerous drawings of Leonardo representing the silver lyre or related to it. Actually, not one of them has anything to do with the silver lyre.

5.35. Francia, two angels, the left one playing fiddle, from *St. Lawrence and St. Jerome*. Hermitage.

5.36. Giulio and Domenico Campagnola, group of musicians in a pastoral setting (H 499.11 Hind).

5.37. Detail of illus. 5.36.

wood. The combination of silver and wood in instruments was not infrequent at the time. We know from the correspondence of Isabella d'Este with her favorite instrument maker, Gusnasco, that silver was combined with various woods. If the sounding board was to face the audience, it was probably this most striking element that was fashioned in the shape of the front of a horse skull, from the noble brow to the soft nostrils. The softly rounded shape of the skull with its almost straight vertical axis of the forehead would offer an ideal basis for stretching bowed strings over it. We can see this flat or, rather, subtly curved front in the Colleoni horse, so familiar to Leonardo from his Verrocchio days (see illus. 5.6). This would leave the side walls and back of the corpus for wood. Perhaps the pegs and the pegbox, or at least its front, may also have been fashioned of silver for visual harmony.

Vasari gives a special reason for using silver: "accio che l'harmonia fosse con maggior tuba[33] e piu sonora di voce" [so that there would be produced a harmony of a larger tone volume and greater sonority of voice]. But he does not say whether this is his own opinion or whether he heard this reason from Giovio or another eye-witness of Leonardo's performances.

33. *Tuba,* originally meaning "trumpet," is used here as a picturesque metaphor for loudness.

CHAPTER SIX

Feste, Theater, and Other Entertainments

The last decade before the dramatic end of il Moro's reign in Milan in 1499 through the occupation by France, the imprisonment of the Duke, and the sack of Milan, was a period of almost incessant glamorous festivities. In addition to the traditional religious feasts and carnival festivities (*spassi carnevaleschi*) there were the celebrations of court and political events such as weddings, births, and conclusions of alliances. There were pageants and masques of all kinds, *giostre, tornei, carri trionfali*, and above all, *spettacoli teatrali*.[1]

What an outburst of artistic creativity if we consider the number of *feste*, the rank of the great artists participating,[2] and the artistic energy of the common people; only a trickle of art objects is left of this splendor in our museums today.

If we mention only the most famous occasions of the celebrations, we have to list:

Sept. 23, 24, 1489: jousting in Pavia offered by il Moro;

June 13, 1490: a great feast in the castle of Milan for the betrothal of Gian Galeazzo Sforza and Isabella d'Aragonia, terminating with a performance of the *Paradiso*;

---

1. A good survey of the varieties of *feste* in the quattrocento and cinquecento can be gained by the 35 pages devoted to the feste by J. Burckhardt in his monumental *Kultur der Renaissance*, pp. 355 ff. There he discusses the kinds of feste, especially processions, traditional in the Renaissance. Among the ecclesiastical ones he mentions reliquary processions, sanctifications, baptisms, weddings, funerals; among the secular events, victory celebrations, state visits (such as the welcomes accorded new ambassadors), pastoral feste, and carnivals. We should perhaps add the festa of the *Nunziata* and the traditional celebrations throughout the church calendar year of the more important saints. Burckhardt also mentions, apparently as characteristic, the institution of the traveling Florentine *festaiuoli* (organizer of feste).

2. Vasari, who in his descriptions of artists often discusses their merits as organizers of feste, also includes feste organized by contemporaries of Leonardo. He describes Brunelleschi's *ingegni del paradiso di San Felice* and his famous *Festa della Nunziata* with a detailed description of the engineering work (*machina*). La Cecca, a Florentine engineer, who in his youth was an excellent carpenter, organized the "festa di San Giovanni a processioni, apparati di feste per ciascuno quartiere," including "Cristo levato di sopra un monte, benissimo fatto di legname, da una nuvola piena di Angeli e portato in cielo [Christ carried upward from a mountain well-fashioned of wood, by a cloud filled with angels and borne to heaven]."

1490: the first performance of Poliziano's *Favola di Orfeo ed Eurydice* in Marmirolo, Mantua, the summer residence of the dukes of Mantua, closely related to Milan by family ties;

Jan. 17, 1491: the wedding of Lodovico Sforza and Beatrice d'Este, the sister of Isabella d'Este, in the chapel of the castle of Pavia, followed by a large feast in the great ballroom;

Jan. 23, 1491: the wedding of Alfonso d'Este and Anna Sforza;

Jan. 26, 1491: jousting in the palace of Galeazzo da Sanseverino, Milan;

1492: feasts for the conclusion of the alliance with the king of France and for the election of the pope;

Jan. 1493: feast for the birth of il Moro's first son, Massimiliano;

end of 1493: the wedding of the Emperor Maximilian Habsburg and Bianca Maria (sister of Gian Galeazzo);

1496: great feast with a performance of *Danaë* in the palace of Giovan Francesco Sanseverino in Milan.

The splendor and glamour of the frequent festivities, pageants, masques and masquerades, triumphal processions, jousts and tournaments, balls, and mock architecture, all this with a great variety of themes from the sacred and pagan—mythological to the satirical and jocular—can hardly be imagined today, although we have reports of guests and visitors, correspondence between the courts, letters from participants to friends, and other documents in archives. In some cases the commissions, orders, and instructions to the theaters and other workshops and cooperating artisans, as well as expense estimates and bills, provide valuable insights.

And even if verbal reports convey at least some idea of the visual splendor, how can we today evoke the mood and impact of the music that permeated all these feasts?

There is, however, a source of information that has not yet been exhausted; the feasts left an echo or a reflection in many paintings of great and lesser artists, and it is these works that could be consulted much more than heretofore to evoke the flavor.[3]

The court of the Sforzas favored lavish entertainments, and it would have been strange if a person such as Leonardo, with so many accomplishments in the visual arts and music, had not participated in many of them. As for musical performance, we have above all the word of Vasari that Leonardo as an improviser excelled all other musicians at the court, implying frequent performances there. For his organization of plays, feasts, masquerades, and processions, we have significant documents: a number of important sketches of stage settings, theatrical machinery and costumes, and the contemporary voice of Paolo Giovio, "Fuit ingenio valde, comi nitido, liberali, vultu autem longe venustissimo; et cum elegantiae omnis delitiarumque maxime theatralium mirificus inventor ao arbiter esset, ad liramque scyte caneret, cunctis per omnem aetatem principibus mire placuit."

Translated into modern Italian it is: "Aveva un' indole molto affabile, brillante, generosa, un aspetto bellissimo e poiché era giudice e mirabile inventore di ogni cosa

---

3. See Emanuel Winternitz, *Les Fêtes de la Renaissance,* I (Paris: Editions du Centre National de la Recherche Scientifique, 1956; reprinted as chap. 16 in *Musical Instruments and Their Symbolism in Western Art,* 2d ed. [New Haven: Yale University Press, 1979]).

bella, specialmente nel campo degli spettacoli teatrali, e (per di più) cantava accompagvandosi abilmente colla lira, egli fu straordinariamente caro per tutta la vita a tutti i Principi."[4]

My English translation is: "He had a very affable, brilliant and generous temperament, an extremely attractive appearance, and, since he was a connoisseur and marvelous inventor of all beautiful things, especially in the field of stage performances, and (in addition) sang masterfully to his own accompaniment on the lira, he was beloved by all princes through his whole life."

The prolific historian Paolo Giovio, born in 1543, thirty-one years after Leonardo, wrote repeatedly about Leonardo, long before Vasari. I chose the remark quoted above because of its emphasis on Leonardo's occupation with music and stage performances. Giovio, a born Comasco, possessed in Como a sumptuous palazzo, decorated with frescoes by his young friend, Giorgio Vasari. It was on this occasion that Giovio, who had established a large collection of portraits of artists and also written several biographies of artists, including a short one of Leonardo, persuaded Vasari to begin his famous *Le Vite degli Artisti.*[5]

It is interesting that Giovio referred also to Leonardo's occupation with stage performances. He credits him with much inventiveness, especially in the field of organizing stage performances ("... raro e maestro inventore d'ogni eleganza e singolarmente di dilettevoli ad teatrali spettacoli, possedendo anche la musica esercitata sula lira, in canto dolcissimo..."). But we have reliable information about his participation in only two complex stage performances (*Paradiso* and *Danaë*) and indirect evidence about his role in the performance of Poliziano's *Favola di Orfeo ed Eurydice* in Mantua. Leonardo's participation in theatrical spectacles illuminates his range of musical interests because these spectacles were permeated by music, vocal and instrumental, and could be regarded in more than one sense as forerunners of opera.[6] They also employed in leading roles improvising virtuosi who accompanied their own recitations on the lute and lira da braccio. We will focus only on the three stage events mentioned above.

On June 13, 1490 the performance of the *Paradiso* took place in the Castello Sforzesco in Milan to celebrate the wedding of Gian Galeazzo Sforza to Isabella d'Aragon. The text for the performance was written by Bernardino Bellincioni, the court poet of il Moro, a fertile and an adaptable author of poems for special occasions. Bellicioni's introduction to the *Paradiso* mentions that this title was chosen because "the performance included a paradise created with great genius by the Florentine master, Leonardo da Vinci."

Bernardo Bellincioni was born in 1452 in Florence and in his youth became a protégé of Lorenzo Magnifico. He lived for a while at the Gonzaga court in Mantua and finally, at the court of Lodovico Sforza in Milan, where, as the official court poet,

---

4. This admirably simple translation of Giovio's stilted Renaissance Latin was sent to me by Augusto Marinoni.

5. See Vasari's biography of himself in *Le opere di G. Vasari,* ed. Milanesi (1906), vol. 7, p. 682.

6. The traditional overestimation of the Camerata at the end of the fifteenth century as the birth hour of opera does not do justice to the importance of improvisation in the quattrocento.

he became a rather facile maker of adulatory and unctuous verses including many political, satirical, amorous, and facetious sonnets—not living up to the promise of his youth.

Bellincioni's text of the *Festa del Paradiso* was nothing but an occasion for Leonardo's brilliant stage machinery and showmanship. Witness the title of Bellincioni's festival poem, if poem it be, given in the first line of the text: "'Festa' or 'Rappresentazione' entitled 'PARADISO,' which was commissioned by Signor Moro in honor of the Duchess of Milan, and which was so entitled because it has been organized by the great genius and artistry of Master Lionardo Vinci, the Florentine, with all the seven revolving planets; and the planets were represented by men in the form and garb as described by the poets, and all speak in praise of the aforementioned Duchess Isabella."[7]

The performance was introduced by the sound of "pifari e tromboni" (shawms and trombones), followed by the roll of drums accompanying a Neapolitan dance in which the bride participated, and then a long line of masques conveying the wishes of the royal houses of Spain, France, Poland, Hungary, the emperor, and others. Then, after an "international" dance, the performance of the play itself began. Paradise was symbolized by a gigantic hollow hemisphere, all gilded inside, with many luminous stars and several fissures in which the seven planets were inserted in the order of their magnitude; on the rim appeared in full illumination the twelve signs of the zodiac.

There were heard "molti canti et soni molto dolci et suavi," and an angel appeared—as was customary in sacred plays (*sacre rappresentazioni*) of the Annunciation. To prepare the audience "to see great things to honor Isabella and her virtue," Jupiter sings the praise of the Duchess Isabella, "the most beautiful, lovely, graceful, and splendid woman," whereupon Apollo, who considered himself the most beautiful creature of the universe, felt slighted. But he is reprimanded by Jupiter, who now descends from the Paradise together with all the other divine representatives of the planets, takes his position on top of a mountain, and dispatches Mercury to inform Madonna Isabella that he had come here with all his retinue to bring her the three Graces and the seven Virtues. There is now great coming and going of Mercury and the Graces and the seven Nymphs, until Apollo offers the duchess and the guests a booklet with sonnets composed, of course, by Bellincioni. The Graces sing the praise of the duchess, and then the seven Virtues rise to sing and finally accompany Isabella into the bridal chamber.

Two comments may be necessary. The traffic inside the Paradise happens not on a horizontal stage but in the vertical, defeating the normal laws of gravity, and it is here that Leonardo could excel with his stage machinery.[8] Also, all the lauding and

7. "FESTA ossia rappresentazione che fece fare il Signore Lodovico in laude della Duchessa di Milano, e così chiamasi, perché vi era fabbricato con il grande ingegno ed arte di masetro Lionardo Vinci Fiorentino IL PARADISO con tutti li sette pianeti che giravano, e li pianeti erano rappresentati da uomini nella forma ed abiti che si descrivono dai poeti, e tutti parlano in Lode dela prefata Duchessa Isabella."

8. A detailed analysis of the stage machinery and its intricate engineering problems is beyond the dimensions of this book, even more so since Kate Steinitz has given many of the essential expla-

praising are to be imagined not in spoken language but as sung by choir or soli, and probably all with instrumental accompaniment, the soli, for instance, with lute or lira da braccio.

No sketches from Leonardo's hand have survived that can clearly be connected with the preparation of the stage machinery or scenery of the *Paradiso*, but we may assume that Leonardo used contrivances similar to those that we know were used in the preparation of the *Danaë* in 1496. At any rate Brunelleschi's machine to transport the Annunciation angel through the air must have been well known to him from his years in Florence.[9]

The story of Danaë is not an easy topic for dramatization. Danaë was the only child of Akrisios, King of Argos; according to an oracle of the Delphian god, he would be killed by the son of his daughter; therefore, he locked his daughter in a bronze chamber in the court of his palace. Through an aperture in the roof Jupiter approached her as golden rain. When it became clear that Danaë was pregnant, Akrisios locked her up again, to dispose of her after the child's birth; the child was Perseus. Akrisios, who had escaped to Larissa, was killed there by Perseus.

The audience was treated to the following presentation. First, instrumental music was sounded behind the scene. Then, "beautiful sky became visible, with Jupiter and the other gods, and infinite lamps for stars." Mercury descended from Olympus with an amorous message, like the Annunciation angel in well-known sacred representations, and informs Danaë, imprisoned in the tower, of the ardor of Jupiter. The latter transforms himself into gold and creates a golden rain. Next, Danaë becomes a star—one sees her ascending to heaven "to music so loud that it seems the palace would collapse"—and the nymphs, going hunting and observing the new star with its own music, beg Jupiter to explain this to them. By order of the god, she was made an immortal goddess, whereupon she herself, in midair, explains the mystery, reports the birth of Perseus, and becomes rejuvenated to console King Akrisios. Thus the cruel end of the mythical story, the murder of King Akrisios by his grandson Perseus, the child of Danaë, is replaced by an arbitrary sort of happy ending more fitting for a wedding celebration, and no one was surprised when Apollo with his lira descended to earth and sang ("canta lungamente"), ending his strophes with the praise of Il Moro.

Since 1918 the Metropolitan Museum of Art has owned a precious leaf with drawings and text that clearly refer to the play of Danaë[10] and was probably written and designed in preparation for this feast (illus. 6.1).[11]

nations in her ingenious Vinciana lecture, *Leonardo Architetto Teatrale e Organizzator di Feste*, IX Lettura Vinciana (Vinci-Biblioteca Leonardiana, 15 Apr. 1969). On a more frivolous note, it is difficult to repress the question: What could the theatrical engineering and the showmanship of a Leonardo have done to solve the perennial embarrassment of Bayreuth: the Rhine Maidens?

9. Brunelleschi defeated gravity two generations earlier with the same engineering skill when he sent his Archangel Gabriel down through the air at the Feast of the Annunciation at the Piazza S. Felice in Florence, where a complex and an enormous apparatus was constructed showing two circles with angels circling the celestial sphere, from which Gabriel flew down in an almond-shaped machine for the Annunciation.

10. *Metropolitan Museum of Art Bulletin* 13 (1918): 214.

11. Marie Herzfeld, *La Rappresentazione della "Danaë" Organizzata da Leonardo* (Raccolta Vinciana XI, 1920–22), pp. 226–28.

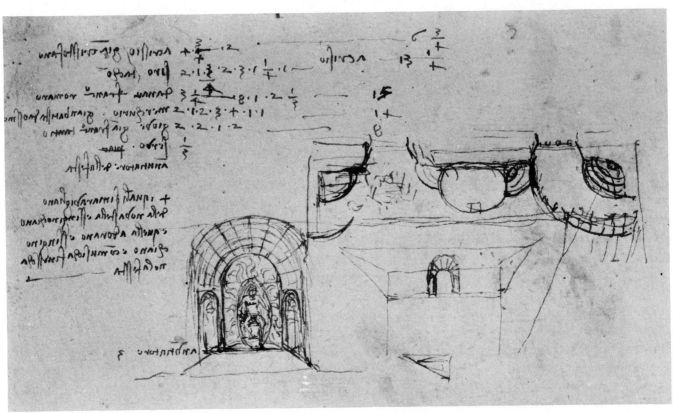

6.1. Drawings and text by Leonardo for the performance of Danaë including a niche for Pluto. Metropolitan Museum of Art, New York.

The upper part shows a list of dramatis personae. On the right are numbers and fractions of numbers, which are interpreted by Kate Steinitz as computations of the costs of the costumes for single actors.[12] The right half of the page shows the ground plan of the stage with the tower of Danaë and the terrace in the foreground, where Danaë is supposed to be when she converses with Mercury. The large window in the tower seems to repeat the architectural motif drawn in the center of the page.[13]

The niche mentioned, drawn near the middle of the page, shows in its center an enthroned deity in a mandorla surrounded by flames. This middle part is crowned by an elaborate vault and flanked by two niches, a pet motif of Leonardo, as we will see later.

The grotto or vault with side niches is reflected not only in this flaming mandorla (Metropolitan Museum of Art)[14] but also in related technical stage designs

12. Steinitz, *Leonardo Architetto*, p. 12.
13. See the detailed explanation in ibid., p. 13, and the deviating interpretation by Pedretti. For the opinion of the latter see also Steinitz, *Le Lieu Theatral a la Renaissance* (Paris, 1964), pp. 39–40.
14. Dr. Marie Herzfeld is the first scholar to point out, in *La Rappresentazione della ''Danaë,''* p. 226, the relation between the drawing by Leonardo of the flaming mandorla and his participation in the organization of the performance of *Danaë* by Baldassare Taccone in Milan. She also enumerates passages in the play related to musical accompaniment.

(Arundel 231v and Arundel 224r) and in distant areas of Leonardo's interests, that is, in church architecture (CA 37 r) and the anatomy of the human heart (Quaderni d'Anatomia II 10 r).

Arundel 263 (BM) 231 v (illus. 6.2) shows an open grotto with a person in the center between two columns that are evidently the hinges for moving the complex machinery for opening the mountain to reveal Pluto. A detailed description of the complex machinery is not necessary here because it has been worked out by Kate Steinitz in *Leonardo Architetto Teatrale e Organizzatore di Feste,* in IX Lettura Vinciana, 15 Apr. 1969. Leonardo's comments to his sketches say: "The mountain opens—Pluto appears in his residence ... as soon as the paradise of Pluto opens, there should be devils who play on pots to create infernal noises—there should be death, the Furies, Cerberus, and many naked, weeping putti; there are also fires made in various colors; dances follow." Leonardo, to remind himself, drew in miniature two of these pots, at the right edge of the page just above the last text section. Small as the sketch is, it shows clearly the characteristic shape of these noisemakers and the two sticks inserted into the membranes. Such visual memos are characteristic of Leonardo's working technique.[15]

The next sketch, Arundel 263 (BM) 224 r (illus. 6.3), shows more details of the stage construction and moving mechanism, and the mountain itself in a closed and an open state. The open mountain is symmetrically conceived, with a large vaulted central cavern and two small lateral entrances into corridors or galleries. We recall the smaller pattern in Arundel 263 (BM) 231 v.

The example from architecture, CA 37 ra, shows one of Leonardo's many sketches with sections through a polygonal church (illus. 6.4). The example from anatomy, Quaderni d'Anatomia II 10 r, shows one of Leonardo's sections through the human heart (illus. 6.5). One wonders on which of the many levels of creative consciousness such analogies of design—Leonardo may have preferred to call them *figure* or *figurazione*—take shape, designs that clearly exceed the region of merely aesthetic similarity.[16]

The delights for eye and ear devised for the entertainment of noble guests at weddings, receptions, and other public occasions are overshadowed by one single spectacle on a much higher level, a real drama and the imaginative rebirth of an ancient legend, the fateful history of Orpheus' love for Eurydice: Poliziano's great *Favola.* It most likely exerted a remarkable influence on contemporary stage performances. The precise date of the first performance of Orpheus in Marmirolo, Mantua, has been controversial for many years but it seems today that the prevailing opinion is 1490.

15. MacCurdy misunderstands and places the devils in twelve pots to resemble the mouths of hell, not a very convincing architecture for the gates of hell. He overlooks that *olle* (pots) mean very common folk instruments that produce a shrieking noise. A more detailed explanation of these *caccarelle* or Rommelpots is given in chap. 9.

16. See Emanuel Winternitz, "Anatomy the Teacher: On the Impact of Leonardo's Anatomical Research on his Musical and Other Machines," *Proceedings of the American Philosophical Society* 3, no. 4 (Aug. 1967): 234–47.

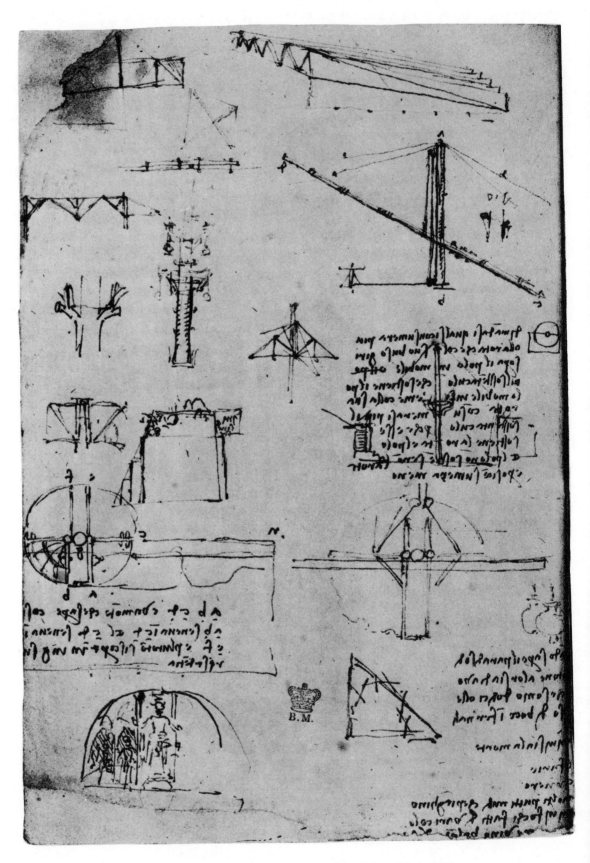

6.2. Drawings and text by Leonardo for the stage machinery for Danaë. Arundel 263 (BM) 231 v.

6.3. Leonardo: drawing with sketches for stage construction and a mountain opening and closing. Arundel 263 (BM) 224 r.

6.4. Leonardo: cross section through a polygonal church. CA 37 ra.

6.5. Leonardo: cross section of a human heart showing "vault," "nave," and "aisles."
Quaderni d'Anatomia II 10 r.

It has been said that such theatrical spectacles were paid for by the courts and served for such functions as state celebrations, and therefore had to be of a light, cheerful character. Nothing could be further from the truth, if we consider Poliziano's *Favola*. The sudden death of Eurydice, bitten by a snake, the visit to Hades, the parting forever, the fruitless argument with the Furies to be admitted the second time to Pluto; the mourning and retreat to the wilderness, the chase by the bacchantes and ensuing decapitation—in short, fear and sorrow, tears and blood—provided little to amuse a bridal couple.

Nothing is known of Leonardo's direct participation in the famous and epoch-making first performance of Poliziano's *Orfeo* in Mantua. But Leonardo must have known Poliziano from his years in Florence, and the performer of the role of Orpheus, who improvised on the lira da braccio, had been a disciple and friend of Leonardo: Atalante Migliorotti.[17]

The performance set a shining example and shows more than any other spectacle of the time the intimate interweaving of a text with vocal and instrumental music.

The music accompanying the performance of Poliziano's *Orfeo* has not come to us, mainly because much of it was improvised. Yet there is a way to assess how central a role it must have played in this drama: to list methodically the stage directions requiring music, and to focus on other musical matters woven into the text

6.6. Woodcut depicting Orpheus teaching the beasts by playing the lira da braccio. From an edition of Poliziano's *Cose vulgare*, Bologna, 1494.

17. See Vasari's remark about the arrival of Leonardo, together with Atalante, at the Milan court.

(for example, the various musical instruments mentioned) that contributed symbolically to the atmosphere. Also, it is often not the stage directions that betray the use of music but the situation itself and the dramatic context in comparison with similar contexts in the contemporary sacre rappresentazioni. For instance, at the words "Mercurio annunzia la festa" we recall the Archangel Gabriel introducing himself in sacred plays as the bearer of the divine message.

It goes without saying that in the illustrations of Poliziano's *Legenda,* Orpheus is often depicted playing the lira da braccio, as in the title page of an early edition of the *Legenda* (illus. 6.6), and is mentioned by the announcer of the play, Mercurius, as entering Hades singing ("Orfeo cantando all' inferno la tolse"). In the conversation of the three shepherds Aristo calls for the "zampogna" (bagpipes) to make Eurydice sing, and in the famous *canzona* "Udite selve, mie dolce parole" has a dialogue with his dear zampogna. Orpheus appears on the mountain top "Cantando in su la lira" (singing and accompanying himself on his lyre—no doubt the lira da braccio); his Latin verses do not fail to invoke "lyra," "cantus," and "citharam"; likewise, his lament for the death of Eurydice invokes "sconsolata lira" and the "dolce cetra" (kithara).

When "Orfeo cantando giunge all' inferno," Pluto's first words are "Chi è costui che con si dolce nota Muove l'abisso e con l'ornata cetra? [Who is it who can move with such sweet sound the black abyss with an adorned kithara?]."

I will not continue this gathering of musical allusions but will draw attention to the climax: the confrontation between Pluto and Orpheus, a confrontation between the power of dominion and the power of music, both represented by unsurpassable poetic condensation in the opposition of the fateful symbols, the sceptre and the plectrum. In the yielding words of Pluto:

I' son contento che a si dolce plettro
S' inchini la potenzia del mio scettro.

I'm satisfied that the power of my sceptre
Bows to the sweetness of your plectrum.

We turn now to the many sketches by Leonardo, who evidently served in the preparation of pageants, most from the Windsor Catalogue and one from the Madrid Notebooks. In these sketches the tailoring and structure and decoration of the fabric, and the shape of the hats and shoes, are so marked that they amount to instructions to the technicians in charge of the pageants or stage performances.

Illustration 6.7 (Windsor 12573 r) is a drawing in black chalk that shows an elderly prisoner with a short beard, in tattered garments, with shackled wrists and feet, supporting himself with a heavy stick and extending his left hand, perhaps begging.

There seems to be no doubt that the drawing was made for a masquerade costume, but the date and actual occasion are controversial. A masque in the house of Galeazzo da San Severino on June 26, 1491, has been suggested by Seidlitz and Bodmer; a masque at Amboise after 1515 by Popp.[18]

18. See the list of suggestions as to the date and occasion in the Windsor catalogue, p. 111.

6.7. Drawing by Leonardo: prisoner with shackled feet and wrists. Windsor 12573 r.

6.8. Drawing by Leonardo: youth on horseback. Windsor 12574.

6.9. Drawing by Leonardo: rider on horseback camouflaged as a bagpipe. Windsor 12585.

Illustration 6.8 (Windsor 12574) is a drawing in pen and ink over black chalk that shows a youth on horseback in an elaborate masquerade costume of a great variety of fabrics, with feathers and ribbons. He is armed with a sword and lance and wears spurs.

Seidlitz suggests the masque in the house of Galeazzo da San Severino, 1491; Müller-Walde suggests a date as early as 1475 for a joust of Giuliano de Medici. See other suggestions in the Windsor Catalogue, pp. 111, 112.

Leonardo also drew a fantastic horseback rider, Windsor 12585 (illus. 6.9). This drawing has nothing to do with the many figures suggesting rich costumes of different textiles for the workshops of pageants. It is rather a specter-like phantasm, an excursion into the realm of fairy tales, certainly as much acclaimed and laughed at by the spectators as it was uncomfortable for the actor. His body has turned into his instrument, the bagpipe; his belly into the bag, his nose into the chanter. Player and instrument are fused into one creature.[19] This drawing has often been misinterpreted.

Bernard Berenson describes the figure as a "boar-headed man on horseback, playing on a horn" (probably for a masquerade and possibly the one of Galeazzo da San Severino in January 1491).[20] Gerolamo Calvi calls the sketch an allegory;[21] Waldemar von Seidlitz describes the figure as a monster on horseback playing a

6.10. Bagpipe player backward on horseback. Woodcut by Barthel Beham. J. Muller, *Kritischer Katalog* 1958, no. 120.

19. Some allegorical bagpipes are discussed in the following chapter on acoustics.
20. *Drawings of the Florentine Painters* (New York, 1903), p. 62.
21. *Un'allegoria di Leonardo* (Milan, 1904), p. 482.

clarinet;[22] and Edmondo Solmi calls the creature a figure on horseback who sounds a reed pipe with his own nose.[23] Heinrich Bodmer identifies the monster as "omo salvatico" without further explanation.[24] Sir Kenneth Clark interprets the drawing as follows: "A masquerader seated on a horse, which is walking in profile to left. He wears a head like an elephant, with long ears like bat's wings, a curly horn like a gramophone, and a trunk, on which he is playing as if it were a flute. He also appears to have a pot belly, and a curly tail."[25] No mention is made of a bagpipe. Giuseppina Fumagalli, in a very interesting article, reviews the earlier interpretations and declares, with cogent and elaborate reasons, that our bagpipe man is one of the "omini salvatichi."[26]

A much coarser and more jocular sketch dealing with a bagpipe is found in the north: a hunchbacked bagpiper backward on his horse (illus. 6.10) in an undated woodcut by Barthel Beham.[27] Here, bagpipe and man are not magically united as by Leonardo—the instrument is realistically represented with two drone pipes.

Illustration 6.11 (Windsor 12575), a drawing in pen and ink, and wash over black chalk, shows a young man striding in a masquerade costume with fluttering sleeves, a cap with feathers, and a rich doublet. His right hand holds a lance, his left wrist is on his hip. For the date and occasion, see the many controversial suggestions in the Windsor catalogue.[28]

Illustration 6.12 (Windsor 12576) is black chalk on white paper. A youth standing with his legs apart, his left wrist on his hip, his right hand holding a palm, his bodice consisting of interlaced ribbons, the sleeves with parallel ribbons.

Illustration 6.13 (Windsor 12577) is a female figure in black chalk on white paper. Her left arm, covered with a cloak, is on her hip; her right arm is covered by a sleeve made of ribbons.

The hypnotically magic female figure in illustration 6.14 (Windsor 12581), mysterious in gesture and expression alike, is certainly not a study for costumes to be used at feasts. It has nothing of the matter-of-fact delineation of the various brocades, velvets, and ribbons to guide the tailors in the workshops. Rather, her costume is subtle and impressive with its smooth fall of drapery. However, this drawing may very well have been a study for an allegorical figure appearing on one of the processional cars in a feast, or even on the stage.[29] The little cascade of water in the left foreground, harmonizing with the only lightly suggested landscape,

22. "I disegni di Leonardo da Vinci a Windsor," *L'Arte* 14 (1911): 286.

23. "La politica di Lodovico il Moro nei simboli di Leonardo," *Scritti varii di erudizione e di critica in onore di R. Renier* (Turin, 1912), pp. 71–72.

24. *Leonardo* (Stuttgart, 1931), p. 203.

25. *Catalogue of Drawings of Leonardo da Vinci in the Collection of His Majesty the King at Windsor Castle* (New York and Cambridge, 1935), p. 99.

26. "Gli Omini Salvatichi di Leonardo," *Raccolta Vinciana* 18 (1960): 129–57.

27. Jean Muller, *Barthel Beham Kritischer Katalog* (1958), no. 120.

28. Kenneth Clark, *The Drawings of Leonardo da Vinci at Windsor Castle*, 2d ed., 1968, revised with the assistance of Carlo Pedretti, vol. 2, p. 112.

29. The Windsor Castle catalogue quotes Meller's suggestion that this figure is Matelda, Dante's guide through Purgatorio, until Beatrice appears.

6.11. Drawing by Leonardo: youth with
lance in fancy costume. Windsor
12575.

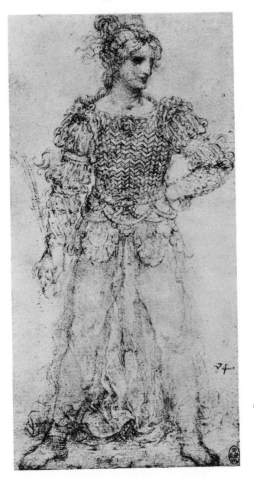

6.13. Drawing by Leonardo: female figure with cloak. Windsor 12577.

6.12. Drawing by Leonardo: youth holding a palm. Windsor 12576.

6.14. Drawing by Leonardo: allegorical figure pointing. Windsor 12581.

6.15. Drawing by Leonardo: costumed
youth with a three-tiered hat.
Madrid MS II folio 76 r.

recalls Leonardo's liking for the melody of falling water in gardens, as stated in his
notebooks as a suggestion for his garden architecture. For instance, in L 78 r he
says, ''Make a harmony with the different falls of water, as you have seen at the
fountain of Rimini.''

In Madrid MS II folio 76 r, a charming little figure is jotted down with a few
rapid strokes in the center of the page (illus. 6.15). Unfortunately the instrument
played by this youth is not recognizable. It might be the little organ shown in the
sketch to the right of his head or the viola mentioned twice in the text. In any case
he is a musician in fancy garb; his three-tiered hat,[30] short pleated tunic with square
neck, and shepherd buskins characterize him as a participant in a masquerade or
stage entertainment.

Among Leonardo's contributions to the divertissements of the court are the
rebuses, or picture-puzzles.[31] Both sides of one large leaf in Windsor Castle are

30. My colleague at the Metropolitan Museum, Dr. Olga Raggio, chairman of the Department of
European Sculpture and Decorative Arts, has kindly led my attention to the fact that similar hats occur
in the embroideries after designs by Pollaiuolo in the Museo dell' Opera del Duomo in Florence. See
Sascha Schwabacher, *Die Stickerien nach Entwürfen des Antonio Pollaiuolo in der Opera di S. Maria del Fiore
zu Florenz* (Strassburg, 1911), especially plates xix, xxxi. The designs for the biblical scenes depicted there
may also have been used for or inspired by the performances of sacred plays.

31. The first and pioneering book on this subject is Augusto Marinoni's *I Rebus di Leonardo da
Vinci, raccolti e interpretati* (Florence: Olschki, 1954), together with his essay ''Una Virtu Spirituale.'' The
illustrations following are reproduced from his book.

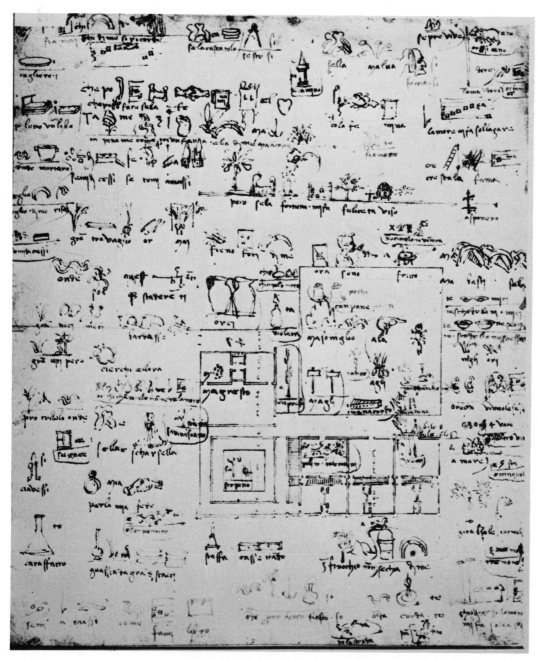

6.16. Rebus by Leonardo. Windsor 12692 v.

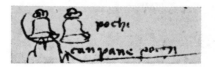

6.17, 6.18, and 6.19. Musical instruments
(viola, bells, "monacordo") used in
rebuses by Leonardo. From Augusto
Marinoni, *I Rebus di Leonardo da Vinci*,
nos. 106, 107, and 123. Windsor 12692 v.

6.20. Rebus by Leonardo. Marinoni, no.
94. Windsor 12692 v.

6.21. Rebus combining musical score
with words. Marinoni, no. 88.
Windsor 12692 v.

full of them (12692 r and 12692 v). The second (illus. 6.16) includes a number of musical instruments that must have been familiar to everyone, for example, the *viola*, the *campane* (bells), and the *manocordio*. A brief explanation may suffice to show how they are used in the puzzles:

Marinoniex. 106, p. 206 (illus. 6.17): This shows a typical lira da braccio characterized by the heart-shaped peg leaf, which at the time of Leonardo was simply called *viola*. This, together with the written addition *ta*, results in *violata*, that is, "violated" or "raped."

Marinoni ex. 107, p. 206 (illus. 6.18): After the picture of two bells is written "pochi," which results in "campane pochi" or "ne campa pochi," which, alluding to phrases or quotations such as "l'uomo non vive di pane solo" (man does not live by bread alone), may mean "bread does not suffice for life."

Marinoni ex. 123, p. 214 (illus. 6.19): The third instrument illustrated in picture puzzles is a *monocordo*, the venerable one-stringed research instrument of the Pythagoreans, which later in the form of manocordio also means the several-stringed *clavicordio*. "I 'mo n'accordo" suggests "I am in accord" or "in agreement."

Much more important for the purposes of this book are his musical examples or, rather, examples of musical notation, especially because these are the only specimens of musical writing by Leonardo that have been preserved. We have pointed out before that neither Leonardo nor any other improviser of his time wrote down his own music.

Marinoni ex. 94, p. 199 (illus. 6.20): The rebus shows from left to right the following pictures: a tree, actually a pear tree ("pero"); a saddle ("sella"); a woman with a sail ("fortuna"); a notation of two musical syllables (mi, fa); a fern ("felce"); two letters ("ta") followed by a human face ("viso"); and a black spindle ("aspo nero"). The words in parentheses above, if read in one sentence, say: "Pero se la fortuna mi fa felice tal viso asponero." (But if fortune makes me happy, this face will be shown to you.)

Marinoni ex. 88, p. 195 (illus. 6.21): This more complex rebus begins with a fishhook ("amo"), continues with five musical notes (re, mi, fa, sol, la), and ends with two written letters ("za"). Read as a sentence, the result is: "L'amore mi fa sollazar." (Loves makes me cheerful.)

At Leonardo's time in Italy the most popular method of designating the tones of the scale was not the traditional medieval Guidonian hand expressing every note by one letter but the solmization (solfeggio) that expresses every tone by a syllable: do, re, mi, fa, sol, la, si.

PART III

THE THINKER

Scientist, experimenter and
pioneer in acoustics, inventor
of new and fantastic instruments

CHAPTER SEVEN

Research on Acoustics

INTRODUCTION

Leonardo's notebooks contain many ideas about acoustics. Some are apparently derived from older authors, many are new ideas, and a large part are the result of experiments. To report on all of them in a systematic way—for instance, arranging them in a logically progressive order as if each observation corrected or improved the preceding one—would amount to a falsification because the chronology of Leonardo's various statements often is not certain.

A great number of analyses of acoustical phenomena in Leonardo's writings are in many ways related to his ideas about musical instruments. Some of his basic acoustical experiments are carried out with the help of musical instruments such as bells, pipes, and stringed instruments. Some inventions of new musical instruments are in fact intended to overcome a basic flaw of music, "la malattia della musica," the all-too-quick fading of the tone.

Considering the variety of Leonardo's observations, one also may be tempted to discuss them against the background of modern acoustics, a formidable and complex body of knowledge indeed, dealing with the origin, source, and behavior of sound, its reflection and refraction, pitch and timbre, as well as the physiology and psychology of hearing. But such fitting-in of Leonardo's remarks would serve little purpose. It should not be forgotten that the present book is not a chapter in the history of acoustics or a description of a phase in the history of science.[1] It is meant only to contribute to our knowledge about Leonardo's mind and personality, his personal way of integrating and interweaving numerous, seemingly divergent interests and curiosities, interlacing his artistic creativity with his deep-seated passion for conceiving the universe as a homogeneous organism.[2]

---

1. The reader who wants to inform himself about the status of physics in Leonardo's time may turn to Roberto Marcolongo, *Leonardo da Vinci Artista–Scienziato* (Milan: Höpli, 1950).
2. One may wonder why Leonardo's sheer incredible sharpness and rapidity of observation of phenomena do not lead him to a myopic approach; yet I believe that he is protected from this by two of his habits. One is his tendency toward using analogies as a method of research. The other is that he is

This is, then, an assessment of the problems as Leonardo saw them, and in his own words, and with his own sketches and diagrams, including the ancient sources he knew. We study the mind of Leonardo as a mirror or reflection of his own notions of the interrelated and converging laws of nature. Therefore what is needed is not a pedantic enumeration and scrutiny of Leonardo's sometimes repetitious observations within the framework of the modern theory of sound, but a selection of symptomatic ideas showing his quick mind freely leaping from one area of acoustics to another, connecting the different realms of the senses—the worlds of sound, sight, and smell—uncovering some of their hidden relations, and thus in his own way contributing to his credo of the unity and organic structure of the universe.

I have preferred to list Leonardo's statements by grouping parallel or similar ones together, including repetitious statements, commenting occasionally on inconsistencies or contradictions, and commenting more extensively on the value of some notions that stand out by their originality or unorthodox imagination, or because they throw an interesting light on other areas of sensory perception by way of analogy even if the analogy is sometimes incorrect or exaggerated.[3]

The reader will observe that in many of the explorations of the phenomenon of sound, the analysis is undertaken by comparison of sound with other phenomena, such as light, water waves, or scent. Sometimes Leonardo evidently had planned such chains of analogies before confiding his formulation to paper. At other times the analogy, or analogies, came to his mind as an afterthought. It looks as if his curious mind could not detach itself from an observation without the question: If this was true, how is it with other seemingly similar phenomena or senses or media? Do they behave according to identical rules, or at least similar or in some way comparable laws?

Apparently obsessed by the initial observation, he may overdo and exaggerate the comparison. One example of this is the drawing which consists of a whole chain of sketches that illustrate similar types of behavior of nature: light, the force of a blow, sound, magnetic force, and odor.

Because analogies permeate his writings it may be appropriate to show their scope and character by a few striking examples. I will quote three examples showing sound as a phenomenon in air compared with other phenomena occurring and fading in air, such as smell, and with phenomena in other media, such as water, and also the spread of light.

---

obviously urged to react to exciting observations by trying to create functional objects, gadgets, machines, or mechanisms that immediately embody and, as it were, crystallize his sensual experience into something functional. It is characteristic that in his study of the flight of birds, he constructed many different and elaborate flying machines long before he intensified his initial observations of flying birds by the systematic study of their many varieties and phases, and recorded these observations in countless small sketches and explanatory remarks in his precious little volume on the "Volo degli uccelli." In F 41 v, he contemplated the subject in four sections: (1) the nature and resistance of air; (2) the anatomy of the bird and its feathers; (3) the action of the feathers in the movement of flight; and (4) the behavior of tail and wings in flying with the wind.

3. Some of these ideas have been analyzed by G. Panconcelli-Calzia in his original and interesting book *Leonardo als Phonetiker* (Hamburg: Hansischer Gildenverlag Joachim Heitmann, 1943), which, however, has no bearing on music itself or on Leonardo as a musician.

1. CA 270 vc:

A programmatic statement begins with the sun as the center of our hemisphere and discusses "how there are images of its form in all the parts where it reveals itself, and you see how in all these same places, there are also the images of its radiance, and to these must also be added the image of the power of its heat; and all these powers proceed from the same source by means of radiant lines which issue from its body and end in the opaque objects *without it thereby undergoing any diminution.*"

   Later on the same page the question of diminution, that is, the diminution of the substance of the body, is tranferred to the medium of air by asking: What will the people say of musk, which always keeps a great quantity of the atmosphere charged with its odor, and which, if it be carried a thousand miles, will permeate a thousand miles with that thickness of atmosphere without any diminution of itself?[4]

2. CA 126 ra:

Here, Leonardo compares the behavior of several spreading or rebounding media or forces, such as a hammer-blow, light, sound, magnetic attraction, and smell, in a row of nine neat drawings (illus. 7.1). Three of them concern sound: the penetration of a wall; the penetration of a hole in a wall; and echo. The explanatory text on the left of each of these drawings runs as follows:

   1. figura—Come le linie, o ver razzi luminosi, non passan se non corpi diafani.
   2. figura—Come la basa [ruiv] x o, sendo allumata dal punto p, genera u[na] piramida che fini[ch] sce nel punto c, e ricausane un'altra basa in r S, e so[ss]tto sopra riceve cio che e in x o.
   3. figura—Come 'l punto e cagione della basa, e metti un vetro colorito dinanzi a ciacun lume, e vedrai la basa tinta in quello.
   4. figura—Come le linie del colpo passa ogni muro.
   5. figura—Come trovando un foro, li si causa molte linie, piu debole ciacuna che la prima.
   6. figura—La boce d'eco.
   7. figura—Come le linie della calamita e quelle del ferro si passan il muro, ma quel ch' e piu leggieri e tirato dal piu grave.
   8. figura—Sendo di pari peso, la calamita e 'l ferro si tirano a un modo.
   9. figura—L'odore fa quel medesimo che 'l colpo.

   1. How the lines, or rather the rays of light go only through transparent bodies.
   2. How the basis XO, when illuminated from p. creates a pyramid that ends at c. and results in another basis at r S, and conversely receives what is marked XO.
   3. How the point produces the base; place a colored glass before each light and you will see the base colored by it.
   4. How the lines of the blow penetrate every wall.
   5. How, when it finds a hole, it causes many lines, each weaker than the first.
   6. The voice of echo.

   4. Not the loss of substance of an aromatic body, but the mathematical rules of fading sound—or, rather, the perspective of sound—is parallelled without any verbal explanation but merely by a suggestive drawing of fragrant flowers in L 80 r (p. 126).

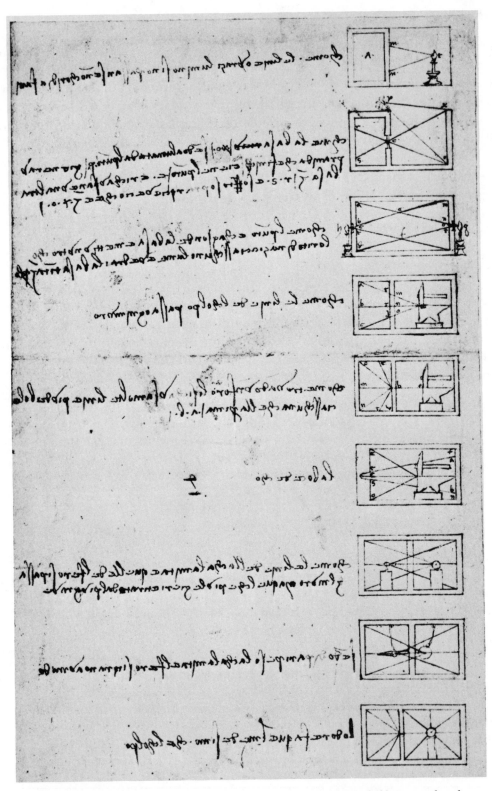

7.1. Set of 9 schematic drawings illustrating the behavior of light, the force of a blow, sound, and magnetism. Detail from CA 126 ra.

7. How the lines of a magnet and those of the iron penetrate the wall, but the lighter of the two is attracted by the heavier.

8. If of equal might, the magnet and the iron attract each other equally.

9. Smell behaves like blow.

3. A 60 r:

This very long paragraph begins with a question in the title and is followed by a comparison of two media, air and water:

> What Causes the Eddies of Water
> All the movements of the wind resemble those of the water.

Then in A 61 r the analysis of complex movements of water continues with the title:

> The Eddies at the Bottom of Water Move in an
> Opposite Direction to Those Above
> The reason of this is that, if the circles which above are large become reduced to a point as they are submerged, and then continue their movement in the direction in which it began, the water will at the bottom make a movement contrary to that above when it separates itself from its center.

Then again the imaginative leap to another medium occurs, from water to air:

> Although the sounds which traverse the *air* proceed from their sources by circular movements, nevertheless the circles which are propelled by their different motive powers meet together without any hindrance and penetrate and pass across one another, keeping always their causes as their centers. [MacCurdy, vol. 2, p. 28]
> Since, in all cases of movement, water has great conformity with *air*, I will offer it as an example of the above-mentioned proposition.

Here Leonardo neglects to say expressly that sound, unlike the circular two-dimensional eddies in water, spreads in space three dimensionally in all directions (that is, in the form of a sphere), but he returns to the analysis of water evidently for didactic or illustrative reasons: water movements, different from sound and air, are visible and therefore easier to follow.

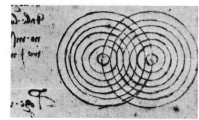

7.2. Concentric circles in water.
Detail from A 61 r.

Then Leonardo turns to a detailed description of the intersection of two concentric circles in water caused by two pebbles (illus. 7.2):

I say that, if at the same time you throw two small stones into a large lake of still water at a certain distance one from another, you will observe two distinct sets of circles form round the two points where they have struck; and as these sets of circles grow larger they come to meet together and the circles intersect one with another, always keeping as their centres the spots which were struck by the stones. The reason of this is that although some show of movement may be visible there, the water does not depart from its place because the openings made there by the stones are instantly closed; and the movement occasioned by the sudden opening and closing of the water makes a certain shaking which one would define as a quivering rather than a movement. That what I say may be more evident to you, just consider those pieces of straw which on account of their lightness float on the surface of the water and are not moved from their position by the wave that rolls beneath them as the circles widen. This disturbance of the water, therefore, being a quivering rather than a movement, the circles cannot break one another as they meet, for, as all the parts of water are of a like substance, it follows that these parts transmit the quivering from one to another without changing their place, for, as the water remains in its position, it can easily take this quivering from the parts near to it and pass it on to other parts near to it, its force meanwhile steadily decreasing until the end.[5]

It is highly characteristic that Leonardo's interest is not restricted to the phenomenon of smooth interference of the circles and their intersection. He is interested in keeping distinct two forms of movement: one, the advance and intersection of the circles; and the other, which he defines as a "quivering" (tremor) in connection with a similarly trembling but not advancing straw. It is clear to him that the individual water molecules forming the circular rings and shaking the straw cause do not participate in the actual movement of the constantly expanding circular waves; they just push their neighbor molecules, communicating the tremor to them. It is also clear that Leonardo applies per analogiam this observation of water to the explanation of the spread of sound in air as a combination of longitudinal and transversal waves (to use modern terms), anticipating much later developments in acoustical theory.[6]

The great classical treatise of Helmholtz, *Lehre von den Tonempfindungen* (Heidelberg, 1862), contains a very similar description of these phenomena. The list of contents in his book simply says: "General characteristics of wave movements; while the waves advance continuously the particles of the medium through which they advance perform periodical movements." Because Helmholtz's whole book is devoted to the exploration of invisible phenomena such as sound, he, like Leonardo, found it practical to give the illustrative comparison with the circular water waves. He emphasized that "the occurrence in the air is essentially the same as that on the water surface, the basic difference being only that sound in the ocean of air extended in space expands in all directions as in a sphere, whereas waves on the surface of water can only advance in the form of rings."

5. English translation here by Edward MacCurdy, *The Notebooks of Leonardo da Vinci* (London: Jonathan Cape, 1938), vol. 2, p. 28. For Richter's version in modern Italian (J. P. Richter, *The Literary Works of Leonardo da Vinci* [London: Oxford University Press, 1939], vol. 2, p. 232), see Appendix below.
6. To my knowledge it has not been observed how original some of Leonardo's observations in the field of acoustics have been. V. P. Zubov's highly original book, *Leonardo da Vinci* (Cambridge: Harvard University Press, 1968), examining Leonardo as a scientist, omits acoustics entirely; there are not even entries in the index on "acoustics," or subjects such as "ear," "hearing," "sound," "voice," or "echo," while Leonardo's ideas about the various meanings of harmony are discussed, pp. 258 ff.

Helmholtz does not reveal the source of the origin of his observations. Could he have read Leonardo? This is extremely improbable. The earliest systematic publication of Leonardo's codices did not begin before the end of the nineteenth century, except for *Il Trattato del Moto e Misura dell' Acqua* (Bologna, 1828).

What about a common source? One recalls Vitruvius's ten books, *De Architectura,* and the chapter on the acoustics of the theater, in which he felt obliged to deal with the problems of echo and sound in general. The work was published in Rome in 1486 and soon after in Venice and Como. There is little doubt that Leonardo had access to it.[7] He refers to Vitruvius repeatedly in his notebooks, for instance, in G 96 r concerning methods to measure distance through the revolutions of carriage wheels; the proportions of augers (L 53 r–53 v); the proportions of the limbs of adults and children (TP 108, 125, 126, 136); in one quick note (K 109 v), Leonardo reminds himself of the address of a gentleman who possesses "a Vitruvius."

Vitruvius, in chapter 3 of his book V, entitled *De theatro ejusque salubri constitutione,* deals with the acoustical requirements of theater rooms and continues:

Etiam diligenter est animadvertendum ne sit locus surdus, sed ut in eo vox quam clarissime vagari possit. Hoc vero fieri ita poterit, si locus electus fuerit, ubi non impediatur resonantia.

Then follows a sentence of lapidary brevity, forming a bridge toward a theory of the expansion of sound: "Vox autem ut spiritus fluens aeris, et actu sensibilis auditu [Now the voice is like a flowing breath of air, and is actual when perceived by the sense of hearing]." This is immediately illustrated by the comparison ("uti si") between the propagation of waves in water and of sound.[8]

7. On Leonardo's knowledge of Latin, especially in texts of science, see ibid., pp. 42, 43, and Augusto Marinoni, "Leonardo's Literary Legacy," in *The Unknown Leonardo* (New York: McGraw-Hill, 1974), pp. 67–69, 75–77.

8. *Vitruvius on Architecture,* edited from the Harleian MS 2767 and translated into English by Frank Granger (London: Heinemann; and New York: Putnam, 1931), vol. 1, pp. 266–69:

Ea movetur circulorum rutundationibus infinitis, uti si in stantem aquam lapide inmisso nascantur innumerabiles undarum circuli crescentes a centro, quam latissime possint, et vagantes, nisi angustia loci interpellaverit aut aliqua offensio, quae non patitur designationes earum undarum ad exitus pervenire. Itaque cum interpellentur offensionibus, primae redundantes insequentium disturbant designationes. Eadem ratione vox ita ad circinum efficit motiones; sed in aqua circuli planitiae in latitudine moventur, vox et in latitudine progreditur et altitudinem gradatim scandit. Igitur ut in aqua undarum designationibus, item in voce cum offensio nulla primam undam interpellaverit, non disturbat secundam nec insequentes, sed omnes sine resonantia perveniunt ad imorum et ad summorum aures. Ergo veteres architecti naturae vestigia persecuti indagationibus vocis scandentis theatrorum perfecerunt gradationes, et quaesierunt per canonicam mathematicorum et musicam rationem, ut, quaecumque vox esset in scaena, clarior et suavior ad spectatorum perveniret aures. Uti enim organa in aeneis lamminis aut corneis *echeis* ad cordarum sonitum claritatem perficiuntur, sic theatrorum per harmonicen ad augendam vocem ratiocinationes ab antiquis sunt constitutae.

It is moved along innumerable undulations of circles; as when we throw a stone into standing water. Innumerable circular undulations arise spreading from the centre as wide as possible. And they extend unless the limited space hinders, or some obstruction which does not allow the directions of the waves to reach the outlets. And so when they are interrupted by obstacles, the first waves flowing back disturb the directions of those which follow. In the same way the voice in like manner moves circle fashion. But while in water the circles move horizontally only, the voice both moves horizontally and rises vertically by stages. Therefore as is the case with the direction of the waves in water, so with the voice when no obstacle interrupts the first wave, this in turn does not disturb the second and later

The conception that the expanding circular waves on the water surface represent only a section of the sphere in which sound waves spread was clear to Vitruvius: "... in aqua circuli aqua planicie in latitudenem moventur: vox in latitudenem progreditur, & altitudinem gradatim scandit... [In water the surface rings move in breadth: sound progresses in breadth, and gradually rises in height...]."

But Leonardo's thoughts on the circular propagation of waves in water and in air exceed those of Helmholtz and Vitruvius. He introduced one more analogy in the Codice Atlantico: the parallel with light.[9]

In CA 108 va, he sums up his theory in general form: "The movements of water within water proceed like those of air within air."

Here one must relate separate statements to one another: CA 108 va, CA 9 v, and CA 347 ra.

One word at least should be said here about Leonardo's choice of expressions for various kinds of sounds. He is not entirely consistent, but in general he distinguishes expressions for sounds with definite pitch and others without. To the first group belong *voce*, *sono*, and *tono*, which could approximately be translated by "voice," "sound," and "tone." To the second group belong words such as *strepido* and *romore*, translatable, respectively, as "roar," "blast," or "boom," and "din" or "noise." A differentiation between the two seems suggested by A 52 v: *strepido* as a very loud, sudden, explosive noise, for instance, caused by large mortars (*bombarde*), while *romore* stands for a somewhat less violent, longer-lasting loud sound.

A 52 v:

Dello strepido
—iltono della bonbarda tratto verso lacqua amazera. tutti lianimali chessi troverano. inessa. acqua

The tone of the bombard directed against water kills all animals that find themselves in the water.

---

waves, but all reach the ears of the top and bottom rows without echoing. Therefore the ancient architects following nature's footsteps, traced the voice as it rose, and carried out the ascent of the theatre seats. By the rules of mathematics and the method of music, they sought to make the voices from the stage rise more clearly and sweetly to the spectator's ears. For just as organs which have bronze plates or horn sounding boards are brought to the clear sound of string instruments, so by the arrangement of theatres in accordance with the science of harmony, the ancients increased the power of the voice.

9. Leonardo has been credited with the invention of the wave theory of light, analogous to the transverse wave motion in water, by Domenico Argentieri in the chapter on Leonardo's optics, which he contributed to the volume *Leonardo da Vinci* (New York: Reynal & Co., 1956), pp. 405 ff. An analysis of his opinion would require the comparative study of the many different concepts of Leonardo of the images of all objects spread out in luminous air to be perceived by eyes, in several of the codices, especially CA 270 vc ("Every body fills all the surrounding air with its image"), and CA 345 vb. Such a study is beyond the limits of the present chapter on Leonardo's interest in acoustics. Seneca, *Natural Questions* 12.2, compares the widening circles in water directly with light: "All light is round," but omits the analogy with sound.

Del romore

—settorai uno vaseletto oaltro vasoresonate. e choverchia choncharta vitellina. bagniata epoi chesecha ficha vna chordetta incierata inquesto modo ettira chon guanto incierato di pocha pegola evldirai strano more [romore]

If you take a little vessel or another resonant receptacle and cover it with soaked calfskin, and if it is later equipped with a small waxed cord, and if you pull it with a glove coated with a little tar, it will produce a strange "romore."

This is a neat and exact description of the shrieking friction drum played traditionally at the Piedigrotta festival in Naples, and known also in the Netherlands as *Rommelpot,* in Germany as *Brummtopf* or *Waldteufel,* and in France as *Cri de la belle-mère.* About its many other omomatopoetic names, see H. Balfour, *The Friction Drum.*[10]

We also quote here part of a long and detailed description in Triv. 18 v (Tavola 44a), full of descriptions of the sensations of loud sound:

The Nature of the Effect of the Roar of the Mortar [*Bombarda*]:

The rumbling [*romore*] of the mortar is caused by the impetuous fury of the flame beaten back by the resisting air, and that quantity of the powder causes this effect because it finds itself ignited within the body of the mortar; and not perceiving itself in a place that has capacity for it to increase, nature guides it to search with fury a place suitable for its increase, and breaking or driving before it the weaker obstacle it wins its way into spacious air; and this not being capable of escaping with the speed with which it is attacked, because the fire is more volatile than the air, it follows that as the air is not equally volatile with the fire it cannot make way for it with that velocity and swiftness with which the fire assails it, and therefore it happens that there is resistance, and the resistance is the cause of a great roar and rumbling of the mortars [*grande strepido delle bombarde*].

But if the mortar were to be moved against the oncoming of an impetuous wind it would be the occasion of a greater roar [*magiore tronito*] made by reason of the greater resistance of the air against the flame, and so it would make less rumbling [*minore romore*] when moved in the line of the wind because there would then be less resistance.

In marshy places or other wide tracts of air the mortar will make a louder report [*magiore romore*] close at hand. . . ."

10. (London, 1910). For further discussion of the Rommelpot, see p. 183.

ORIGIN OF SOUND

Celestial Harmony: F 56 v

Whether the friction of the heavens makes a sound or no:

Every sound is caused by the air striking a dense body, and if it is made by two heavy bodies one with another it is by means of the air that surrounds them; and this friction wears away the bodies that are rubbed. It would follow therefore that the heavens in their friction not having air between them would not produce sound. Had however this friction really existed, in the many centuries that these heavens have revolved they would have been consumed by their own immense speed of every day. And if they made a sound it would not be able to spread, because the sound of the percussion made underneath the water is but little heard and it would be heard even less or not at all in the case of dense bodies. Further in the case of smooth bodies the friction does not create sound, and it would happen in a similar manner that there would be no sound in the contact or friction of the heavens. And if these heavens are not smooth at the contact of their friction it follows that they are full of lumps and rough, and therefore their contact is not continuous, and if this is the case the vacuum is produced, which it has been concluded does not exist in nature. We arrive therefore at the conclusion that the friction would have rubbed away the boundaries of each heaven, and in proportion as its movement is swifter towards the centre than towards the poles it would be more consumed in the centre than at the poles; and then there would not be friction any more, and the sound would cease, and the dancers would stop, except that the heavens were turning one to the east and the other to the north.[11]

CA 267 ra:

In this long passage there are drawings of models for experimentation, with proportion numbers added to them. Leonardo continues: "In these two rules, that is, of the blow and the force, one may employ the proportions which Pictagoras [sic] used in his music." Leonardo, in quoting Pythagoras, sometimes uses "Pitagora" and sometimes "Pictaghora" or "Pictagora." Could we assume that by this playful transformation of the great magician's and musician's name, Leonardo welcomed him across 2,000 years into the company of pictorial pioneers, heirs, and masters of the principles of proportion theory?

Leonardo here evidently refers to the Pythagorean doctrine of the harmony of the spheres, well known in the Italian Renaissance, above all through the "Dream of Scipio" in Cicero's *De Republica*, book VI, which through many copies, prints, and comments had become one of the most famous and influential treatises of the Renaissance.[12]

11. MacCurdy, vol. 1, p. 299.
12. On the influence of the doctrine of the harmony of the spheres on Filippino Lippi's Cappella Strozzi, see Emanuel Winternitz, "Muses & Music in a Burial Chapel: An Interpretation of Filippino Lippi's Window Wall in the Cappella Strozzi," in *Mitteilungen des Kunsthistorischen Institutes in Florenz*, vol. XI (1965) no. 4, and *Musical Instruments and Their Symbolism in Western Art*, 2d ed. (New Haven: Yale University Press, 1979).

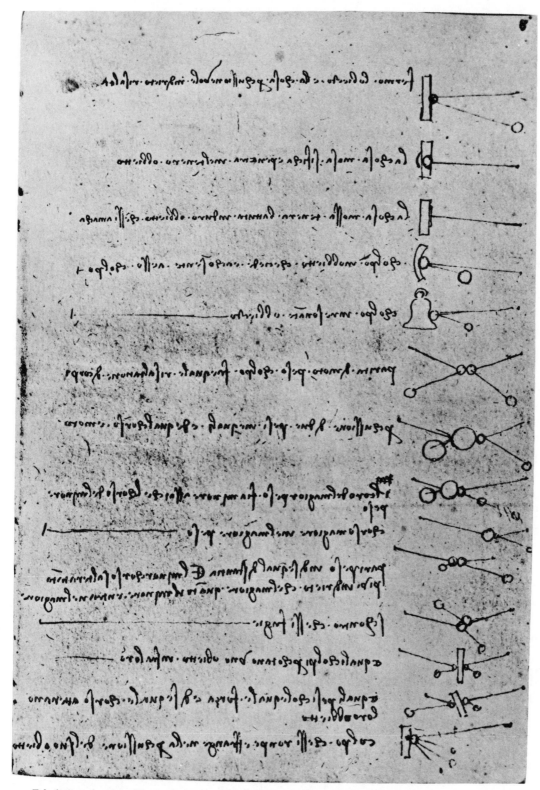

7.3. Tabulation of various blows upon materials of different hardness or softness. A 8 r.

A Blow on a Hard Resonant Object: A 8 r

In A 8 r (illus. 7.3) Leonardo makes a tabulation of various blows or percussions upon materials of different hardness or softness. He lists 14 cases, each described with a line or two of text, and to the right of each, diagrams of which the fifth from the top shows a bell hit by a ball and the angle by which the ball is deflected. Leonardo's caption to this fifth diagram reads: "cholpo in resonante obbiecto [the blow on a resounding object]."

The Time Consumed by a Blow: C 6 v

An interesting examination of the time needed by the blow to produce sound is made in C 6 v (illus. 7.4):

7.4. Sketch of a bell hit by a hammer accompanying the text. Detail from C 6 v.

Of the sound made by percussion:
However near to the ear a sound is produced, the eye would see the blow first. Reason: if we admit that the time of the blow is indivisible, that the nature of the blow does not produce without time its impact upon the body that has been struck, that no body struck can sound while the thing that has struck is touching it, and that the sound cannot travel from the struck body to the ear without time, then you must admit that the thing which strikes is separated and divided from the thing struck before this thing struck can itself produce sound; and not producing it, it cannot convey it to the ear."[13]

Duration of a Blow—Suspended and Nonsuspended Objects: Triv. 36 r (Tavola 64 a) and Triv. 43 r (Tavola 73 a)

In Triv. 36 r (Tavola 64 a) Leonardo examines the duration of a blow, the vibration of suspended and nonsuspended objects, and the question of whether the tone is in the hammer or anvil.

What is sound made by the blow?
The time in which a blow is produced is the shortest thing that can be achieved by man, and no object is so large that when suspended it would not react to a blow by an instant movement; this movement shakes the air, and the air begins to sound as soon as it touches the vibrating object. [Adapted from MacCurdy, vol. 1, p. 282]

Whether sound lies in the hammer or in the anvil:
I say that an anvil not suspended in air cannot resound; it is the hammer that resounds

13. This is a much corrected version of MacCurdy's translation (vol. 1, p. 285).

in rebounding after the blow, and if the anvil were to echo the sound made on it by every small hammer, as the bell does when every different thing which strikes it with the same depth of tone (pitch); but since you hear different notes with hammers of different sizes, it follows that the note is in the hammer and not in the anvil.

Why an object that is not suspended does not sound, and when suspended every slight contact removes the sound from it: the bell when struck makes a sudden tremor and this tremor causes it to strike the surrounding air which instantly resounds. If the bell is prevented by any slight contact (damped) it does not make the tremor or the strike, and so the air does not resound.[14] [Adapted from MacCurdy, vol. 1, p. 282]

In partial contradiction to the statement quoted above from Triv. 36 r (Tavola 64 a) is another observation in Triv. 43 r (Tavola 73 a): "The blow given on the *thick* object will keep its sound longer than on a *thin* object, and that will be of longest duration which is made upon an object that is suspended and *thin*." But Leonardo's eager mind did not pause to clarify the contradiction but hurries on to one of his beloved heuristic analogies, this time with the phenomenon of light: "The eye keeps within itself the images of luminous objects for a certain interval of time" (translation by MacCurdy [vol. 1, pp. 282–83], who uses number TR 73 r).

Dust and Tone Figures: F 61 r

As a musician, Leonardo was naturally occupied with the factors that determine musical pitch, and he experimented with vases of different shapes and apertures. Although he could not foresee its implications, another of his observations had musical importance. When he struck a table with a hammer, small heaps of dust of geometric patterns formed on its surface:

Of the local movements of movable arid [particles of dry matter], that is, dust and smaller [ones], I say that if a table is struck along diverse lines, the dust [lying] on it concentrates [or organizes] in various shapes of hills and small mountains, and this originates from . . .

The dust which divides itself into various mountains on the struck table descends from the hypotenuse of these mountains, enters under their bases and rises again around the axis of the region under the top of the mountain, and so moves with the movement of the orthogonal triangle[15]—and this originates from . . .

And when the dusty table is struck on one side, notice the manner in which the motion of the dust begins towards the creation of the mentioned mountains and in which manner the dust rises towards the mountain top.

The axis of the angle of incidence . . . ends over the corpuscles by a vertical line, by whatever aspect all around[?]—

14. See comments on CA 267 ra for an application of the musical proportions "used by *Pictagora*" to the rules of the blow and the force (p. 106). For Leonardo's deliberately peculiar Italian, see Appendix.

15. The French translation radically misunderstands Leonardo's observation by changing Leonardo's orthogonal triangle "triangolo ortogonio," a triangle with a right angle, into "triangle octogon," an octagonal triangle, although Leonardo's reference to "hypotenuse" suggested the right-angle triangle.

Describe the mountains of flexible arids [particles of dry matter], that is, the creation of the waves of sand carried by the wind and the creation of their mountains and hills as it happens in Libya, you will see an example of it on the large sand stretches of the Po and of the Ticino and other great rivers.

This is an extraordinary observation of Leonardo, as overwhelmed by the novelty of his idea, he puts it down in jerks, beginning several sentences over again and not finishing them.

It is unfortunate that of the two translations into English of this page, Richter and MacCurdy, each concentrates on a different section of Leonardo's statement. MacCurdy is interested only in the behavior of moving dust, and the experiment with a table that is covered with dust and struck, organizing the dust upon it into regular little mountains.[16] Richter, translating movable dust with "shifting deserts" and "the formation of wind-shifted waves of sand," is interested in the origin of geological formations.[17] Hereby both miss the comprehension of Leonardo's basic idea reaching from a small experiment with dust organized into geometrical figures by hammer strokes on a table, to a question of cosmogony, resulting in one of the most striking among his many analogies. One could entitle it: "A little home experiment for exploring the creation of the Universe."

Leonardo's discovery must have had special significance for him since it constituted an easily observable correspondence between the auditory and the visual realms.

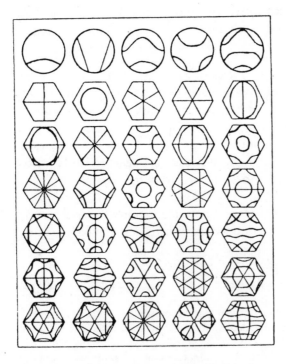

7.5. *Klangfiguren* from Chladni.

16. MacCurdy, vol. 1, p. 559.
17. Richter, vol. 2, p. 207.

It is not generally known that this experimentation with dust on a struck table anticipated by three hundred years a discovery by the famous physicist and creator of experimental acoustics, Ernst Florens Friedrich Chladni. Chladni was born in 1756 in Wittenberg and died in 1827 in Breslau. Famous for his treatise on acoustics, in his *Entdeckungen über die Theorie des Klanges* (1787) he described the discovery of "Klangfiguren" (tone figures): sand distributed on the surface of flexible plates forms into geometrical figures if the plate is hit or set into vibration by a fiddle bow (illus. 7.5).

Spirits Have No Voice: B 4 v

At times Leonardo's meditations on sound tempt him to enter surrealistic, if not magical, territories: If corporeal things can exert blows and therefore produce sounds, how can disembodied or spectral spirits communicate?

In B 4 v, Leonardo states:

There can be no voice where there is no movement or no percussion of air; one cannot have percussion of the air when there is no instrument [tool]; but an instrument cannot be incorporeal. Therefore, a spirit cannot have either voice or form or force; if it assumes a [material] body, it will not be capable of penetrating or entering where the doors are locked. [18]

PITCH

Entries in many notebooks made at different times show that Leonardo made many experiments to study the effect of various factors upon pitch. Putting them together, one admires the encyclopedic intention:
  a. effect of size or volume of the vibrating body
  b. effect of size of vibrating wings
  c. effect of length and width of pipes
  d. effect of shape of vessel
  e. effect of speed of air stream
The contraction of trachea rings belongs to the physiology of voice production.

a. Effect of size or volume of the vibrating body: Forster III 5 r

If you make two bells of the same proportion but one of the same weight but double size, the bigger one will be twice as low in pitch.

18. In general, Leonardo's opinion of the corporeality of spirits can perhaps best be seen in Windsor AN. B 19048r (B31r) and the comments to these statements in Zubov, *Leonardo da Vinci*, p. 96.

b. Effect of size of vibrating wings: Windsor AN. B. 19032 v (B 15 v)

The sound made by flies originates in their wings and you will see this by cutting them a little or, even better, by smearing them a little with honey in such a way as not entirely to prevent them from flying, and you will see that the sound made by the movement of the wings will become hoarse and the pitch will change from high to deep in proportion to the diminution of the free use of the wings. [MacCurdy, vol. 1, p. 288]

c. Effect of the length of pipes: Quaderni d'Anatomia IV 10 r

You should describe and illustrate how the varying, modulating, and articulating of the singing voice is a simple function of the rings of the trachea,[19] which are moved by the reversive nerves. In this the tongue is not used.

And this remains proved by what I have proved before, that the pipes of the organ do not become lower or higher in pitch by changing the fistula (that is, the place where the voice is produced) in making it wider or narrower, but only by the change of the pipe itself in making it wider or narrower or longer or shorter, as one sees in the extension or retraction of the trombone ["astensione o ractractione della tronba torta"].

MacCurdy's translation (vol. 1, p. 184), "expansion or compression of the winding trumpet," is misleading. Leonardo clearly means a slide instrument of which part of the tubing can be extended and retracted. Likewise, the word *winding* is misleading: Leonardo meant by *torta* not large, round coils as in the baroque hunting horn but small coils that permit folding back into parallel tubes to use telescopic sliding. Since I could not use a literal translation such as "slide trumpet" [the slide trumpet did not exist in Leonardo's time], I used "trombone," the familiar sliding instrument of his day.[20]

Resuming the quotation of Leonardo's text:

Furthermore, in a pipe unchangeable in width and length, the sound is varied by introducing the air with more or less force, and this change happens not in the objects which are struck with major or minor impact, as one perceives with the bells hit by smallest or biggest beaters, and the same happens with guns [*artelerie*] similar in width and different in length; but here the shortest makes a louder and lower noise than the longer one, and on this I will not linger since I have treated this in my book on musical instruments ["nel libro dellj strumenti armonjcj ne ho trattato assai chopiosamente"].[21]

d. Effect of the shape of the vessel: L 63 r

Why will the sounding vessel with a smaller mouth have in its percussion a much deeper and lower sound than with a wider mouth? [translation by the author].

19. Here Leonardo, who was not familiar with the vocal cords, is apparently influenced by his profound knowledge of wind instruments. See entry *e* below.

20. The slide trumpet (*tromba da tirarsi*) was not invented before the eighteenth century; the principle of the slide in the trombone can be traced back as far as the fifteenth century. See Adam Carse, *Musical Wind Instruments* (London, 1939), pp. 236 ff., 251.

21. For a discussion of the book mentioned here, see the preface, above.

[Perchè il vaso sonoro di minor bocca arà [probably "avra"] nella sua percussione molta più grave e più bassa voce colla sua bocca stretta che essendo larga.]

e. Effect of speed of air stream: E 4 v

Why the swift wind passing through a reed makes a high sound.

The wind passing through the very same reed will make a sound so much lower or higher in proportion to its slowness or swiftness. And this is seen in the changes of sounds made by trumpets or horns without fingerholes and also in the winds which with their sound penetrate the chinks of doors or windows. This sound originates in the air where the sound emerging from the instrument fills the space and proceeds to spread more or less according to the degree by which the air is pushed by a greater or lesser force. One can prove this. [Adapted from MacCurdy, vol. 1, p. 285. The last two sentences are freely translated to make sense in English.]

PROPAGATION OF SOUND

Quaderni d'Anatomia III 12 v

I have provided (p. 101) a description of Leonardo's analysis of the intersection of two circles in the water caused by the impact of two pebbles (in A 61 r). An application of this experience is found in the behavior of water in Quaderni d'Anatomia III 12 v, which shows a simple but ingenious contraption for testing the expansion of fragments of circular water waves as a model for the behavior of sound waves (illus. 7.6).

Go into a barque and construct the enclosure [outside the boat in the water] m, n, o, p, and put therein two pieces of board, s, r, t, r; then cause the percussion "a" and see whether the broken wave with its segment reaches up to "b, c." And this experiment with the wave cut by the wave which is cut off from the [normal, full] circular wave [see "a"] will make you understand the wave of air passing through a hole through which passes the human voice enclosed in a box, as I have heard at Campi of somebody who was locked up in a keg open only at the vent.

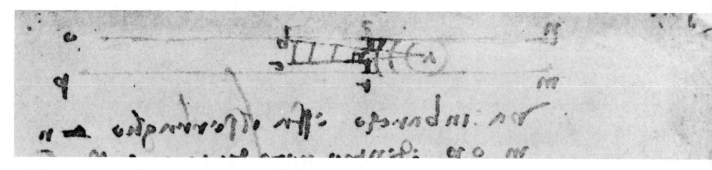

7.6. Diagram of a contraption for testing the expansion of fragments of circular water waves as a model for the behavior of sound waves. Quaderni d'Anatomia III 12 v.

It is tempting to compare this sketch of Leonardo's with the famous "Young's diagram" published in 1801 by the physicist Thomas Young (illus. 7.7), which shows the behavior of concentric light waves passing through an aperture and diverging there.

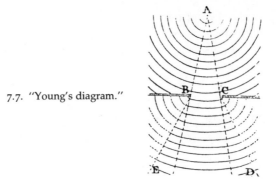

7.7. "Young's diagram."

CA 199 vb

The spread of sound, and especially of the human voice, is explored in CA 199 vb (illus. 7.8):

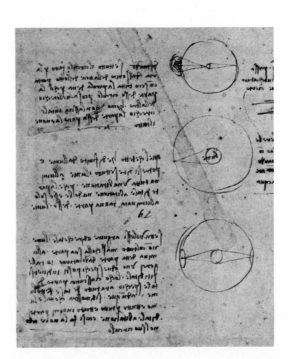

7.8. Three diagrams accompanying the discussion of the spread of sound. Detail, CA 199 vb.

Whether the whole circle formed by the *sound* of the human voice carries with it the whole word spoken because part of the circle striking another man's ear does not leave in that ear a part of the word but the whole.

What we have said is clarified by light, and you would be able to say that if the light as a whole illuminates the whole of the room because a part of this room would not be illuminated by only part of this light.

If you wish to argue and to say that this light illuminates the room not as a whole but only with its part, then I would explain that with one or two mirrors placed in different locations in the room, each part of the mirror will have in it the whole of the illumination mentioned; thus this shows that the light is all in all and also all in each part of the room; and this is also the case with the voice in its circle. [MacCurdy, vol. 1, p. 279]

B 6 r

The spread of sound, not in air but in another medium, water, is treated in B 6 r:

If you cause your ship to stop, and place the head of a long tube in water, and place the other extremity to your ear, you will hear ships at a great distance from you.

You can also do the same thing by placing the head of a tube upon the ground, and you will then hear anyone passing at a distance from you. [MacCurdy, vol. 1, p. 284]

REFRACTION OF SOUND: ECHO

Leonardo's thoughts on the phenomenon of refraction of sound present us with a dilemma. Several longer statements each combine many observations, for instance, on the geometric implications of refraction such as the angle of rebounding, the speed of echo, the effect of the various shapes of the wall causing the rebound, and others. To split these complex descriptions and to recombine their content into lists of the various special problems would rob them of their freshness and repress the élan so characteristic of Leonardo's panoramic curiosity and impatient energy. Thus, we will quote some of them unmutilated and then turn to examples of his discussions of single problems in coherent groups.

CA 77 vb

CA 77 vb (illus. 7.9) gives a description of unsurpassed conciseness, with hardly a superfluous word in the Italian text (see Appendix), of the conduct of the sound of echo in its varieties including even a case in which the ear is deceived about the actual origin of the echo.

The sound of the echo is continuous or discontinuous, single or accompanied, of brief or long duration, of finite or infinite tone, immediate or from far.

It is continuous when the surface where the echo is generated is uniformly curved. The sound of the echo is discontinuous when the place where it is generated is irregular or interrupted. It is single when it is generated in one spot only. It is accompanied when it is generated in several spots. It is brief or long when it circles or zig-zags in a struck bell, or in a cistern or other hollow place, or in clouds in which the sound holds back in degrees of space or of time, always regularly growing fainter and behaving like a circular, expanding wave in the ocean.

Often one perceives the sound not from the place where it actually originates, but from a phantom ["simulacro"]; such a thing happened at Ghiera d'Adda when a fire that took the town produced in the air twelve phantom apparitions of sound ["toni"] in twelve clouds, and one could not perceive the cause. [Adapted from MacCurdy, vol. 1, p. 279]

7.9. "The Voice of the Echo." Detail, CA 77 vb.

7.10. Creating a chain of echoes.
Detail, B 90 v.

7.11. Rebounding sound deceiving
the ear as to its origin. C 24 r.

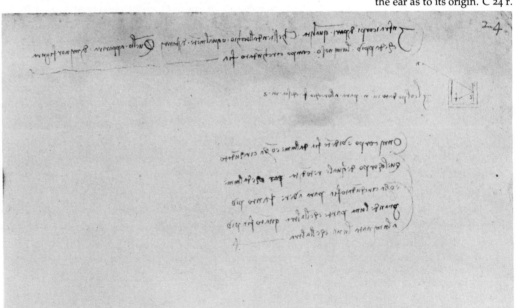

B 90 v (Illus. 7.10)

The sound emanating from the man and rebounding from the wall will escape upward. If there will be a ledge above this wall with a right angle, the surface above will send the voice back toward its origin.

How one could lead the sound of the echo, whatever you may say, so that it will be repeated to you in many voices.

150 braccia from one wall to the other. The voice which issues from the horn takes shape at the opposite wall and rebounds from there to the first, as a ball that leaps between two walls, which diminishes its leaps and therefore diminishes the sound itself. [Adapted from MacCurdy, vol. 1, p. 284]

[The sketch refers only to the last paragraph.]

To study and explain the functioning and phenomenon of echo, Leonardo constructs with his pen a contraption consisting of two opposite stairs. The left has five, the right four steps; each step is covered by an overhanging ledge to catch the sound beneath it and prevent it from radiating upward. The effect is a chain of echoes. If the horn player sitting at the foot of the right stairs sends the sound nearly horizontally toward the opposite stairs, directing it at the point beneath the third step, the sound bounces back toward the point beneath the projecting ledge of the second step (from the top) and from there again toward the corresponding point of the opposite stairs, and so forth.

C 24 r

Leonardo often indulges in analogies between deceptive sensations received by the eye and by the ear. In the notes shown in illustration 7.11, chiefly on visual matters, there is an insert in smaller handwriting concerning an acoustical problem. He wrote all the notes, as he so often did, from right to left. It may be that the remark on echo with the small diagram was inserted later when the analogy occurred to Leonardo (see Appendix for Leonardo's Italian).

Among bodies of similar kind and equally distant from the eye, that one which appears of smaller shape is the one that is surrounded by a field of great luminosity.

The stroke delivered at *"n"* appears to the ear, *"f,"* as [if] delivered in *"s."*

Every visible body is surrounded by light and shade. A body of uniform roundness which is surrounded by light and shade appears to have one of its regions larger than another if it is more strongly illuminated.

C 5 v (illus. 7.12)

Sound

If the sound is in *"m"* and the listener in *"n,"* the sound will be believed to be in *"s"* if the court is enclosed at least on 3 sides against the listener.

[Voce

Se la voce fia in *"m,"* e'l uditore d'essa sia in *"n"* essa voce liparira in *"s"* se'l chortile sara serato ilmeno da 3 bande diveso esso ulditore.]

7.12. Ear of the listener deceived by a rebounded sound. Detail, C 5 v.

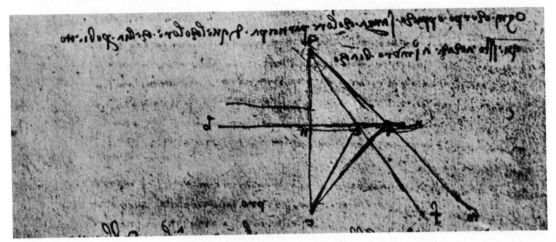

7.13. Reflection of an object by a mirror comparable to the rebounding of sound by a wall. Detail, A 19 v.

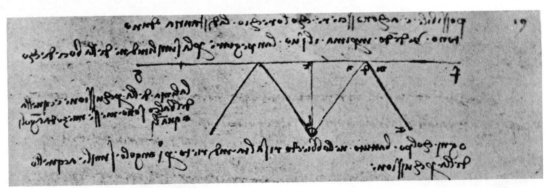

7.14. Explanation of the rebounding of a ball and of the human voice from a wall at certain angles. Detail, A 19 r.

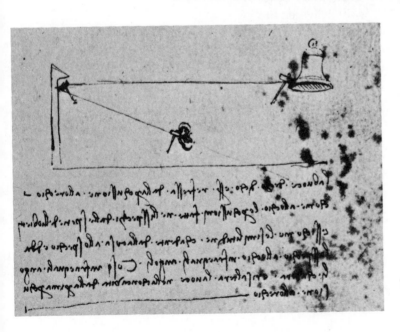

7.15. Diagram of the impact of the sound of a bell toward a wall and reflected from there to the ear. C 16 r.

A 19 v, A 19 r, and C 16 r

Among the observations of and experiments with echo, analogies between seeing and hearing again play a great role.

One tempting although not quite exact comparison is stated in A 19 v. To avoid translating literally Leonardo's rather long-winded and repetitious presentation, it may be simply stated that the comparison is between the reflection of an object by a mirror and the rebounding of sound by a wall, together with an examination of the angles by which light and sound are refracted.

In the diagram accompanying the text (illus. 7.13), *a-b* means the mirror. Just as *c* sees all parts of the mirror, so all parts of the mirror see *c*; therefore *c* is wholly in all of the mirror because it is in all its parts; but it is also wholly in all parts because it can be seen from that many different parts according to the different locations of the observer. If an object, *c*, is seen at point *n* on line *a-b*, it also seems to be inside in the same measure that it is outside; one will therefore see *c* in *d*; if the observer stands at *f* and looks at *d*, he sees it in a straight line at point *e* of the mirror; if he stands at *m*, he will see the object *d* at *t*.

Let us take as an example the sun, which, if you walk along the bank of a river and see the sun mirrored in it for so long as you walk along the bank of this river, it will seem that the sun walks with you and this is because the sun is all in the whole, and all in the part. [MacCurdy, vol. 1, p. 283]

These explanations of refraction by Leonardo have to be considered together with his statements in A 19 r (illus. 7.14) and C 16 r (illus. 7.15).

A 19 r: The line of the impact and its response are between equal angles.
Each impact inflicted upon the object leaps back in an angle similar to that of the impact. The proposition appears clearly; in effect, if you hit a wall with a ball it will leap back by an angle similar to that of the impact, that is, if the ball *b* is thrown at *c* it turns back on the line *c-b* because it is forced to leave the wall *f-g* at equal angles [*sic*]; and if you throw it on the line *b-d* it will turn back along the line *d-e*, and so the line of the impact and the line of the leap back form an angle with the wall *f-g* located between the two equal angles as it appears between *m-n*. Therefore if one stays in *b* and shouts, the voice is wholly in the whole and throughout the whole length of the line *f-g*; thus the one standing as I have said in *b* and shouting will believe to hear his voice in *c* and that it returns to his ear along the line *c-b*, and at the same time to somebody who find himself in *e* it will appear that he hears the voice *b* in the place *d* and coming over the line *d-e*.

C 16 r: The voice of the echo, I say, is reflected from the percussion toward the ear, just as percussions[22] made upon the mirrors by all kinds of objects are reflected to the eye; and as the image falls from the object upon the mirror, and from there upon the eye by equal angles, so sound will fall and bounce back from the original concussion to the concavity[23] and to the ear.

22. Leonardo uses *percussione* here in a wider sense, which could perhaps be translated by "impact," a term applicable to the visual field as well as to the audible.
23. MacCurdy translates as "within the hollow"; see the small projecting edge on top of the wall in the illustration.

RESONANCE

The problem of resonance is touched upon by Leonardo in two passages:

MS 2037 Bib. Nat. 1 r: (illus. 7.16)

If you wish to find out where a mine runs, set a drum over all the places where you suspect the mine is being made and on this drum set a pair of dice, and when you are near the place where the mining is, the dice will jump up a little on the drum through the blow given underground in digging out the earth. [Richter, vol. 2, p. 229]

A 22 v[24]

A stroke on a bell will cause a response and move somewhat another bell similar to the first one, and the string of a lute when played will cause a response and move another string of similar sound[25] in another lute, and this you will see if you place a straw on the string similar to the one that is played.

To Leonardo, the virtuoso on the lira da braccio, the phenomenon of resonance (or sympathetic vibration) must have been very familiar because of the open strings on his instrument.

VOLUME AND FADING OF SOUND

Triv. 7 v

It may be helpful to begin a presentation of Leonardo's thoughts on the volume of sound and fading with his significant observation, in Triv. 7 v (Tavola 12a), that small and large sounds are not simply small or large but have to be judged with respect to the distance they have traveled:

I ask whether a small sound from near can seem as loud as one large sound from far. [translation by the author]

Domando . sel romore picholo . dapresso . po . parere . grande quanto . vno . grande . dallontano

As a sought-after technical adviser on artillery and especially as the military engineer for Cesare Borgia, Leonardo was familiar with all aspects of firearms, including, of course, the acoustical aspects of firing cannons, particularly the effect of the length of the gun on the volume of the sound produced and the impact of the atmosphere, misty or clear, on the loudness.

24. This is only one paragraph in A 22 v; other statements on this page refer to the phenomenon of the afterimage.
25. Leonardo says *simile voce*. Richter (vol. 2, p. 231) translates this as "voice" and MacCurdy (vol. 1, p. 284) as "tone." A free but probably most congenial translation would be "pitch."

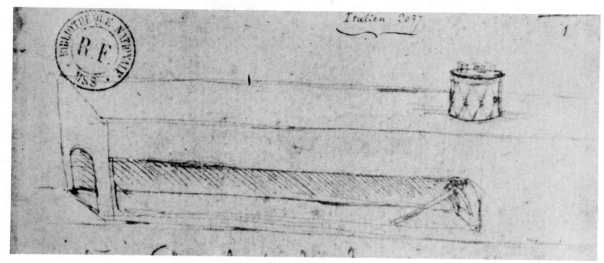

Italien 2037

1

7.16. Drum used as acoustical detective. Detail, MS 2037 Bib. Nat. 1 r.

7.17. Short mortar. CA 9 ra.

I 85 (37) r (illus. 7.17 [CA 9 ra])

"Why the *short* mortar makes a louder explosion when fired than a *long* one, as one hears it in drawing the breech[es] of the small cannon."

Forster II 69 r

The ball of the bombard shot through the mist makes a much shorter course and less percussion than that which is shot through the pure thin air; but it still makes a considerably louder report.

Leonardo is interested in the use of existing holes or ditches for amplification of wind instruments (K 2 r):

The shepherds in the Romagna in the Apennines use large hollows (concavities) in the mountains in the shape of a horn, and put in a real horn so that this small horn becomes part of the concave space. In this way they produce an enormous sound.

A somewhat similar device in using the existing terrain for musical performance is frequently found in the Swiss mountains. Players of the alpenhorn choose their position with respect to a vertical opposite rock at an appropriate distance so that the wall throws back the melodies in a carefully calculated time lag. In the Eiger region I often heard an alpenhorn player performing canons with the echo of his melody.

Forster II 32 v, which is based not on observation of musical practices or local customs but on acoustical experiment, will be discussed later.

Two entries, Triv. 43 r (Tavola 73 a) and the much longer CA 360 ra, touch on the phenomenon of the lingering of sound:

Triv. 43 r (Tavola 73 a)

I say that every body moved or struck keeps in itself for some time the nature of this blow or movement, and keeps it so much more or less in proportion as the power or the force of this blow or movement is greater or less.

Example:
Observe a stone ejected from a bombard, how much it preserves the nature of the movement. The blow given on a thick body will keep its sound longer than on a thin body, and that will be of longest duration which is made upon a body that is suspended and thin. The eye keeps within itself the images of luminous bodies for a certain interval of time.[26]

This analogy of Leonardo's implies a confusion of two phenomena that appear as the lingering of sensuous impressions. One is the continuing vibration in the

---

26. MacCurdy (vol. 1, pp. 282–83) quotes this passage under the wrong number (TR 73 a). It is TR 43 r, Tavola 73 a.

sounding object, which is a physical occurrence and has nothing to do with the receiver of sound, the ear; the other is the afterimage retained in the eye after it has received an impact of light. The latter is a physiological phenomenon; it occurs only in the receiving organ, the eye, and not in the luminous body sending forth light.

CA 360 ra

A longer whole catalogue of observations is found in CA 360 ra. It starts with the phenomenon of sound, especially in "bells and suchlike things" and widens the circle of analogies by including "the radiance of the sun or other luminous bodies" and the circling of the firebrand "remaining in the eye"; the raindrops are perceived as "continuous threads" by the retaining (retentive) force of the eye. Mirrors, however, as unsensitive objects, cannot, unlike the eye, preserve impressions. Yet— again the circle of analogies more widely expands—other objects are capable of preserving impressions, such as water waves, the eddies of water, winds, and a knife stuck into a table and set quivering. Finally, the voice is mentioned traveling through the air without displacing it, impressing itself upon objects, and returning to its source.

Every impression is preserved for a time in its sensitive object; and that which was of greater power will be preserved in its object for a longer time, and for a shorter time with the less powerful.

In this connection I apply the term sensitive to such object as by any impression is changed from that which was at first an insensitive object—that is one which, while changing from its first state preserves within itself no impression of the thing which has moved it. The sensible impression is that of a blow received upon a resounding substance, such as bells and suchlike things, or like the note in the ear, which, indeed, unless it preserved the impression of the notes, could never derive pleasure from hearing a voice alone; for when it passes immediately from the first to the fifth note the effect is as though one heard these two notes at the same time, and thus perceived the true harmony which the first makes with the fifth; but if the impression of the first note did not remain in the ear for an appreciable space of time, the fifth, which follows immediately after the first, would seem alone, and one note cannot create any harmony, and consequently any song whatsoever occurring alone would seem to be devoid of charm.

So, too, the radiance of the sun or other luminous body remains in the eye for some time after it has been seen; and the motion of a single firebrand whirled rapidly in a circle causes this circle to seem one continuous and uniform flame.

The drops of rain water seem continuous threads descending from their clouds; and so herein one may see how the eye preserves the impressions of the moving things which it sees.

The insensitive objects which do not preserve the impressions of the things which are opposite to them are mirrors, and any polished substance, which, so soon as ever the thing of which it bears the impression is removed from before it, becomes at once entirely deprived of that impression. We may, therefore, conclude that it is the action of the mover pressing against the body moved by it which moves this body in the direction in which it moves.

Among the cases of impressions being preserved in various bodies we may also instance the wave, the eddies of the water, the winds in the air, and a knife stuck into a table, which on being bent in one direction and then released, retains for a long time a quivering movement, all its movements being reciprocal one of another, and all may be said to be approaching towards the perpendicular of the surface where the knife is fixed by its point.[27]

The voice impresses itself through the air without displacement of air, and strikes upon the objects and returns back to its source. [MacCurdy, vol. 1, pp. 534–35]

One point in this long entry deserves special comment because of its importance to musical aesthetics and the psychology of the perception of harmony. Leonardo states that the ear, "unless it preserved the impression of the notes, could never derive pleasure from hearing a voice alone." He describes the melting of a fading tone into the inception of its successor, which permits the perception of harmony in listening to a melody. One is tempted to ask how deeply he followed this notion in his discussions with Gaffurius.[28]

Forster II 32 v

With Forster II 32 v begins a series of explorations of the fading of sound, especially the ratio of fading in relation to the volume of the vibrating body and the distance between it and the ear:

If a bell were to be heard two miles, and then it were to be melted down and recast into many small bells, certainly they would never be heard at as great a distance as when they were all in one single bell. [MacCurdy, vol. 1, p. 288]

A 23 r

In Forster II 32 v Leonardo cautiously refrains from indicating a precise mathematical ratio between the duplication of bells and the diminution of the distance between the sounding body and the listening ear. The same is true ("could not be heard as far") in A 23 r:

Of the Voice.

Whether many tiny voices joined together will make as much noise as one large one; I say "no," for if you were to take ten thousand voices of flies all together, they could not be heard as far as the voice of a single man, and if such voice of a man were split into ten thousand parts, none of these parts would be equal to the loudness of the voice of one fly. [Adapted from MacCurdy, vol. 1, p. 284]

A 43 r

In A 43 r, Leonardo comes at least near to posing the possibility of mathematical ratios: "*twice* as strong . . . *twice* as far."

27. A sketch of such a vibrating knife was drawn by Leonardo in C 15 r for an investigation which does not concern us here.
28. See p. 6 on Gaffurius.

Whether a sound that is twice as strong as another will be heard twice as far. I say that it will not because if it were so then two men shouting would be heard twice as far as one; but experience does not confirm this. [MacCurdy, vol. 1, p. 284]

But the last remark, that "experience does not confirm this," keeps the explorer away from any commitment to ratios.

L 79 v

In L 79 v (illus. 7.18) Leonardo finally takes the last step and tries to establish strict mathematical proportions between the loudness of a sound at its origin and its range, the distant point in space up to which it can be heard.

The diagram shows a triangle with its base indicating the initial volume of the voice, and with its apex the end of its range; the triangle is divided into four sections indicating that in half the distance the volume is reduced to one half. In comparison, both of the two smaller triangles begin with half the initial volume of the longer triangle, and therefore reach only to half its range.

The fading of voice through distance.

At the distance *a b* the two voices *m n* are diminished by half; consequently although there are two half voices they are not as powerful as one whole voice but merely as a half.

And if an infinite number of halves should find themselves at such distance they would only amount to a half.

And at the same distance the voice *f* which is double *n* and *m* having lost the fourth part of its power remains consequently as a voice and a half, and surpasses in three times the power, so that at three times the distance, that is at *g*, *f* will be as powerful as *m n* are at the distance *a b*. [MacCurdy, vol. 1, p. 287]

L 80 r

L 80 r goes still further: "Where one voice does not carry, a multiple, however great, made up of voices equal to the aforesaid will not carry" (MacCurdy, vol. 1, p. 287).

The diagram (illus. 7.19) shows seven small triangles, all pointing to the center point not reached by their apexes, evidently the ear.

Neither Leonardo nor any commentator has ever explained the added little ornament consisting of seven six-pointed stars. To the careful student of Leonardo's analogies, the meaning is not hard to find: seven flowers, clearly a bird's-eye view of one of Leonardo's beloved flowers, the star of Bethlehem (*Ornithogalum umbellatum*) (illus. 7.20), a little graphic memo reminding himself to explore whether smell behaves like sound and whether the fading of its range is comparable to that of sound. One thing is strange—that Leonardo introduces, at least in graphic form, an analogy between sound and the olfactory realm but that his often used analogy between sound and light (the realm of vision) is not introduced here or in the previous entry (L 79 v). Actually, it would be just there that a strict analogy exists: the proportions between the loudness of sound and the degrees of its diminution by distance resemble the proportions between the size of a visible object and the degrees of its diminu-

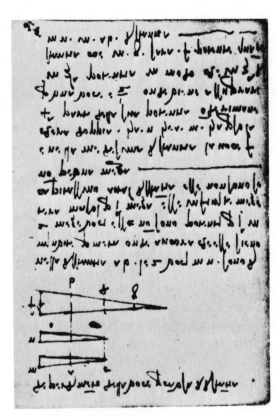

7.18. Diminution of sound in proportion to its distance from its origin. L 79 v.

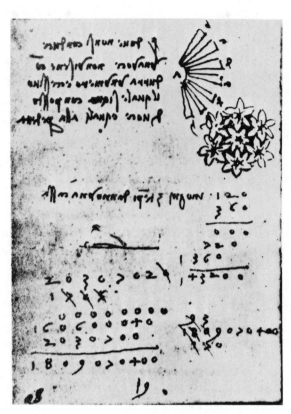

7.19. Seven triangles symbolizing the fading of sound at their apex, the ear, compared with 7 flowers, probably symbolic of the fading of odor. L 80 r.

7.20. *Star of Bethlehem and other plants.* Drawing, Windsor 12424.

tion by distance. In fact Leonardo tried to establish here a theory of the perspective of sound parallel to his laws of linear perspective laid down in his *Trattato della Pittura*.

VELOCITY (SPEED) OF SOUND

Characteristic examples of observations on the speed of sound are found in A 19 r and I 129 (81) v.

A 19 r

One part of A 19 r is based on the well-known comparison between the travel of light represented by the flash of lightning and the travel of sound represented by thunder:

It is possible to recognize by the ear the distance of a clap of thunder on seeing its flash [by seeing first the flash of lightning], from its resemblance to the note [sound] of the echo. [This is only part of a long paragraph, adapted from MacCurdy, vol. 1, p. 283]

I 129 (81) v

The second example, I 129 (81) v (illus. 7.21), states the proportion between units of time and space, couched in the form of a question:

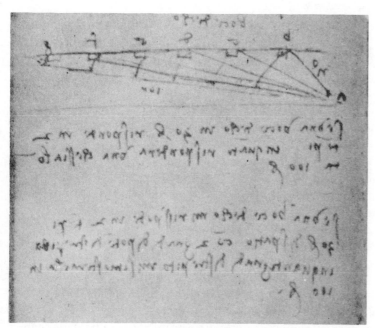

7.21. Proportions between units of time and space. I 129 v.

If the sound of the echo answers in two divisions of time at thirty braccia, in how many divisions will it answer if it is a hundred braccia away? [MacCurdy, vol. 1, p. 286]

(If it travels 30 feet in 2 seconds, how many seconds will it take to travel 100 feet?) This is only the first part of a long note, the remainder of which is devoted to the problem of the volume of sound.

LOSS OF SUBSTANCE THROUGH EMITTING SOUND

CA 270 vc

Objects that lose substance by emitting sound are treated by Leonardo as one of several cases where substance or power is lost through the emission of rays. The loss of power, substance, or shape by an object that sends forth rays making an impact on the eye, the ear, the olfactory sense, or the human organs sensing heat, is discussed by Leonardo in CA 270 vc in the form of questions to the reader or to himself—since the observations recorded in the notebooks were not necessarily meant for publication.

Here we have a multiple analogy between various senses: sight, heat, sound, and odor. The first is vision. Leonardo discusses the problem of "emanations" from objects to the eye in the form of "likenesses" or images in great detail in the Codice Atlantico and in MS D. Because our chapter deals not with light but chiefly with sound, we cannot follow up Leonardo's theory on the eye and on light here but may only briefly state that he bases some of his theories on the eye and the images on the ancients, especially Democritus and Lucretius, and some also, although with different results, on the Stoics.

The following quotation from CA 270 vc shows that an object surrounded by an infinity of its images does not involve a diminution of its substance. Leonardo mentions that the sun does not suffer loss of *h e a t* through its radiance, or the north star a loss of shape:

Qualities of the Sun

The sun has body, shape, motion, splendor, heat, and generating force, all things which stem from it without diminution.

I say that the power of vision extends by means of the visual rays as far as the surface of bodies which are not transparent, and that the power possessed by these bodies extends to the power of vision, and that every similar body fills all the surrounding air with its image. Each body separately and all together do the same, and not only do they fill it with the likeness of their shape, but also with that of their power.

Example

You see the sun when it is at the center of our hemisphere, and how there are images of its form in all the parts where it reveals itself, and you see how in all these same places there are also the images of its radiance, and to these must also be added the image of the power of its *h e a t*; and all these powers proceed from the same source by means of radiant lines which issue from its body and end in the opaque objects without undergoing any diminution.

The north star remains continually with the images of its power spread out, becoming incorporated not only in thin but in thick bodies, in those transparent and those opaque, but it does not on this account suffer any loss of its shape.

These statements are followed by a tentative "confutation" by mathematicians dealing with a possible diminution of the power of vision by beholding the stars:

Confutation

Those mathematicians, then, who say that the eye has no spiritual power which extends to a distance from itself, since, if it were so, it could not be without great diminution in the use of the power of vision, and that though the eye were as great as the body of the earth it would of necessity be consumed in beholding the stars: for this reason they maintain that the eye takes in but does not send forth anything from itself.[29]

Then follow two other examples, examining the odor of *m u s k* and the sound of *b e l l s* with respect to the possible loss of substance by the emitting objects:

Example

What will these say of the musk which always keeps a great quantity of the atmosphere charged with its *o d o r,* and which, if it be carried a thousand miles, will permeate a thousand miles with that thickness of atmosphere without any diminution of itself?

Or will they say that the sound which the *b e l l* makes on its contact with the clapper, which daily of itself fills the whole countryside with its *s o u n d,* must of necessity consume this bell?

Certainly, it seems to me, there are such men as these—and that is all that need be said of them. [MacCurdy, vol. 1, pp. 249–51]

One wonders whether Leonardo really does expect or hope to meet "such men," or does he only express his uneasiness for having fallen prey to his similemania?

THE INACCESSIBLE INNER EAR AND THE PHYSIOLOGY OF VOICE PRODUCTION

One may ask why Leonardo, who was profoundly interested in the eye and its function, paid little attention to the ear, its anatomy and physiology. The reason is not that he was primarily a painter and therefore devoted to the phenomenon of vision and its rationalization, linear perspective, but that the time was not yet ripe for a methodical examination of the inner ear. The small, complex apparatus of the inner ear is deeply embedded in the massive bone structure of the skull, and there were neither appropriate tools available for its removal and dissection nor sufficient refrigeration and chemicals to preserve the delicate and minute mechanism for any length of time from decomposition.

29. For Leonardo's Italian for this passage, showing how by graphic means he tries to achieve the utmost brevity in his script, see Appendix.

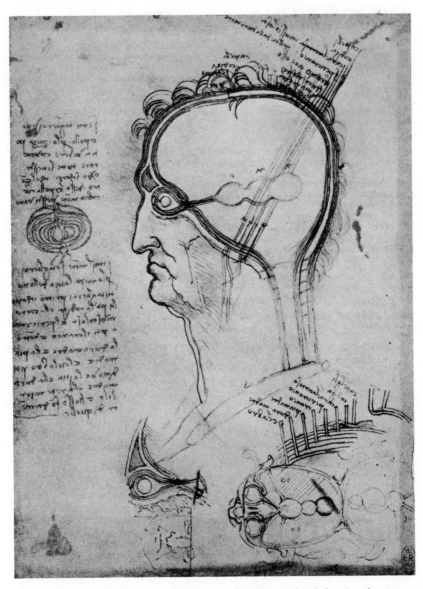

7.22. Cross section of an onion and diagrams of the human head showing the *sensus communis*. Quaderni d'Anatomia V 6 v.

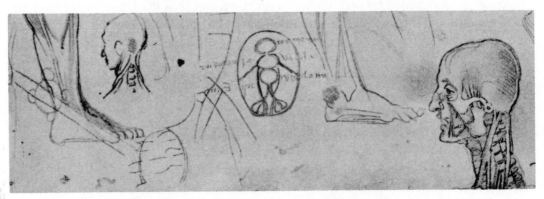

7.23. In the center, cross section of the brain showing the vesicles. Detail, Quaderni d'Anatomia V 15 r.

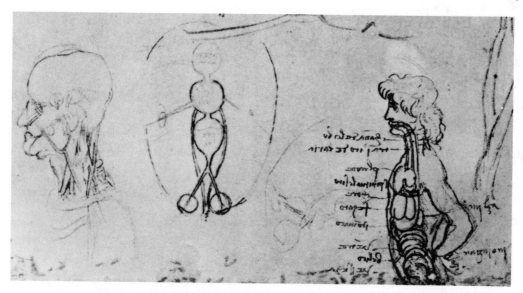

7.24. In the center, cross section of the brain showing vesicles. Detail, Quaderni d'Anatomia V 20 v.

The comparatively primitive status of the knowledge of ear anatomy at Leonardo's time is admirably sketched in the pioneering book *Leonardo da Vinci, the Anatomist* by J. Playfair McMurrich (Baltimore: Carnegie Institute, 1930), to which all later treatises on Leonardo's anatomical research are indebted or should admit indebtedness. Only one of his quotations from Leonardo's notebooks pertinent to the inner ear may suffice to illuminate the situation: "To hear the sound of a voice it is necessary that it should resound in the concave porosity of the petrous bone, which is to the inner side of the ear, whence it is carried to the *sensus communis*" (Windsor AN. B. 19019 [B 2 R], McMurrich, p. 217). It is significant that among the hundreds of accurate and ingenious anatomical drawings by Leonardo there is not a single one of the inner or middle ear—not even a diagrammatical or hypothetical one. In the drawings of the cranium the location of the ear is left blank, and among the several sketches of the brain and cranial nerves there are only a few in which, besides the optical nerves, the acoustical nerves are at least marked as they lead from the outer ear to the center of sensation, called by Galen and in medieval terminology the *sensus communis*. The groping approach of Leonardo, harking back to ancient and medieval notions, is of great interest. It reveals how he, dissatisfied with the state of anatomy he found, tried to free himself from traditional notions of the five senses and their location in the body and to proceed to a more consistent solution.

The most characteristic diagrams showing the location of the acoustical nerve and the other sensory nerves in the brain are the following three:

Quaderni d'Anatomia V 6 v, Windsor 12603r, O'Malley 142 (illus. 7.22)[30]

The diagram on the left shows an onion cut through the middle for comparison with the layers in the sagittal section of the head in the large drawing in the center of the

30. Charles D. O'Malley and J. B. Saunders, *Leonardo da Vinci on the Human Body* (New York: Henry Schuman, 1952).

page. In this large drawing the optic nerve runs from the eye to the anterior of the three brain vesicles receiving the sensory nerves and therefore called the sensus communis; the ear is not shown. In the lower right corner of the page we see the horizontal section of the head. Here, the acoustic nerves are also shown, leading from the ear lobes to the sensus communis, but the apparatus of the ear itself is not shown at all.

Quaderni d'Anatomia V 15 r, Windsor 12626r, O'Malley 159 (illus. 7.23)

Here a diagrammatic cross section of the brain shows the optic nerves passing to the anterior vesicle but the acoustic nerves as well as the olfactory nerves passing to the middle vesicle. The inner ear is not shown.

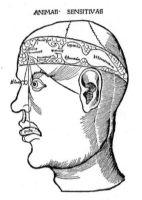

7.25. Diagram of the brain and the location of the senses from G. Reisch's *Margarita Philosophiae* (Strasbourg, 1504).

Quaderni d'Anatomia V 20 v, Windsor 12627r, O'Malley 160 (illus. 7.24)

Here we find the same location of the sensory nerves as in Quaderni d'Anatomia V 15 r: the optic nerves attached to the first vesicle ("imprensiva"), the olfactory and the acoustic nerves to the second vesicle ("conoscimento"). Again, the inner ear is not shown.

To show one example of the general level of knowledge of brain anatomy in Leonardo's day, especially of the connection between the ear and the brain, we reproduce one example from a well-known book on anatomy from that time (G. Reisch's *Margarita Philosophiae* [Strassburg, 1504] [illus. 7.25]). The drawing is entitled *animae sensitivae;* the tongue is marked "gusto," the upper part of the nose "olfactory"; these two senses together with the optic and acoustic pass to the frontal vesicle, which bears the inscription "fantasia" and "imaginativa." The middle vesicle is inscribed "cogitatio" and "estimatio"; the posterior vesicle is inscribed "memoranda." Here, as in Leonardo's various diagrams of the auditory nerve passing from the ear to the brain, the inner ear is completely omitted.

It remains to examine Leonardo's sketches of the voice-producing organs such as the trachea and larynx. A study of his phonetics, that is, of the speaking and singing voice, its production, and the anatomical and physiological factors involved, would amount to a whole treatise and would exceed the scope of the present volume. Furthermore, such a book already exists: the excellent volume *Leonardo als Phonetiker* by G. Panconcelli-Calzia (Hamburg, 1943).

But we can be very brief. For several reasons, Leonardo took as models for his sketches not human organs but parts of animal bodies—pigs, oxen, and dogs; human bodies for dissection were not always obtainable, and as with the inner ear, there were no chemicals to preserve the delicate vocal cords. He also, again, leaned heavily on earlier authors on anatomy, from Galen to those of his own day. It is obvious from his notebooks that he was unaware of the vocal cords, and this led to his erroneous interpretation of the function of the trachea in changing the pitch of the human voice through widening and narrowing of what he called "anule della trachea" (cartilage rings of the trachea). For further discussion of this subject, see p. 192 concerning his invention of the glissando flute.

LINGERING OF SOUND IN THE OBJECT PRODUCING IT; AFTERIMAGES AND ANALOGIES WITH LIGHT AND SMELL

CA 332 va

Leonardo examines the phenomenon of the seeming lingering of sound in a bell after it has been struck, and mentions two possible causes: (1) a slowly fading afterimage in the listening ear, and (2) a gradual weakening of the actual vibration of the bell.

Strangely enough, he treats the two reasons as alternatives, not allowing for the coexistence of both.

Of the Sound Which Seems to Remain in the Bell after the Stroke

"That sound which remains or seems to remain in the bell after it has received the stroke is not in the bell itself but in the ear of the listener, and the ear retains within itself the image of the stroke of the bell which it has heard, and only loses it by slow degrees, like that which the impression of the sun creates in the eye, which only by slow degrees becomes lost and is no longer seen."

A proof to the contrary

If the aforesaid proposition were true, you would not be able to cause the sound of the bell to cease abruptly by touching it with the palm of the hand, especially at the beginning of its strength, for surely if it were touched it would not happen that as you touched the bell with the hand the ear would simultaneously withhold the sound; whereas we see that if after the stroke has taken place the hand is placed upon the thing which is struck the sound suddenly ceases. [MacCurdy, vol. 1, p. 280]

We have discussed the two forms of lingering of sound before (p. 108) (Triv. 43 r [Tavola 73 a]) and found that Leonardo sometimes confuses the physical phenomenon, the vibration of the bell continuing after the stroke, with the physiological–psychological phenomenon, the impression of sound continuing in its receiver, the ear, after the sound itself has stopped. The just quoted statement (CA 332 va) suffers from the same confusion ("impression of the sun . . . in the eye" becoming lost "by slow degrees"). The "proof to the contrary" is not a valid argument because both phenomena, the lingering of sound in the producing object, the bell, and the lingering of sound in the receiving organ, the ear, can happen simultaneously.

Triv. 43 r (Tavola 73 a)

The noise preserved in the bell is used by Leonardo as one of several examples of the general principle of the preservation of the impact of a blow: "Observe a blow given on a bell how much it preserves in itself the noise of the percussion."

Leonardo's choice of examples is not consistent since it exceeds the field of mechanics. (See p. 108, for quotation and discussion of Triv. 43 r [Tavola 73 a]). The examples of bell, bombard projectile, thick and thin bodies, and the influence of suspension, all concern the lingering of force within the substance of the struck body. However, images of luminous bodies preserved in the eye are typical afterimages and, as such, physiological phenomena.

A 22 v

The first phrase of A 22 v deals with the phenomenon of the afterimage, namely, the sensory impressions left behind by the object producing them. Leonardo tries here a daring triple analogy among the bell, the sun, and a smell-producing object: "The stroke in a bell will leave behind its likeness impressed just as the sun in the eye or the smell in the air, by placing your ear to the surface of the bell after the blow.[31]

But here Leonardo is far from consistent. The triple analogy would work only if one could assume placing the eye near the sun and the nose near the cheese.

IMAGINATION STIMULATED BY VISUAL OR ACOUSTICAL SENSATIONS

MS 2038 Bib. Nat. 22 v

A Way of Stimulating and Arousing the Mind to Various Inventions:
I cannot refrain from mentioning among these precepts a new device for study which, although it may seem but trivial and almost ludicrous, is nevertheless very useful in arousing the mind to various inventions.

And this is, when you look at a wall spotted with stains, or with a mixture of different kinds of stones, if you have to invent some scene, you may discover a similarity with different kinds of landscapes, embellished with mountains, rivers, rocks, trees, plains, wide valleys and hills in varied arrangement; or, again, you may see battles and figures in action or strange faces and costumes, and an endless variety of objects which you could reduce to complete and well-drawn forms.

It happens with this confused appearance of walls as it does with the sound of bells in whose jangle you may find any name or word you can imagine. [translation by the author]

31. Richter's translation (vol. 2, p. 231, #1129A) omits the end of the phrase, from "air" to "blow."

Leonardo's observations about blots have often been mentioned in the literature. The well-known Rorschach test, using a symmetrical configuration of inkblots, is based on a similar process of imagination. But less attention has been given to Leonardo's comparison of a visual stimulation with an audible one, the triggering of verbal association by the sound of bells. A similar observation was made by the fifteen-year-old Mozart in a letter that he wrote from Milan to his sister in Salzburg, on August 24, 1771. He mentions the terrible heat during his journey to Milan and continues with a description of his lodging: "On top of us is a viol player; beneath us, another one; next door is a singing teacher who gives lessons; in the last room is an oboist. This puts one into a good mood for composing, gives one many ideas."

It is remarkable that Mozart, when composing, was not at all disturbed by participation in noisy pastimes such as bowling, and, especially, his most beloved game, billiards.[32] In 1787, during a bowling party in the garden of his friend, the composer Duschek, in a suburb of Prague, Mozart composed several pieces for his opera *Don Giovanni*. When his turn came, he arose, but as soon as it was over, he immediately continued composing without being disturbed by the talking and laughing company. As for billiards, Nissen reports:

In 1791, while Mozart wrote the coronation opera, *La Clemenza di Tito*, he visited almost daily with his friends at a coffee house near his home, in order to play billiards. One could observe that for several days during playing, he repeatedly hummed one motif softly to himself, took out a little booklet from his pocket while his partner played, glanced quickly into it, and played again. How astonished everybody was when Mozart, in the house of Duschek, played on the piano for his friends the beautiful quintet from *The Magic Flute* of Tamino, Papageno, and the three ladies, which begins with the same motif that had occupied him during the billiard game.[33]

SYMBOLIC ASPECTS OF SOUND

I 65 (17) r: A "Prophecy"

The wind plays a role in one of the many riddles called "prophecies,"[34] written by Leonardo for the entertainment of the Milanese court: "The wind passing through

---

32. See E. Winternitz, "Gnagflow Trazom: An Essay on Mozart's Script, Pastimes, and Nonsense Letters," in *Journal of the American Musicological Society* 11, nos. 2–3 (1958).

33. Leitzmann, *W. A. Mozarts Leben*, p. 113. The quotation is from Georg Nikolaus von Nissen's biography of Mozart:

Mozart, während er 1791 die Krönungsoper "La Clemenza di Tito" schrieb, besuchte fast täglich mit seinen Freunden ein unweit seiner Wohnung gelegenes Kaffeehaus, um mit Billardspielen sich zu zerstreuen. Man bemerkte einige Tage lang, dass er während dem Spielen ein Motiv ganz leise für sich mit "hm hm hm" sang, mehrmals, während der andere spielte, ein Buch aus der Tasche zog, flüchtige Blicke hineinwarf und dann wieder fortspielte. Wie erstaunt war man, als Mozart auf einmal seinen Freunden in Duschets Hause das schöne Quintett aus der "Zauberflöte" zwischen Tamino, Papageno und den drei Damen, das gerade mit demselben Motive beginnt, welches Mozarten während des Billardspielens so beschäftigt hatte, auf dem Klaviere vorspielte.

34. To characterize the kind of forecasts and riddles collected under the name "prophecies," I will

the skins of animals will make men leap—that is, the bagpipe, which makes people dance [Il vento passato per le pelli delli animali fará saltare li omini; cioé la piva che fa ballare]."

H 67 r: Three Elements and the Soul

Sometimes Leonardo used the phenomenon of sound as one item of several within a comprehensive analogy, for instance, in a comparison of the three elements of water, sound, and fire with the mind (soul, spirit).

> Of the Soul
> Movement of earth against earth pressing down upon it causes a slight movement of parts struck.
> Water struck by water creates circles at a great distance round the spot where it is struck; the sound in the air goes further; still further in fire; mind ranges over the universe but, being finite, does not extend into infinity.[35]

Windsor An. A 19012 v (A 13 v): Finger Nerves and the Mind of the Organ Player

Leonardo's anatomical exploration of the mechanism of the hand and the function of the median and ulnar nerves reminds him of the needs of the organ player: "See if you understand that this sense [of touch] is employed by the player of an organ, and that the mind at such time is attentive to the sense of hearing."

Triv. 40 v (Tavola 71 a): Soul and Sound beyond Corruption

The importance of the wind and breath as carriers of sound and symbols of the soul is very alive in Leonardo, a symbolism perhaps suggested by the relation between the words *spirito* and *inspirare* and *inspirazione*. "The soul can never be infected by the corruption of the body, but acts in the body like the wind which causes the sound of the organ, wherein if one of the pipes becomes spoiled, no good effect can be produced because of its emptiness."[36]

---

quote two more although they do not deal with music: (I 65 r) "Men will deal bitter blows to that which is the cause of their life—in thrashing grain." "The skins of animals will rouse men from their silence with great outcries and curses—balls for playing games."

35. "De Anima. Ilmoto della terra contro allatera ricalcando quella poco simove leparte percosse. Lacqua perchassa [percossa] dallacqua facir culi dintorno alloco perchosso per lunga distantia lavoce infrallaria piv lunga infral foco piv lamen te infralluyverso maperche le fini ta nonsastende infra llonfinito."

Leonardo's reference to the friction of the heavenly spheres and their harmony has been discussed in "Origin of Sound, F 56 v" (p. 106).

36. "Lanima mai si puo chorrompere. nella coruttion del corpo ma ffa nel corpo assimilidine del vento che chavsa del sono del organo che quasstandosi van chana non resultava per quella del voto buono effectto."

CHAPTER EIGHT

New String Instruments and the Viola Organista

It is odd that the many sketches for musical instruments and musical machines contained in the pages of Leonardo da Vinci's notebooks have never found a thorough and systematic interpretation. It is true that some look rather fantastic, at least to us today, and others are clearly only quick embodiments of passing ideas put down on paper by Leonardo to aid his own memory. However, nearly all the sketches reveal themselves as most interesting, and many as ingenious new inventions, if they are scrutinized and analyzed in the right context: that is, against the background of the instruments existing at Leonardo's time, with a knowledge of clockworks and other mechanical devices used by Leonardo outside the field of musical instruments, and examined in the light of Leonardo's leading ideas for instruments which can be distilled from a comparison of all the drawings and his many remarks on music, musical aesthetics, and acoustics.[1]

For their help in my study of the wide range of musical instruments invented by Leonardo (see chapter 8, below), I wish to express my profound gratitude to my old and good friends: the late Professor Ladislao Reti, and Professors Augusto Marinoni and Carlo Pedretti. Professor Reti, who in 1967 discovered the 700-page manuscript of Leonardo that had been lost or misfiled in the Biblioteca Nacional in Madrid, informed me without delay of sketches of musical instruments in these codices showing mechanized drums (MS I folio 91 v and folio 160 r), unusual bellows operated by the elbow (MS II folio 76 r), and bells with a damper mechanism (MS II folio 75 v), all discussed in this chapter. Professors Marinoni and Pedretti both brought to my attention the two sketches for musical instruments in the Codice Atlantico (213 va and 34 rb), which had not been considered in my article "Leonardo's Invention of the Viola Organista" for the Raccolta Vinciana in 1964. Pedretti pointed this out in his Richter Commentaries (*Commentary on the Literary Works of Leonardo da Vinci*, p. 216), rightly suggesting also that I should consider H 104 v as related to CA 34 rb, and that these illustrations should be printed in an upright rather than sideways view. He also suggested that both instruments are operated by a leg of the walking player, or by an arrangement of a belt and straps attached to the body of the player; Pedretti also helped me to clarify a tentative chronology of the codices. I was also greatly helped by discussions with Bo Lawergren, composer and professor of physics at Hunter College, New York, whose knowledge of theoretical and applied mechanics in historical perspective led to clarification of the mechanics in CA 213 va and 34 rb.

1. Leonardo's many notebooks attest to his insatiable curiosity about what nature could tell him and what he could learn from books. In the preceding chapter on acoustics there are not only numerous examples of his own experiments but also references to the authority of Vitruvius, for instance, con-

Among the many musical instruments and machines contrived by Leonardo—string instruments, drums, bells, and wind instruments—the viola organista is by far the most complicated. No fewer than ten different pages in the notebooks show sketches for it: fol. 28 r, 28 v, 45 v, 46 r, and 104 v in codex H; folio 50 v in codex B; folio 34 rb, 213 va, and 218 rc in the Codice Atlantico; and folio 76 r in the Madrid MS II.

None of them are precise drawings for an instrument builder, and some are not even completely thought through since several details would probably have been found impracticable in actual construction. However, to anticipate the outcome of our analysis, they are all concerned with the idea of a stringed instrument with keyboard in which the strings are set into vibration by a mechanical device—a wheel, a bow with a back-and-forth motion, or a belt of hair moving across the strings as a sort of endless bow. Such an instrument would fill a big gap in the multitudinous array of instruments not only of Leonardo's time but also of ours today. It would combine the polyphonic possibilities of the keyboard with the tone color of strings and thus would be something like an organ with string timbre instead of wind timbre.

The mechanical obstacles confronting the builder of such an instrument are obvious. The bow in the hand of a fiddler selects the string wanted; it can easily turn from one string to another or even press against two strings simultaneously and, in the case of the early viol with a flat bridge and soft bow, against three strings at the same time. The bow can travel either quickly or slowly and exert heavy or light pressure upon the strings. But if a mechanical bow is to be used, the problem immediately arises as to how to select, in turn, the strings which are supposed to sound, and how to press them against the vibrating device, be it a friction wheel, a belt of hair, or a shuttling bow.[2]

Instruments with friction wheels existed before Leonardo's time and were still popular in his day although their mechanism and musical capacity were incomparably simpler than his elaborate contrivances, which amounted to nothing less than a one-man orchestra. In connection with these other instruments we must mention, above all, the hurdy-gurdy—known variously as the *ghironda*, *vielle à roue*, and

---

cerning the study of echo. But did he also consult contemporary literature on music and musical instruments, such as the famous, enormous encyclopedia by Giorgio Valla, written in sumptuous, humanist Latin, "Giorgii Vallae Placentini viri clarissimi *De Expetendis et fugiendis rebus* . . ." (Venice, 1501), *Things to Seek and Things to Avoid?* Valla (1447–99) lived for many years in Milan, and Leonardo had a copy of the encyclopedia, if we can so interpret the inclusion of Valla's name in Leonardo's inventory of his own books (in Madrid MS II 75 v).

Valla's encyclopedia with its 49 books in 2,119 chapters includes no fewer than five chapters (58 pages) on music. They all treat of the mathematical aspects of musical theory and contain no discussion whatever of musical instruments and their practice in his and Leonardo's time. Augusto Marinoni, who very kindly sent me a summary of these five chapters, believes that Leonardo never read them.

2. In the twentieth century, only some ingenious ideas of Emanuel Moór, the inventor of the Moór duplex piano, include suggestions for an instrument combining the bowing of many strings with a keyboard. See Max Pirani, *Emanuel Moór*, p. 91: "During the winter of 1919–1920 he made experiments with a horizontal instrument based on the principles of the violin . . . to be used for orchestral purposes and intended to replace not only violins, but all the members of the string family."

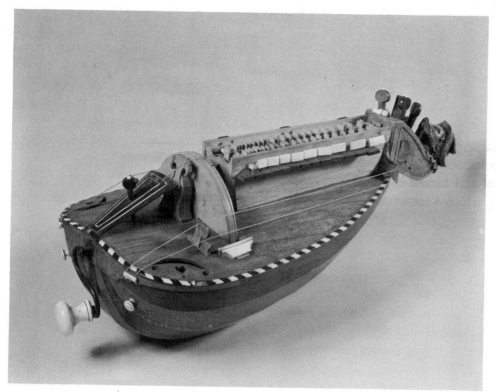

8.1. French hurdy-gurdy in lute shape,
eighteenth century. Metropolitan
Museum of Art, The Crosby Brown
Collection.

8.2. Wheel and stopping mechanism of
a French eighteenth-century
hurdy-gurdy in guitar shape. Metropolitan Museum of Art, The
Crosby Brown Collection.

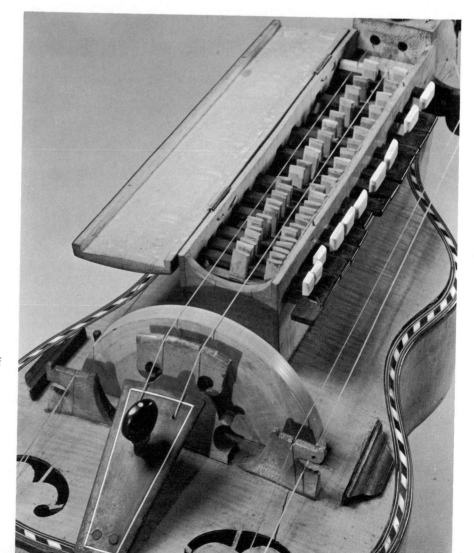

Drehleier—a sort of mechanical fiddle of venerable history. This instrument was already popular in the Middle Ages and appeared at that time almost all over Europe, and it is still being played today as a folk instrument in certain regions of France.[3]

The hurdy-gurdy can have different shapes: its sound box may resemble a lute, guitar, or fiddle, but the strings stretched along it are neither plucked nor bowed, being set into vibration by a wooden wheel revolving in the middle of the sound box and turned by a crank at its tail end (illus. 8.1). The smooth edge of the wheel, which is coated with resin, serves as an endless bow. Like the pipes of the typical bagpipe, the strings differ in kind and function: there are stopped ones (the melody strings, or *chanterelles*) running along the middle of the sound box and open ones (the drones, or *bourdons*) running on either side. The melody strings are stopped by a primitive key mechanism, a set of stopping rods (naturals and sharps) equipped with little projections that press inward against the strings when the rods are pushed in (illus. 8.2). Thus, a full scale can be produced. When released, the rod falls back of its own weight. Consequently the hurdy-gurdy is held and played with the keyboard down. As the two melody strings are tuned in unison, each rod has two projections simultaneously stopping both strings. When there are two drones, they are tuned in octaves; when there are more, the octave is strengthened by an added fifth.

8.3. Organistrum played by two elders end of twelfth century. Portico de la Gloria of the Cathedral of Santiago de Compostela.

3. For an account of the origin of this instrument, its function, evolution, and colorful changing history as a representation of religious and pastoral symbolism, see my article "Bagpipes and Hurdy-gurdies in their Social Setting," *Metropolitan Museum of Art Bulletin*, Summer 1943, pp. 56–83; reprinted in *Musical Instruments and Their Symbolism in Western Art*, 2d ed. (New Haven: Yale University Press, 1979).

A construction of this kind gives the instrument three distinctive features. First, it is mechanized: that is, the strings are touched neither by plucking fingers nor by a bow but by an intervening mechanical device, the friction wheel. Second, the hurdy-gurdy, through its wheel, makes possible something which not the lute or the violin or the harpsichord can render—a continuous sound; the wheel overcomes the pauses between the single strokes of plucking or bowing. The third distinctive feature is the accompaniment of a melody by an invariable bass, the drone.

The early history of the hurdy-gurdy is beyond the scope of this book because it has no bearing on Leonardo's invention. Thus it should only briefly be mentioned that the hurdy-gurdy developed from the organistrum of the tenth, eleventh, and twelfth centuries: a large box with a wheel and a crank turned by one player, while another manipulated a primitive stopping mechanism. Organistra are depicted in the sculptures of Romanesque churches such as the cathedrals of Moissac and Santiago de Compostela (illus. 8.3). By the time of Giotto the smaller and handier one-man instrument, the hurdy-gurdy, had replaced the organistrum. As has been pointed out, the mechanism of the organistrum and of its successor, the hurdy-gurdy, did not allow the selection of single strings to be sounded alone due to the action of the wheel rubbing simultaneously against all the strings. It was, in fact, just this limitation which gave this instrument its charm as a vehicle for that characteristic drone music which is still familiar today, even to musical laymen, through the large family of bagpipes.[4]

But while the drone principle is a very ancient one—for instance, in the music of western Asia, and also of importance in the development of occidental polyphony—it plays no role in the invention of Leonardo which we are discussing here. On the contrary, Leonardo's invention aimed at a machine of maximum freedom and flexibility, offering to the player precisely that choice of tones or chords wanted at the moment. A drone, humming on continuously, would have been only an undesirable restriction of the harmonic possibilities of an instrument such as the viola organista.

Before turning to the analysis of the single drawings it should be pointed out that their interpretations support one another since several elements such as keys and pushbuttons occur in several of the drawings. Lacking any external indications as to their chronology, I have arranged the order according to the inner logic of the development of one solution from the preceding, less satisfactory one.

Codice Atlantico 218 rc (illus. 8.4) is completely filled with several sketches concerned with different machines. For convenience I will call them A, B, C, D, and E, from top to bottom.

A and B cover the upper third of the narrow page. There is one thing which immediately strikes the eye in B—a precise sketch for the typical bow for the viol or the lira da braccio of the time. The bow is placed over an oblong box without any

---

4. On the historical relation between hurdy-gurdies and bagpipes as equivalent providers of drone music, see ibid.

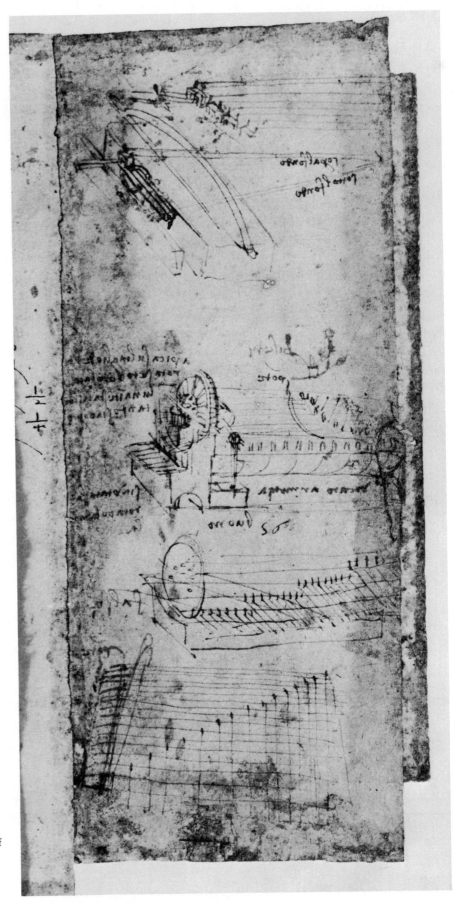

8.4. Sketches for different versions of
the viola organista. CA 218 rc.

clear indication as to how it is attached. It is crossed by two sets of double lines; the upper set, marked "sopra 'l fondo," is drawn more heavily than the lower set, which is marked "sotto 'l fondo." These two double lines converge toward the right, the upper set being drawn strictly parallel to the side walls of the box, and the lower set at a marked angle. This latter fact alone, in view of the unerring sense of perspective habitual with Leonardo even in his smallest sketches, seems to exclude the assumption that the lower double line indicates vibrating strings.

But the upper set evidently does represent a double string, for we can see these two lines fastened at the left end to two pins, evidently tuning pins which protrude from a cube. A clearer idea of this fastening method is gained from sketch A, which is apparently a detail for B. There we notice four sets of double strings with their tuning pins, which are inserted in four little individual doors or frame-shaped bridges. We may ask why the tuning pins are not fastened directly to a wrest plank, as it is done in harpsichords or spinetti. The answer, it seems to me, is connected with the problem of selecting the strings which should actually sound: that is, to bring the proper string into contact with the hair of the bow. A device was needed to grasp the proper string and lower or raise it against the bow, from its resting position, in order that the string might be set into vibration. If we look at the uppermost of the four little "doors" or frames, we note, protruding from it, three lines strongly suggesting a key. A glimpse at the corresponding area of sketch B confirms this assumption. There must, therefore, have been a keyboard acting through some intermediate levers or wire loops on the strings. But we consult the drawing in vain for such a device.

If we assume the existence of keys, as suggested, we must also assume double strings, as mentioned above, and not single strings, because the supposed key in the drawings corresponds to one set of double strings. Double strings for the purpose of giving a louder tone were common in the hurdy-gurdy, as it has been described, with its two melody strings tuned in unison and its several bass drone-strings tuned in unison and sometimes at the octave and the fifth, in addition. Which leads to the question of how many strings Leonardo's machine was meant to have. I believe that the four double strings in A give only an idea of the arrangement but I do not exclude the possibility that there were more than four pairs. To construct such a complex machine for only four double strings, each sounding only one tone, would hardly have been worth the trouble unless there were also a stopping device, perhaps similar to the tangents of a fretted clavichord or the teeth on the stopping rods of the hurdy-gurdy, which made it possible to produce more than one tone from each string. But although these devices in the clavichord and hurdy-gurdy are simple and easy to construct, in our machine where the keys would be busy in pressing the strings against the bow, any stopping mechanism subdividing each string for the proper pitch would have been a cumbersome affair and would require more fingers than God has given to one man.

There remains, finally, another question that is likewise, alas, not sufficiently answered by the drawing—the method of moving the bow. As we stated before, no device is visible for fastening the bow to the box. In principle, two ways would be

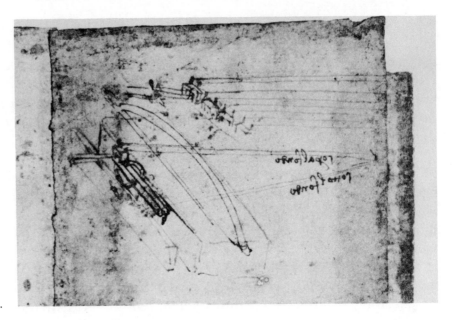

8.5. Detail of illus. 8.4.

feasible, either to move the bow against the strings or to move the strings against the hair of a stationary bow. The only clue is the device drawn in the middle of the long side of the oblong box in B (illus. 8.5). But here the drawing is too muddled to be reliably interpreted. It may perhaps indicate a sled, gliding on top of the narrow box or log to the left of the big box. But whether this was to move the bow or the set of strings cannot be decided. One can only say that moving the strings sideways under the bow would have been practical with only a few strings; with a considerable number, let us say as in a small spinetta, it would have been difficult even if we do not take into account the problem of having to move the keyboard along with the strings and, at the same time, manipulate its keys. Thus, the method of moving the bow back and forth seems more probable. But then again, this method would be very close to what a fiddler does, without any complicated mechanism. In many pages of his notebooks Leonardo was thinking aloud (so to speak) with pencil in hand, amending and replacing again and again his verbal statements and explanations, and often abandoning them in favor of a different formulation. Why should he have done otherwise in his sketches of novel mechanical conceptions? It may have been precisely the difficulties described which prompted him to abandon the idea of an actual bow and turn to a more practical device—the friction wheel.

Drawing C (illus. 8.6) in the middle of the page shows an elaborate mechanism with a large spoked wheel. The idea of the bow in B has apparently been abandoned as impractical, and the vibrating element here is a wheel. Leonardo was, of course, familiar with the popular ghironda of his time, which was then, in its simplest form, a peasant instrument and yet noble enough in more elaborate forms to be played by angels.[5] A beautiful ghironda is played by an angel in the Sforza *Book of Hours* (plate

5. Ibid.

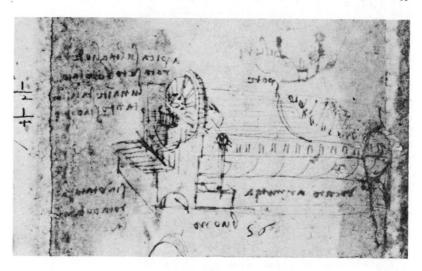

8.6. Detail of illus. 8.4.

xxix), written precisely at the time when Leonardo was in Milan (illus. 8.7); an even more beautiful one is played by one of the numerous angels in Gaudenzio Ferrari's fresco in the cupola of the church of Santa Maria Novella in Saronno, north of Milan (illus. 8.8).

In the present drawing the wheel is set into the front part of a large sound box which carries the strings. The curved bridge (*ponti*) and several hitch pins (*bischeri*), to its right, are clearly drawn. The large wheel has spokes and a central disk with pins that tally with the sticks of a revolving vertical drum. The wheel is evidently kept in motion by a horizontal cylinder partly seen at its right, whose axis terminates in a little wheel which, in its turn, is moved by ropes extending down into a little box where we may assume there is a spring as "prime mover." Such springs were used by Leonardo in similar devices such as, for instance, in his flying machine (cf. B 74 r). Instead of springs, the force could of course be supplied by a foot pedal or a weight.

There are two mechanical problems which would have to be solved in a mechanism such as this. The first concerns the contact between the strings and the edge of the wheel, and the shape of the sounding board thereby required. Our drawing gives only an ambiguous answer. If the wheel is really a friction wheel, the strings rubbed by its edge have to be placed on a plane curved correspondingly, that is, on a concave soundboard. Would the whole sound box then have to be curved? The seven or eight little curves visible over the words "vocato armonico" seem to indicate a rounded bottom of the sound box. But how about the shape of the sound-board itself? The curved double line indicating the bridge, and marked "ponti," does not answer our question since the bridge, as every harpsichord builder knows, may be curved in the horizontal plane, corresponding to the different lengths of strings from treble to bass. Also, a large soundboard of concave shape would not be easy to build although Hans Hayden's Geigenklavizimbel, built about 1600 in Nuremberg and illustrated in Praetorius's *Syntagma Musicum*, II, "De Organographia" (1618), had a soundboard of five concave sections corresponding to its five friction wheels (illus. 8.9). It may be even more instructive to compare Leonardo's sketch and the

8.7. Angel playing a hurdy-gurdy.
Sforza Book of Hours, plate XXIX.

8.8. Angel playing a hurdy-gurdy. From
the cupola fresco by Gaudenzio
Ferrari in the Santuario at Saronno.

illustration of Hayden's instrument with pictures of the only surviving old Geigen-werk built in 1625 by Fray Raymundo Truchado and preserved in the Mahillon Collection of the Conservatoire in Brussels. Illustration 8.10 shows the whole in-strument, with the keyboard deeply set in at the front, the crank protruding at the rear, and the strings running over wheels set into the soundboard. Illustration 8.11 gives an oblique view of the arrangement of the wheels and bridges and the hooks that force the strings against the edge of the wheels.[6]

The other mechanical problem concerns again, as we saw in the first drawing, the way in which the player selects the strings.[7] In the hurdy-gurdy this was no problem—the wheel rubbed all of them at the same time. But Leonardo's elaborate machine was evidently meant to produce more complex music than the pastoral music of the hurdy-gurdy, with its never silent melody in the treble and incessant drone in the bass. Richer polyphony was to be expected at the time of Isaac, Ag-ricola, and other famous visitors to the court of Milan and therefore a selecting device for each string was needed. As an indication of this device we must consider the keyboard at the left, for thus one should be inclined to interpret the set of parallel lines in front of the architectural structure that carries the wheel and that is, by the way, shaped after the form of an organetto of the time. But how these keys select the strings is not revealed in the drawing.

However, the last two drawings on our page, sketchy as they are, evidently are concerned with this problem of selection (illus. 8.12). In D, which is crossed out and labeled "falso,"[8] we see a concave soundboard with a number of strings running from left to right, and a wheel equipped with strings set into the curve of the soundboard in about the same place as in C. There is no hint of a keyboard as in C, but four sets of diagonal lines cross the strings and terminate in short, upright marks just where the farther ends of the lines meet the strings. Of these four sets of lines the first, which is nearest the wheel and reaches the first string, has eight such marks. The second set, touching the second string, has nine marks; the third, reaching the third string, likewise has nine marks; and the last, touching the fourth string, shows five marks although this number may be fewer than for the others merely because the margin of the paper had been reached. When I view this drawing, the only association I can make is with the keys and tangents of a fretted clavichord, in which the keys, which are equipped at their rear ends with little upright metal blades that strike the string, not only make it vibrate but also divide it at the proper point in order to obtain the desired tone.

Leonardo was familiar with the clavichord, called at his time *monocordo* and also *manicordo* (one of the wordplays frequent in the Renaissance). The *monocordo*

6. I took this photograph years ago in bad light and with a small camera. It is slightly blurred yet shows clearly enough the salient features of the wheel mechanism.

7. Even if the wheel mechanism was meant to be an automat, a selective device would have been necessary. All the musical automata known from later times, as illustrated in Athanasius Kircher's *Musurgia Universalis* (Rome, 1650), used the pin barrel as the central device to pluck the strings.

8. Evidently Leonardo, when abandoning sketch D by marking it "falso," added "buono" to sketch C.

8.9. Geigenklavizimbel. Woodcut from Michael Praetorius's *Syntagma Musicum II*, "*De Organographia*," Nuremberg, 1618.

8.10. Keyboard instrument with wheels, built by Truchado, 1625. Brussels Conservatoire.

8.11. Oblique view of the soundboard with wheels from illus. 8.10 (photographed by the author).

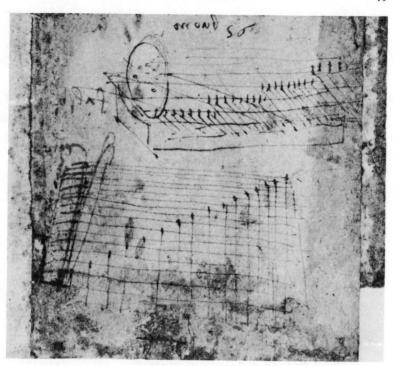

8.12. Detail of illus. 8.4.

of the Renaissance, despite its name, had many strings[9]—the beautiful large clavichord or monocordo represented in the intarsias of Federigo da Montefeltro in his palace at Urbino (illus. 8.13), long before Leonardo's time, had no fewer than twenty-two strings and forty-seven keys.[10] Now if the schematic lines in the drawing suggest the clavichord action at all, the first string nearest us could render eight tones, the second nine, the third nine, and the last at least five: in sum, thirty tones: two octaves and a fourth on a chromatic keyboard.

A different method is followed in drawing E, which shows a scheme for a soundboard in more of a central top view than in the other sketches, with a wheel (or possibly a bow) on the left. Here the arrangement of fifteen strings each crossed by a "tangent," and thus amounting to an equal number of strings and tangents, would correspond to the action of the unfretted clavichord in which each string sounds its whole length (one tone) rather than being subdivided into many tones by the action of several tangents on one string, as in the fretted clavichord described above. If Leonardo really thought of something like a clavichord action, the keys reaching across the strings, with the wheel at the left side of the player, would by means of the tangents press the strings against the wheel or bow. And the keyboard in front of the wheel, such as in C, would have been unnecessary. For this reason I do not think that D and E are merely supplementary sketches to C.

9. In Windsor 12350 Leonardo refers to the light reflected on the strings (*chorde*) of the monochord.

10. See my article "Quattrocento-Intarsien als Quellen der Instrumentengeschichte," *Bericht über den siebenten Internationalen Musikwissenschaftlichen Kongress* (Cologne, 1958); reprinted in *Musical Instruments*.

8.13. Clavichord; detail of the intarsias in the Studiolo of Federigo da Montefeltro in his palace in Urbino.

In looking back at all the drawings on page 218 rc, we find that even if we were to discard everything which is only guesswork and unexplainable detail, the following facts remain: Leonardo begins with the idea of a mechanical bow moving back and forth, similar to the actual hand-moved bow of a fiddle; then he discards this idea and turns to the more reliable device of the friction wheel, adds keys, and evidently begins to grope for a method of how to stop the strings and how to make them touch the wheel. We can now justify why we began our interpretation of Leonardo's musical machines with 218 rc: it includes the most primitive device—the fiddle bow—and one other traditional device known from the ghironda—the wheel. But no satisfactory method seems to have been found. The wheel mechanism comes nearest to a practical solution and in fact, long after Leonardo and certainly without his influence, was incorporated into Hayden's Geigenwerk, which we described earlier. However, we will see in the other drawings discussed here that the wheel idea is likewise abandoned.

Manuscript H 28 v (illus. 8.14) contains three drawings, but before trying to interpret them one must pose the question as to which is the top and which is the bottom of the page. The natural position for the big musical machine seems to be with the flat side down, as if it were to be placed on a table. But in that case the few words written on the page, "tessta della viola" and "tasti della viola," would be upside down. In the facsimile edition of MS H (Ravaisson-Mollien, 1891) the page is reproduced with the writing upside down. It may be, of course, that Leonardo drew the machine that way and made notes later without regard to the position of the

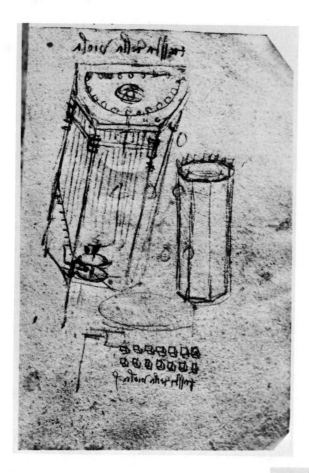

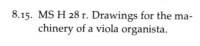

8.14. MS H 28 v. Three drawings for a
viola organista.

8.15. MS H 28 r. Drawings for the machinery of a viola organista.

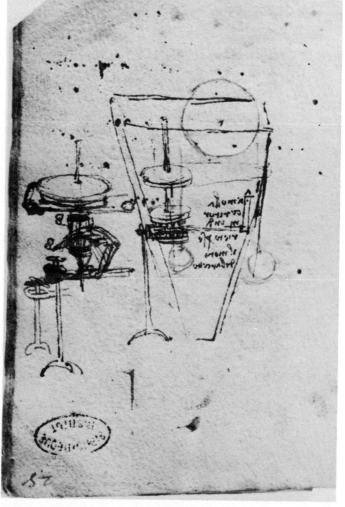

drawings. On the other hand the explanations are done with unusual neatness, aligned with the drawings. Thus, the following analysis refers to the drawing with the writing in upright position.

The large instrument on the left is a polyhedron with a broad flat base and five sides, of which at least two are employed as soundboards. The most striking detail is the friction device: this time a double belt, probably of hair or silk thread, passing over three small spindles at the upper end of the sound box. The spindles are evidently activated by the double wheel shown at the lower end of the sound box, whose source of motion is indicated. Two of the sides of the sound box, middle and left, carry strings; the left also clearly shows a bridge for the hitch pins. The little circles arranged on the upper end of the soundbox may indicate keys or push buttons. If this is so, the line leading down from one of the middle keys to one of the strings may indicate a lever by which the key brings the string in contact with the double belt, or endless bow. And further expanding our assumption that these little objects are keys, their number and arrangement would make one expect that strings would cover all sides of the sound box and not just the two which I have pointed out. But in that case, how would the box be held or placed? This is not clear in the drawing.

Although many details are drawn in only a suggestive manner, Leonardo did take great care to make clear that the bow passes over rather than beneath the strings. Attention should also be drawn to the fact that in this drawing we meet for the first time the name given by Leonardo to this type of machine: viola.

The double wheel device on the lower end of the soundboard can be identified with the help of MSS H 28 r, H 46 r, and H 45 v as part of the motor that furnishes the drive for the endless bow or archetto. However, the way by which it is connected with the archetto is not indicated in the present drawing. The smaller polygonal sound box on the same page is perhaps a passing idea or a variant of the larger instrument.

The drawing of the *tasti* consists of a double row of push buttons in the same cubic shape which we will encounter again in MS H 45 v. They have no visible relation to the instruments on this page. The possibility that the double row may imply a chromatic arrangement must remain an open question.

The opposite side of the same leaf (MS H 28 r [illus. 8.15]) gives more detailed although different versions of the wheel mechanism that drives the endless bow indicated in MS H 28 v. On the left a large wheel is shown, and beneath it is a rod cylinder or pinion cage, whose vertical rods engage horizontal pins of a contrivance which is only sketchily drawn but whose shape reminds one of that part in clockworks which serves to retard and regulate the motion of the wheels. On the right of the horizontal wheel there is an indication of the threads or hairs of the archetto (see MS H 28 v).

The wheel machinery in mid-page is somewhat different although probably only in the shape and dimensions of the structural parts, not in their function. The pinion cage is much larger and more distant from the upper wheel. The drawing of its vertical rods is somewhat obscured by a cluster of horizontal lines which may

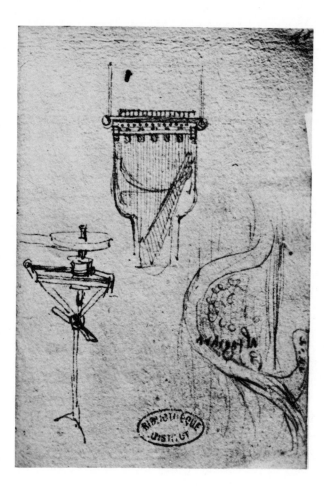

8.16. MS H 46 r. Two sketches relating to the viola organista, and a map of a river, perhaps for a project of canalization.

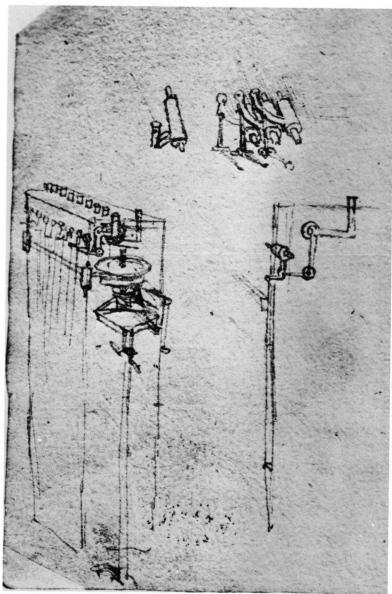

8.17. MS H 45 v. Sketch of a viola organista with details of construction.

again suggest an anchor device. Of greatest interest, however, is the indication of the endless bow, running from the right of the pinion cage toward the spindle (or, possibly, capsule), which contains the spring. The explanation written there says: "a molla ceritor ni indi rieto perse il moto dell'arcetto" (a molla ci ritorni indietro per se il moto dell'arcetto); we may translate this, "toward the spring, returns by itself (automatically) the motion of the bow device." This explanation is important, for it permits some conclusions as to the type of motion of the archetto, whose name, by the way, we find only on this page and in MS B 50 v.

If the thread moving the archetto returns to the spring, it is evidently wound up there on a spindle, and was wound up before at its other end, around the pinion cage. This implies a continuous motion in one direction without pauses rather than the movement back and forth which the fiddle bow performs. (We will come back to this problem in the interpretation of MS B 50 v). When the spring was coiled, the thread of the archetto must have been wound around the pinion cage; when the spring was released, the thread was drawn toward it in a smooth motion, owing to the retarding motion of the anchor, until it was wound up on the spring.

There remains another question: the meaning of the three long rods (with half-moon crutches) extending below the whole machinery. They must be pedal levers to activate—perhaps by winding—the wheel machinery, which in its turn guarantees an easy, regular motion of the archetto. In an earlier interpretation of this page I suggested that the rods were two-pronged handles, shown more clearly if the page were turned so that the half-moons appear on the left side. But this would not be in harmony with the six written lines in the center of the page.

Manuscript H 46 r (illus. 8.16) shows on the left a wheel device for propelling the archetto, similar to the ones in MS H 28 r. The upper drawing shows a bird's-eye view of a mechanism with at least twenty-six strings and a keyboard of sixteen keys. I am not able to explain the two vertical double lines extending from its upper end. The drawing is not precise, for the long oblique bridge that follows the gradation of strings from bass to treble does not cross all the strings. The whole drawing is connected with the viola organista only if one interprets the double line, which crosses the strings at their upper end, as the archetto. But this is just as doubtful an interpretation as saying that at the left and right ends of the double line are revolving cylinders or spindles over which the archetto would pass. Both these interpretations are possible but unfortunately the sketch is too unclear to draw such conclusions with any degree of certainty.

The sketch on the right has no connection with musical instruments. It is evidently a map of a section of a river, perhaps for a project of canalization. The inscription says, "Altagiara."

Manuscript H 45 v (illus. 8.17), as we shall see, is the result of the struggles and attempts embodied in the preceding pages. The sketch on the left shows a perfectly consistent, workable keyboard instrument with an endless bow. The soundboard of the oblong box carries eight strings, corresponding to the eight push buttons or keys (similar in shape to those drawn in MS H 27 v) projecting from the top of the sound box. It goes without saying that there could have been more strings and keys, and the drawing only suggests the construction of the machinery. The double line which marks the archetto, crossing the strings between the two corner spindles, is clearly visible. The archetto is moved by the wheel contrivance developed in MSS H 28 r and H 45 r and is most similar to the latter.

But there is one more important detail about which the preceding pages have given no information: the action of keys on the strings to enable them to make contact with the archetto. The reader would do well to look first at the large sketch on the right, which shows a schematic side view of this device: the levers connecting a single key with a single string; and a longitudinal view of one string running, parallel to the soundboard, toward the rear bridge and from there, with a slight change of direction, toward the hitch pin. If the player pushes the projecting end of the key, a set of two, right angular levers similar to the tracker mechanism used in organs, with their pivots clearly marked, turns a little capsule or cylindrical casing that moves around the horizontal axis. Firmly attached to this casing is another right angular lever terminating in a little circular loop that grasps the string a little distance above the point where the archetto passes over the strings. Upon receiving the impetus from the key, this loop-lever then draws the string against the moving archetto, thus creating the required friction. If the reader turns to the whole instrument with this schematic longitudinal sketch in mind, he will recognize the complete contrivance built in.

The two little sketches at the top are slight variations in the shape of what I have called the contact lever; in the sketch at the left the lever is built with a sharp bend, and in the sketch at the right, showing three levers side by side, it is shown with a slight curve.

With a mechanism such as this, the player would be able to graduate the intensity of friction and thus the volume of tone by varying the pressure of his fingers against the keys. This feature of Leonardo's instrument is of inestimable importance; the harpsichord, the keyboard instrument closest to the present sketch in general shape and construction, with strings running back from the player and each sounding their full length or one tone, was incapable of providing the increase or decrease of tone-volume through the varying of finger pressure. In the harpsichord these dynamic variations could be achieved only by pulling a stop and thus bringing into play one or more additional sets of strings. The clavichord, the only other contemporary instrument with a keyboard, permitted some dynamic shading through its tangent action on the strings, but it had an incomparably smaller tone than that of the harpsichord of Leonardo's time. The modern pianoforte, which, as its name reveals, permits dynamic shading (through hammer action on the strings by means of finger pressure on the keys), was invented only in the early years of the eighteenth century.

All construction sketches for the viola organista with an endless bow examined in the preceding pages are from MS H (28r, 46r, 45v). The last one (45 v) may be profitably compared with a sketch in CA 213 va (illus. 8.18 and 8.19), although 45 v represents the most unified and "logical" solution, whereas CA 213 va presents some difficult puzzles. There is, however, a close relation between the drawing of

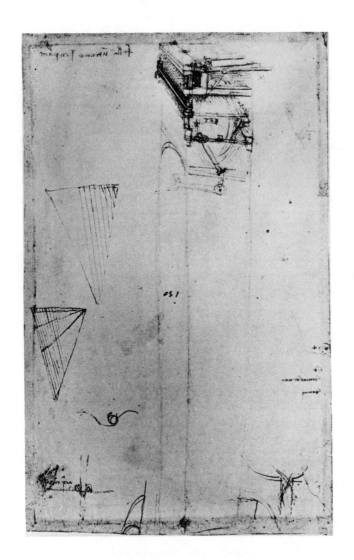

8.18. CA 213 va. Construction details for a viola organista.

8.19. Detail of illus. 8.18.

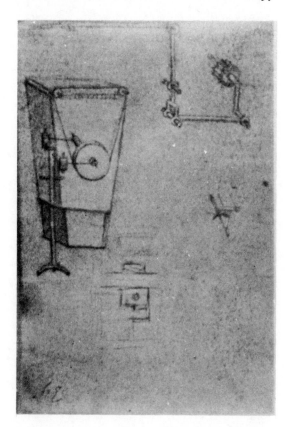

8.20. MS H 104 v. Drawing for a compact
     form of the viola organista.

the endless bow and the push-button machinery in both; also, both show a foot lever
for turning the machinery that operates the spindles moving the archetto. There
even seem to be several archetti, and a very large flywheel. Many details in CA 213
va, however, are so imcomplete or blurred that an interpretation cannot reach an
exact and a comprehensive level.

Manuscript H 104 v (illus. 8.20) shows a compact conoidal form of the viola
organista, perhaps for an itinerant musician in pageants, processions, or stage performances; in front the driving lever is visible, with rollers and center wheel showing
the path followed by the *archetto infinito*. At the top of the page is a diagram of the
machinery moving the archetto.

CA 34 rb (illus. 8.21) is filled with sketches of musical instruments and their
essential elements, no fewer than nineteen in number. Unfortunately the page is
badly mutilated; its left margin, which included parts of drawings and of verbal
explanations, is missing.

The most complete sketch of a whole instrument is at the bottom center. The
massive case is nearly triangular, with something like a keyboard on its top. The case
is to be attached to the chest of the player by a complex arrangement of [leather?]
belts, probably to keep the player's hands free for touching the keys or pushing
levers. There are wide openings for the hips and legs of the player. The distance
between the chest and the sound box is maintained by a vertical metal stick and four
smaller horizontal sticks (see the hinges).

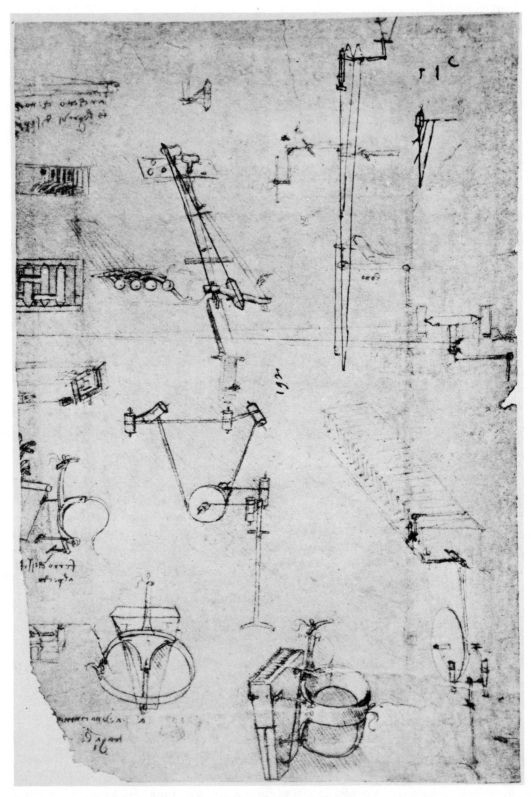

8.21. CA 34 rb. Drawing of viola organista (at bottom) and many other construction details.

Nothing in this sketch reveals the inner mechanism, the method of setting the strings into vibration, or the existence of an archetto infinito, and we cannot find this information in the two other triangular instruments, one to the left of the first, and the other a little higher on the left edge of the page. But we can infer just such information from the large drawing that reaches from the right lower corner toward the center of the page. There a large stick with a curved handle, probably a foot or knee lever, conveys motion over two spindles to a master wheel, from there to other spindles, and, one could guess, to a belt vibrating the strings under the illustrated keyboard. If this is only guesswork we receive clear information from the precise sketch in the lower center of the page. Here the same stick and master wheel direct the belt over the upper horizontal side of the triangular sound box to set the strings into vibration. Thus this belt could not have a function other than that of an archetto infinito.

The reader must keep in mind that here Leonardo does not sketch for publication but for his own memory. When he indulges himself, with pen in hand, in the anatomy of new machines, he does not always feel obliged to show several aspects or views of the same object in strict perspective but while illustrating sometimes expands or varies the main idea of the machine from picture to picture. While searching, he widens the field of research.

The upper half of the page shows a rich assortment of machine parts, all belonging to the viola organista. Some supplement one another; others are slightly different versions of one another. A detailed description and analysis as well as a reconstruction of all alternative versions would amount to a technical monograph beyond the limits of this book and, in a way, to a verbalization of the constant hypothetical conversation of Leonardo with himself and his simultaneous rapid sketching.

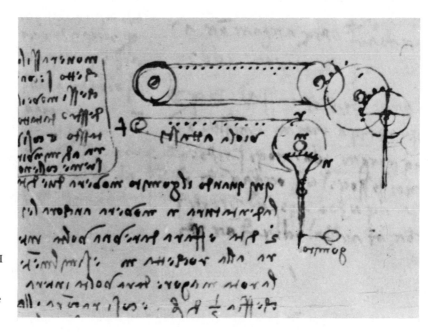

8.22. Lower part of page, Madrid MS II folio 76 r, with sketches for a simplified version of the viola organista (see illus. 10.8 for a whole page).

A page from MS II 76 r, National Library, Madrid (illus. 8.22), includes two different simple sketches of the viola organista. In the upper sketch we have a schematic front view of the instrument that we have seen in H 45 v (p. 153). Sixteen strings are now represented by sixteen dots as seen in cross section. Two interacting cogwheels move the right wheel of the two that turn the archetto. The cogwheels in turn must receive their impulse from some source of energy (mechanical or hand motion of the player or his assistant). We have seen such devices for the viola organista in H 45 v and other pages.

The lower sketch differs from the upper one in several respects. It indicates only eleven dots for strings; beneath the dots is written *viola a tasti* (keyed viol). The left wheel is much smaller and, above all, the device for driving the right wheel is different. Instead of two cogwheels, here only a segment of one is visible; it is operated by a lever with a handle inscribed *gomito*. The use of this wheel segment does not permit a continuous rotary movement of the archetto in one direction but facilitates only a forward and backward movement comparable to that of the actual bow of a viol or any other bowed instrument. All these features point to a smaller and simpler version of the viola organista, and probably to a portable version.

As we have seen, Leonardo used the human body as the source of energy for all the string instruments previously examined, through the motion of a foot, the chest, or an elbow setting a flywheel into motion, which in turn sets the endless bow rotating. There is, however, one exception. In B 50 v we find a clockwork operating an endless bow (illus. 8.23).[11] The clockwork with metal springs appears to be impractical. Metal springs have their caprices—they act strongly at first and then gradually lose power until the exhaustion point. To counteract this disadvantage and to achieve a smooth and an even motion of the archetto, Leonardo evidently searched for a more reliable device. His solution is shown in the left upper corner of B 50 v.

Before studying the entire machine, we should turn to the text—the most elaborate and revealing among all the pages dealing with the viola organista: "Questo e il modo del moto dello archetto della viola organista e se farai le crene della rota de 2 tempi che siano minori l'una quantita de denti che l'altra e che non si schontrino insieme chome apare in a. b. sara all'archetto uno (cho) equale movimento se non e andra a schosse esse farai a mio modo la rochetta f. senpre andera equale." A free translation follows: "This is the way the motion works of the viola organista. If one makes the notches to respond not to the same time but to two different times, so that one set of teeth is smaller in number than the other [on the opposite side of the wheel], and the teeth [on the left] do not correspond [the teeth on one side of the wheel not projecting on the same level as those on the opposite side] as it appears in a. b., the archetto will have an even motion while otherwise it would run in jerks. But if you make it in my way the spindle f. will turn evenly."

11. I am fully aware of the fact that by general consent MS B dates earlier than the other codices discussed in this chapter. Nevertheless I preferred discussing this page from MS B here at the end of this chapter because it concerns an auxiliary mechanism which can be better understood after discussion of the instruments designed in the others.

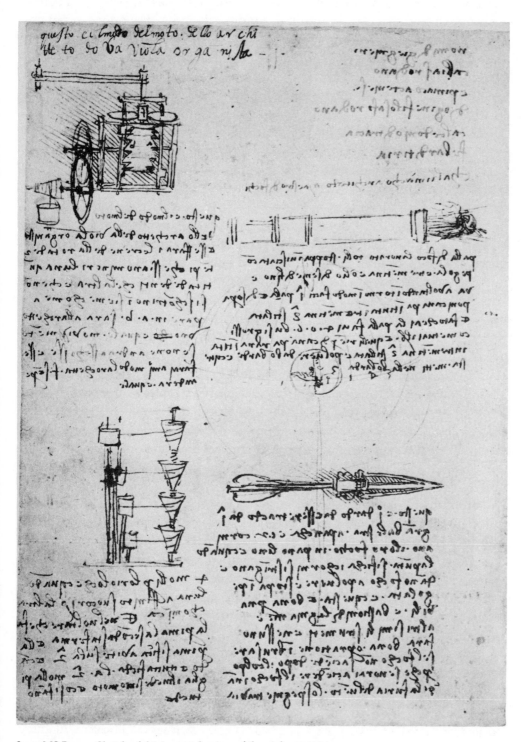

8.23. MS B 50 v. Sketch of driving mechanism of the viola organista.

This text contains some unclear or at least ambiguous passages which I believe become clearer through the study of the drawing, which itself is only a rapid embodiment of the basic idea, leaving some important detail open. Thus we must make the best of the situation and try to understand the drawing and its verbal explanation, each in the light of the other.

The *archetto della viola organista,* that is, the unending bow, is seen at the top of the drawing. It runs over two rolls of which the right-hand one is connected to a lower cylinder just above the large, toothed wheel (marked "a" and "b"). It is marked "f" in the drawing, and is called "rochetta" (roll, or spindle) in the text. The source of motive power is indicated in the lower left corner of the drawing: a round box from which a cord comes and is wound over a horizontal cone. This cone is known as a *fusée*[12] (from the medieval *fusus, fusella,* or *fusata*); it is a form of spindle used in machines driven by spiral springs. When the spring uncoils, its pull gradually decreases; the cord pulled by the spring is wound around the fusée pulling first its thin end with small leverage effect, and proceeding gradually to the wide end, thus counteracting the decrease of the force and producing an even drive. The use of the fusée in our drawing indicates that the cylindrical box or barrel in the drawing does not represent a weight, that time-honored source of motion for clocks and other mechanisms, but is rather an encased spring. This assumption is also supported by the four similar barrels in the lower drawing on the same page. They are all connected with fusées, and there the text expressly mentions "4 molli per l'oriolo" (four springs for the clock). They are staggered in an ingenious way so that the first of the springs, after uncoiling sets into motion the next one, and so forth until the last one has unwound itself. Although the text[13] does not mention any application of this combined spring device to musical machines, it would of course be possible and would give the player a much longer time before he had to rewind the spring.

The arbor (axle) of the fusée carries also a large spoked wheel, which again drives another spoked wheel, probably by means of a toothed drum attached to the upper wheel. This device would impart to the upper wheel a much greater speed of revolution than that of the first wheel. The second wheel shares its arbor with the indented wheel, which shows only its broad rim in the drawing. It is the indented wheel whose teeth ("crene" and "denti") are mentioned in the text. These tooth-like projections on either side of the broad rim are not placed symmetrically but on different levels. The letters "a" and "b" in the drawing make it clear that a tooth on one side corresponds to a recess or indentation on the other.

To understand this asymmetry we must undertake a little digression into the

---

12. I do not know of any earlier representations or descriptions than this. A. Lloyd, in *Chats on Old Clocks* ([New York, 1952], p. 40), considers it possible that the fusée, employed in 1525 in an extant metal clock made by Jacob Zech in Prague, was inspired by Leonardo. However this may be, the fusée appears not only in MS B 50 v but also in several other drawings of Leonardo.

13. Text for the drawing of the four cones, or fesées, in MS B 50 v: "4 molli per l'oriolo, che cquando l'una a ffinito suo corso, l'altra comincia. E nel voltare che fa la prima, la seconda sta ferma, e lla prima si ficca a vite su la seconda e cquando e ttutta ficta, la seconda molla piglia il medesimo moto; e cosi fanno tucte."

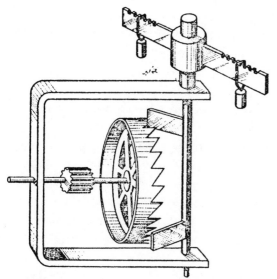

8.24. Escape mechanism of a clock with crown wheel (diagram by the author).

escape mechanism of clocks, particularly what is called the crown wheel[14] or escape wheel, and the verge (also called "balance staff," or simply "rod") (illus. 8.24). The pull of the weight or of the coiled spring in the clock mechanism would create a rapid motion of the wheels unless it was retarded. This can be achieved by attaching, to the arbor of one of the vertical wheels of the clock, another wheel with ratchet-shaped teeth. Near this "crown-wheel" a vertical rod is held so that it can turn back and forth. For this purpose it is equipped with two projecting plates, the pallets, one on top and one down below usually at an angle of about 100 degrees to the top one. These pallets engage alternately with the teeth of the crown wheel. The upper pallet receives a thrust from one of the teeth and turns the verge in one direction, where-upon the lower pallet receives a thrust in the opposite direction and turns the verge back. The result is a continuous swinging back and forth of the verge, permitting the teeth of the crown wheel to slip by one by one and thus to provide a slow and regular motion of the crown wheel. The verge carries a crossbar with a weight on either end, thus increasing the inertia of the verge. The weights can be shifted toward the verge or away from it, to regulate the speed of its oscillation and therefore of the whole clock.

Clocks with this verge escapement existed before Leonardo, who must have been familiar with this device. In the beautiful intarsias made by the school of Fra Giovanni da Verona about 1500 for the choir stalls of Monte Oliveto, south of Siena, which I visited some years ago in order to photograph the numerous musical instruments represented there, I found a depiction of a large clock with crown wheel and verge clearly delineated (illus. 8.25).

The verge escapement in its traditional form, however, would not have been serviceable for Leonardo's idea of an unending bow. As we have seen, the verge

14. The picturesque Italian term for a wheel with such projections is *ruota Caterina*.

moves back and forth in little jerks; the crown wheel, although it revolves in one direction, does so in little leaps whenever one of its teeth is released by one of the pallets of the verge. Neither type of motion provides the constant pull needed for uninterrupted bowing of the strings of a musical instrument. And here is where Leonardo's mechanical inventiveness provided an answer.

He retained the verge mechanism to retard the wheels, but at the same time he transformed it by thickening the crown wheel and equipping it with teeth on either side that project asymmetrically, as he explained in his text. Instead of one verge, Leonardo uses two, furnishing each with one pallet only. In the drawing the verge on the right side has its pallet on the bottom, and the other on the top. A single verge, with one pallet only, would of course have no retarding effect because it would spin in one direction with rapidly increasing speed. Not so with two verges, as drawn in Leonardo's sketch. They cooperate to provide retardation: since one verge has its pallet high and the other is low, both revolve in the same direction and turn the two horizontal wheels, left and right of the spindle "f," of which they are the arbors. These wheels then, by means of engaging teeth (not drawn in the sketch), impart to "f" that constant motion used for the unending bow, which is drawn on top with its right roll directly connected to "f."

As we pointed out at the beginning of this chapter, an instrument controlling a multitude of bowed strings by only the ten fingers of one player must have been a dream of imaginative instrument builders for centuries. Such an instrument would not have been merely a counterpart of the organ, where ten fingers control numerous pipes, but would have surpassed the organ in one significant aspect: that is, in the flexible dynamics permitting the fine gradation of volume. (The "swell" was invented for harpsichords only in 1769 and then, later, adapted for organs). In Leonardo's viola organista the finger pressure on the keys would have also modified the loudness of the tones produced by single strings so that, for example, one middle voice could have been dynamically emphasized such as we are able to do today on the pianoforte. But again, even the pianoforte would have been inferior to the viola organista in one regard. The striking of the hammers produces a tone that immediately begins to fade away or, as Leonardo says in the *Paragone,* "muoie durante la nascita," whereas the bowed strings of the viola organista would produce tones that crescendo and decrescendo but do not die away.

How vivid the dream must have been appears from the fact that from the sixteenth century until the time of the French *Encylopedie,* keyboard instruments were constructed, or rather, invented and re-invented. In 1581 Vincenzo Galilei, in his *Dialogo . . . della musica antica, et della moderna,* published in Florence, mentions a keyboard instrument with bowed strings in fact, as he says, like an "ensemble of viols."[15] In 1618 Michael Praetorius devoted a whole chapter in his *Syntagma*

15. Vincenzo Galilei, *Dialogo della Musica Antica et Moderna* (Florence, 1581), p. 48.

"*Strumento di tasti molto artificioso e bello.* Un'altro esempio d'uno Strumento di tasti, che già l'Elettore Augusto Duca di Sassonia, donò alla felice memoria del Grande Alberto di Baviera, mi

8.25. Clockwork with escape mechanism. From the intarsias in the choir stalls of Monte Oliveto, by Fra Giovanni da Verona.

Musicum, II, "De Organographia." and a beautiful woodcut (see illus. 8.9), to the "Geigenwerck-Geigen Instrument, oder Geigen Clavicymbel." In 1625 Fray Raymundo Truchado built his instrument with four friction wheels. In Italy also the dream must have lingered on. An official inventory of the Medici Collection (23 Sept. 1716) of musical instruments included an instrument with five wheels which, according to the short description given there, must have been a Geigenwerk.[16] Oddly enough this fact has never been noted in the organological literature[17] and this is especially strange because it was this inventory which was signed by Bartolommeo Cristofori, the inventor of the pianoforte, when he was appointed keeper of the Medici Collection. There are certainly good reasons for assuming that this instrument, which must have permitted crescendos and diminuendos by finger pressure, played a role in Cristofori's invention of the pianoforte, whose hammer action made possible the gradation of tone volume by finger pressure.

But it has never been discerned that Leonardo was the first to realize this dream and arrive, after wrestling with various tentative constructive schemes, at a practical solution or, at least, a skeleton for a workable instrument. One is tempted to imagine the Magus putting together a real instrument in Milan or perhaps later in the laboratory given to him by Pope Leo X in the Belvedere behind St. Peter's. That no real instrument has survived to our day does not mean that he did not build one. Musical instruments are fragile—their soundboards, of necessity, are made of soft wood and easily warp, bend, or crack under the tension of the strings and changes in humidity and temperature. And if they are not played and cared for continuously,

---

sovviene in questo proposito, più di ciascuno altro efficace, il quale Strumento ha le corde secondo l'uso di quelle del Liuto, e vengano secate à guisa di quelle della Viola da un'accomodata matassa artifitiosamente fatta delle medesime setole di che si fanno le corde à gli archi delle Viole; la qualmatassa con assai facilità, viene menata in giro con un piede da quello istesso che lo suona, e ne seca continuamente col mezzo d'una ruota sopra la quale passa, quella quantita che vogliano le dita di lui, il quale Strumento, due anni sono che io fui à quella corte, temperai secondo l'uso del Liuto, e faceva dipoi ben sonato, non altramente che un corpo di Viole, dolcissimo udire."

[*A Very ingenious and beautiful keyboard instrument.* Another example of a keyboard instrument which the Elector Augustus, duke of Saxony, presented to the late great Albert of Bavaria, occurs to me in this regard, better than any other. This instrument has strings similar to those of the lute and they are bowed like those of a viola by a strand made ingeniously of the same hairs of which are made the hair of viola bows. This strand can very easily be made to revolve by the foot of the player and strikes (bows), by means of a wheel over which it passes, the number of strings wanted by the fingers of the player. When I visited that court two years ago, I tuned this instrument in lute-like fashion and when well played it produced the sweetest sound, not different from an ensemble of Viols.]

The most telling word in this description is *matassa*, which means also the skein of yarn held by one person as it is being wound, and it therefore describes accurately the position of the belt or unending bow of Leonardo's instrument, particularly as it is shown in MS B 50 v.

16. The description of the instrument: "Un Cimbalo con' tastatura d'avorio, con' invenzione di cinque Ruote per toccar le corde di budella ad'uso d'una ghironda, tinta di rosso, e filettato d'oro, con' riquadrati copti di dommasco rosso, con' suo piede intagliato, tinto color' sim., e dorato, con' sua sopracopta di corame fod.a di tela, seg. N. 29."

17. Curt Sachs, in his *Real-Lexikon der Musikinstrumente* (Berlin, 1913), gives the most complete listing of wheel instruments of this sort after Truchado (under the heading "Streichklavier," p. 360 b).

they soon fall prey, as Leonardo said, to that great consumer—Time. As any connoisseur of the history of instruments knows, many instruments and even whole
collections have disappeared without a trace, and old treatises and illustrations,
even as late as the Baroque, tell us of instruments of which not a single specimen has
survived.

CHAPTER NINE

Melodic and Chordal Drums, Other Membranophones, and Tunable Bells

Leonardo was greatly interested in the construction of drums. Not only did he try to improve their playing technique but he expanded their musical possibilities, such as the range of tones, far beyond the limitations of the conventional instruments of his time. He also gave some thought to the mechanization of military drums, which is not strange if one recalls his interest in devising tools of war from small daggers to gigantic war machines and battlements.

The following pages in his notebooks contain sketches of drums:

CA 355 rc: 319 rb; 306 va;

Arundel 263 (BM) 137 v; 175 r.

CA 355 rc: This large page (illus 9.1) shows three instruments. The ones at the left and at the bottom are only faintly visible: at the left we see an instrument with seven strings, by its shape vaguely related to the hurdy-gurdy (ghironda). Keyboards are placed not only at the side of the neck but also appear strangely at the sides of the body. The function of such keys, if they are keys at all, remains mysterious since such a large number of keys does not seem to correspond to the much smaller number of strings.

The faint sketch at bottom of the page represents a set of twelve small kettledrums graduated in size. Simple as this sketch is, it clearly indicates Leonardo's idea of utilizing the drum as a melody instrument, that is, employing drums for producing all the tones of the scale and thus radically exceeding the role of the drum as primarily a reinforcement of rhythm.

The large drawing on our page represents, in accurate detail, a large kettledrum with the usual screws placed near the rim of the skin, to tighten the latter for tuning. The three beaters are operated by a cogwheel, which is turned by a crank.

A somewhat similar kettledrum of a shallower profile and with no screws is reproduced in Madrid folio 160 r. A crank turns a cylinder whose projections lift four beaters (illus. 9.2).

Codice Atlantico 319 rb (illus. 9.3) shows, besides a number of drawings not related to drums, eight sketches of drums. All these concern drums which are driven automatically by the wheels of their carriages. There are five side views of mechani-

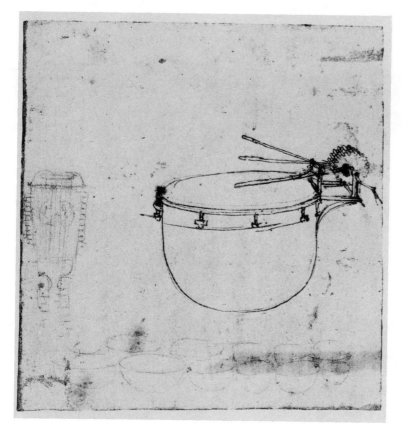

9.1. CA 355 rc. Mechanized kettledrum.

9.2. Madrid MS I folio 160 r. Mechanized kettledrum.

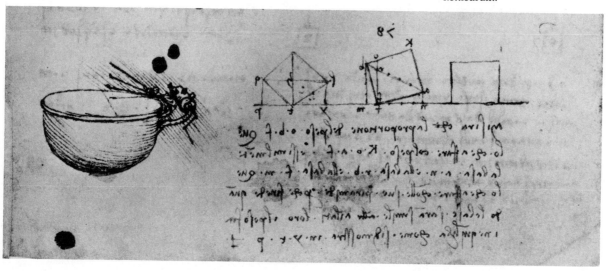

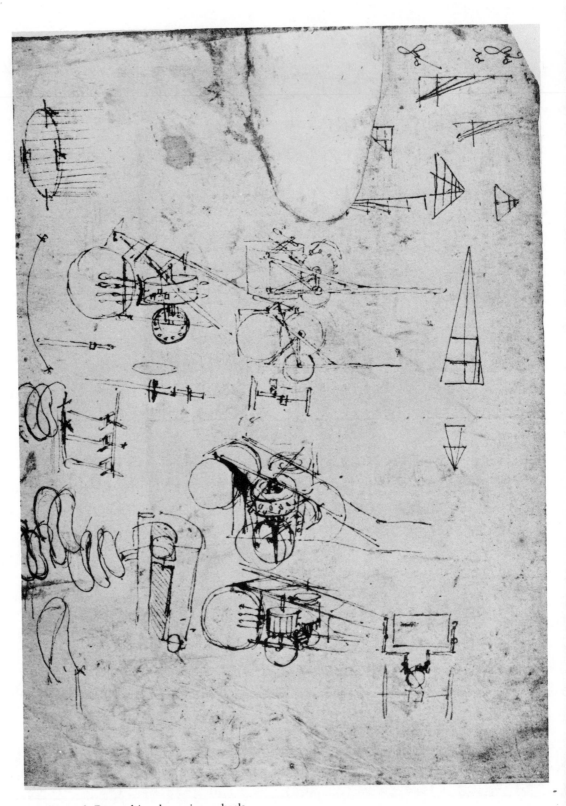

9.3. CA 319 rb. Drums driven by carriage wheels.

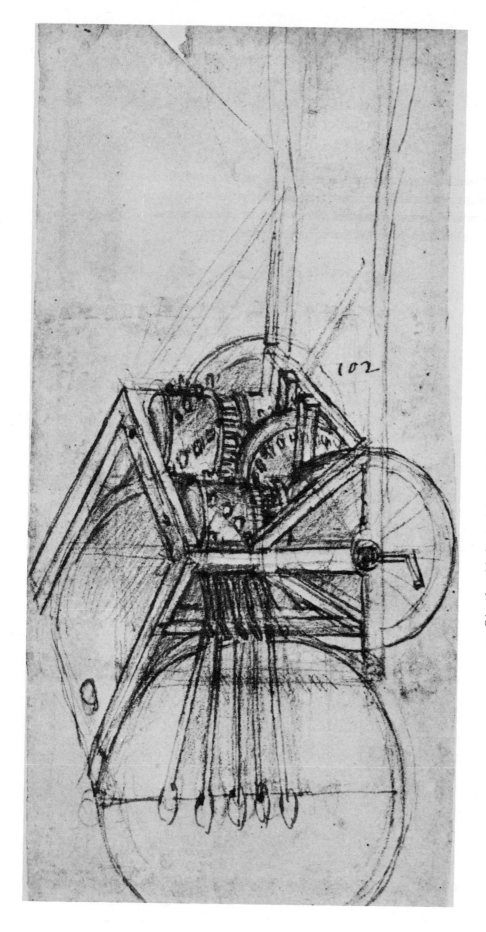

9.4. CA 306 va. Mechanized drum activated by crank and/or carriage wheels.

cal drums, one schematic sketch in front view (bottom of the page), and two diagrams showing the wheels and axle of the carriage. The five side views represent
slightly different versions of the same principle: the axle of the carriage wheel drives
a central cogwheel, or pinion wheel, and this in turn, through other cogwheels or
pinion cages, activates the beaters. In detail, the upper left sketch shows a side drum
with four beaters which are moved in turn by the pins of a horizontal wheel. The
sketch to right of it is a cylindrical drum in vertical position, with its skin on top, and
the beaters work by a large vertical pinwheel. The sketch immediately beneath it
wavers between two ideas: the cylindrical drum in side or vertical position.

The drawing beneath the center of the page is more detailed: here the cogwheel between the two carriage wheels engages two horizontal cogwheels evidently
to beat both sides of the side drum.

The last detailed drawing (middle bottom) seems to employ pinion cages in
place of cogwheels. The use of beaters on both sides is also clearly indicated in the
frontal sketch in the lower right corner of the page.

Codice Atlantico 306 va (illus. 9.4) is clearly a detailed and slightly modified
version of the sketch in CA 319 rb beneath the center. Here the drum has a snare and
five beaters. The teeth of the central vertical wheel engage with vertical rods of two
side cylinders, whose upper surface carry several oblique rows of pins, which in
rapid succession lift the levers that move the beaters. A crank protruding from one of
the carriage wheels indicates that the whole machinery could be operated by hand if
the carriage was not in motion.

Before turning to an analysis of Leonardo's new ideas for the construction of
melodic and chordic drums (Arundel 263 (BM) 137 v and 175 r; CA 355 rc), it will be
necessary to inquire into the general state of drum construction in Leonardo's time,
especially the form and function of kettledrums, which were the noblest and most
elaborate members of the drum family. Only against this background will it be
possible to judge the novelty of Leonardo's inventions and, in some cases, even to
arrive at a reasonable interpretation of his sketches.

Small kettledrums, always used in pairs, entered the Occident from the Islamic
Near East at the time of the Crusades and gradually became indispensable in martial
music together with their inseparable companions, the trumpets. Large kettledrums
came to Central Europe and Italy during the fifteenth century from the Turkish
empire. They could be tuned by turning the screws one after another, which thus
increased the tension of the skin (illus. 9.5).

The simplest and most obvious device to employ drums for playing a scale or a
chord is to use a whole set of gradated drums. I have already mentioned one of
Leonardo's sketches of this invention when I discussed CA 355 rc, a set of small,
gradated kettledrums. Another similar sketch is found in a corner of Arundel 263
(BM) 136 r (illus. 9.6), which is chiefly devoted to a wheel of pipes for producing
musical canons (this will be discussed later [p. 191]). However, in the upper left
corner of this page a little diagram shows five bowl-shaped drums of increasing size
attached by stems to a common base. Two beaters are indicated, one at left and one
at right. The text explains: "tanpa nj sona ti co me ilmo na cordo ovei dolce mele

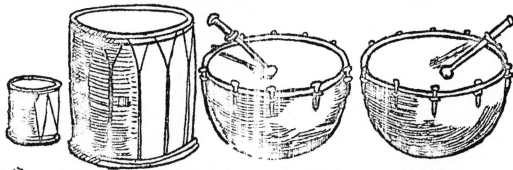

Herpaucken Trume n vnd clein paücklin

Dise baucken alle synd wie sye wellen/ die machen vil cnrüwe den Erbern frum men alten leuten/ den siechen vnd krancken/ den anbechtigen in den clöstern/ die zü lesen/zü studieren/vnd zü beten haßt/ vnd ich glaub vnd halt es für war der teüfel hab die erdacht vnd gemacht dann gann kein heilseligkeit/ nochgüts dar an ist/ sunder ein vertempfung/ vnnd ein nyder truckung aller süssen melodeyen vnd der gantzen Musica/ Darumb ich wol geachten kan/ das dz Tympanü vil eynander ding mü ß gewesen sein/ das man zü dem dienst gottes gebraucht hatt/ dann yetz vnser Bauck en gemacht werden/ vnd das wir on billich den namen de tüfelischen instrument zü geßen/ das doch nit wirdig ist zü der Musica zü brauc
D

9.5. Pair of kettledrums and two cylindrical drums. From Virdung, *Musica getutscht*, Basel, 1511.

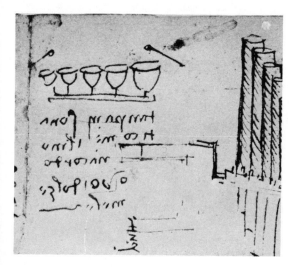

9.6. Arundel 263 (BM) 136 r. Detail: set of gradated, small kettledrums with beaters.

VNICA CHORDA QVA SONI CVIVSLIBET CONSONANTIÆ SIMVL AVDIRI POSSVNT ·

9.7. Monochord. The two stopping bridges permit two tones to be produced simultaneously on a single string. Woodcut from Lodovico Fogilano's *Musica theorica,* 1529.

[timpani sonati come il monacordo ove il dolcemele] [kettledrums played like a clavichord or dolcimele].''

My translation of *monacordo* by "clavichord" requires a justification. In the fifteenth and sixteenth centuries the word *monocordo* (also written monacordo or manicordo) was used for two different instruments: (1) the monochord, that venerable sound box with one or more strings, used for studying the numerical ratios of stopped strings (illus. 9.7), and (2) the clavichord, which had a larger number of strings stretched over an oblong sound box, and a set of keys that had little flat upright metal plates (tangents) inserted at their rear ends to strike at the same time to stop the strings. The clavichord was already fashionable before Leonardo's time (see illus. 8.13). It was also sometimes called *manicordio*, the word based in free association on *monocordo* but alluding to *mano* ("hand").

The *dulce melos* was another contemporary keyboard instrument, of square shape with jacks standing freely on the rear end of the keys. These jacks had brass hooks that struck the strings when the keys were pressed.[1] At any rate, Leonardo meant to compare his set of drums with a keyboard instrument because the latter could produce melodies and chords.

Arundel 263 (BM) 175 r (illus. 9.8) contains three groups of sketches and observations. One concerning theoretical mechanics, specifically gravitation and the behavior of weights,[2] fills the top and the upper right of the page. The lower part of the

1. The first description of the dulce melos is found in a fifteenth century Latin manuscript in the Bibliothèque Nationale in Paris. Botte de Toulmon first brought attention to it in his *Dissertation sur les instruments de musique au moyen-age* (Paris, 1844), comparing it to a pianoforte. Curt Sachs gave a more convincing description of it in his *History of Musical Instruments* (New York, 1940), p. 343.

2. See the transcription of these passages in Arturo Uccelli, *Leonardo da Vinci: I Libri di Meccanica* (Milan: Höpli, 1940), p. 20.

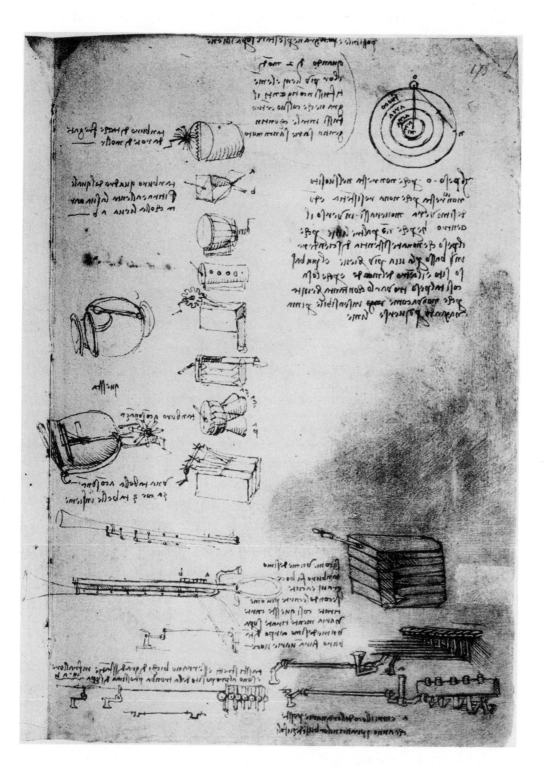

9.8. Arundel 263 (BM) 175 r.

page shows eight sketches for the construction of keyboards for wind instruments.[3] The rest of the page, that is, the upper left half and center, deals with drums, and to this section belongs also the large chordal drum with beater in the lower right section.

The eleven drum sketches represent an astonishing variety in aim and construction. I should like to point out here, before detailed interpretation, that the sequence from top to bottom is not haphazard; the drawings are not isolated aperçus but instead seem to follow a methodical order progressing from group to group, each group dealing with a different problem. Thus I will take them up in my analysis from top to bottom and reflect on the method of the grouping at the end of our analysis.

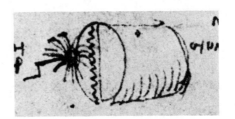

9.8A. Arundel 263 (BM) 175 r. Detail.

9.8A: The body of the drum is clearly a cylindrical snare drum. The problem begins with the indented line vertically crossing the skin, and the concentric cluster of black lines on the left from which a crank evidently protrudes. Leonardo's explanation says: "tamburo di tacche fregate da rote di molle" (at least this is the diplomatic translation in the facsimile edition of 1923, edited by Danesi). In English this would be: "A drum with (a device of) notches scraped by a wheel of springs." With the word *tacche* Leonardo probably indicates a small board with many little saw-like indentations. The *rote di molle* is probably not a wheel in the strict sense of this word but a number of flexible metal sticks arranged like the spokes of a wheel. It is possible, however, to read rot*i* instead of rot*e* and to translate it "fragments" (or little pieces) of springs. The protruding crank is unmistakable, but the way in which the cluster of springs is attached to the drum is not evident from the drawing.

What, then, is the meaning of the whole? Leonardo's explanation gives the technical ingredients of the mechanism, not its purpose. We probably have here a combination of a scraper action (that is, the springs beating against the indentations of the saw) with a cylindrical drum functioning mainly as a resonator or sound reinforcement. The whole achievement then would be moderate: a different timbre and a sort of mechanization through crank action but no revolutionary invention such as we will find in the following sketches.

3. Analyzed on p. 193.

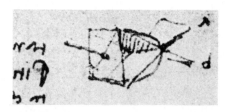

9.8B. Arundel 263 (BM) 175 r. Detail.

9.8B: This sketch is of incomparably greater importance and novelty than A. Leonardo says: "tamburo quadro del quale si tira e allenta la sua carta colla lieva *a b*" (square drum whose skin is tightened and slackened by means of the lever *a b*).

The drum, that is, its body—contrary to Leonardo's words—is not square but its head is. The function of the tightening mechanism becomes clear if the reader's eye separates the outer shape of the drum from the levers which look so:

If the player pushes asunder the ends at the right, perhaps wedging a fist in between, the other ends open, scissor like, thus tightening the skin, while the other hand is beating it. The result is that of a drum with pitch changeable during performance, something which the Occident did not know until the invention of the pedal machine drum toward the end of the nineteenth century.[4] This latter invention enabled the player to change the tuning so fast during performance that even a melody of moderate tempo can be played.

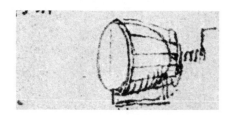

9.8C. Arundel 263 (BM) 175 r. Detail.

9.8C: Here the shape of the instrument is that of a kettledrum, which was well known to Leonardo. Small kettledrums, always used in pairs (*naqqârâ, nacchere, nacaires, nakers*) entered the Occident from the Middle East during the Crusades if not earlier. Large kettledrums (*tympana*) were known in Eastern Europe, especially Hungary and Poland, as early as the fifteenth century. In 1511 Sebastian Virdung, a priest in Basel, complains in his *Musica getutscht* of the "horrible noise of these

4. German patent Apr. 2, 1881 (see *Zeitschrift für Instrumentenbau* XXIII (1903): 636. West Africa and the Far East know the "hourglass drum," whose two skins are connected by external ropes which can be pressed by the player's arm or elbow to increase or decrease the tension of the skins and thereby change the pitch during performance. It is, however, improbable that Leonardo knew this type of drum.

drums, which disturb the pious old people, the sick and the devout in the cloisters, who try to read, to study and to pray," and considers them "an invention of the devil, and the suppression of all sweet melodies."[5]

Virdung's illustration of the kettledrums (illus. 9.5) shows a device which, according to all historic evidence, must have been quite novel at his time: there are ten screws visible that can lower or raise the iron frame by which the skin is stretched, and thereby tighten or slacken the skin. None of Leonardo's drums has this device. The present drum, like the ones in 9.8F and 9.8G show an earlier tightening device, namely, laces. Cords like these either connect the two skins on opposite sides of a cylindrical drum, as for instance in 9.8G, or are slung from the rim of the skin around the body, as in kettle- or pot-shaped drums like 9.8C. For tuning purposes this net of cords can be tightened but this of course takes some time, and a quick change of skin tension during performance is out of the question.

Leonardo's sketch shows an extraordinary feature: the cords running from the circular frame of the drum are not fastened to its round bottom but go beyond it toward a sort of disk or ring to which we must suppose they are attached. From this contraption protrudes—drawn in Leonardo's inimitable shorthand technique—a screw and a crank. The only interpretation that explains all these unusual features is to consider them as a device that can, by turning the crank, change the tension of all the cords simultaneously and thereby change the pitch in a minimum of time. On such a drum, any melody could be played by appropriate manipulation of the crank. This invention, whether Leonardo knew the hoop-tightening screws depicted in Virdung or not, goes far beyond Virdung's device and in fact anticipates the latest development of the modern pedal-tuned timpani or machine drum of the modern orchestra, which dates back no earlier than the middle of the nineteenth century. The screws on the Virdung instrument could be turned only one at a time and therefore would permit only slow tuning. As pointed out above, not until the pedal machine drum of the nineteenth century was a quick, simultaneous tightening of all the screws on the hoop made possible.

In sketch 9.8C, which we are discussing here, the drum apparently rests on a stand; the player could not hold the drum because both his hands were engaged, one in turning the crank and the other in beating the drum. Thus, the presence of a stand would support the assumption that the crank serves to tighten the laces rather than activate a beating mechanism.

It seems appropriate here to at least mention a different interpretation. One may perhaps consider the crank a device for beating the skin in some way from the inside of the body, and there are three sketches where cranks are used to set the beaters or beating springs into motion: 9.8A, 9.8E, and 9.8H.[6] But in all these sketches the connection with the beaters is obvious and the beaters are clearly

5. Sebastian Virdung, *Musica getutscht und ausgezogen* (Basel, 1511), p. 25.
6. The study of cranks in Leonardo's machines is rewarding beyond their use in musical instruments, for they function only if turned counterclockwise, that is, as a left-handed person would turn them. This fact alone would have been a decisive argument in the controversy raging for generations about the reasons why Leonardo used mirror writing.

drawn. Moreover, in sketch 9.8C the crank is attached to a screw which would allow only slow turning as required for tightening, and not for rapid beating. Finally, sketch 9.8C appears as one in a row of five drums (9.8B–9.8F), which all aim at a workable solution of changing pitch during performance.

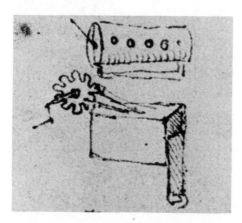

9.8D and 9.8E. Arundel 263 (BM) 175 r. Detail.

Sketch 9.8D is one of the most original solutions of the problem of obtaining a series of different tones from a drum while beating it. Here a snare drum with a long, nearly cylindrical body on a stand has several side holes in flute fashion. Before finally convincing myself that the little circles indicate holes, I decided to experiment and had built a little wooden tube with a skin on one opening and several side holes. The closing of the various holes while beating the skin results in clear pitch differences, and one wonders why in primitive music or for children's toys such a "flute drum" was never used.

Sketch 9.8E shows a square box with a ratchet wheel worked by a crank. The several slightly curved lines on top of the upper side of the box seem to indicate springy tongues attached at one end to the surface of the box while the free end is lifted in quick succession by the spokes of the wheel, to snap back against the surface. The way in which the wheel is attached to the box is not shown unless one of the lines just mentioned indicates such a connection.

The unusual feature of this instrument is the flat oblong board on its right side, which is softly shaded while the square above it is strongly shaded. The board is, in my belief, a slide and the square above it a hole which can be opened or closed by moving the slide. The purpose would again be to obtain a change in pitch during playing. To verify my interpretation I again built a model whose performance fully corroborated my assumption. Notice also the little projections on the bottom end of the slider, which can hardly be anything else than loops or handles for moving the slide.

There is still the question of whether this instrument is a "drum" in the strict sense of this term, that is, an instrument with a membrane. We must rather assume that its upper surface is of wood since only this would provide the right basis for the springy tongue of the ratchet mechanism.

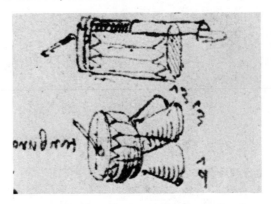

9.8F and 9.8G. Arundel 263 (BM) 175 r. Detail.

The drum in sketch 9.8F is evidently based on the same principle as 9.8E: the slide action. Here the body is that of a conventional cylindrical drum with laces. The side hole and slide are on top, and the right end of the slide again has some sort of handle for pulling. This drum has no mechanical beating machinery but an ordinary beater.

The next sketch introduces a group of three drums (9.8G–9.8I) that are based on another method of expanding the function of drums: the production of simultaneous tones or chords by combining several drums into one compound instrument. Sketch 9.8G shows an instrument which is a combination of a side drum with snare, and several cones inserted into its base. Three cones are visible but it is possible that there may be more, hidden behind. However, there are marks added at the right of the cones that may be the symbols for tones according to the Guidonian system of solmization, which designated the tones of the scale by syllables such as ut re mi fa sol la. This seems probable also from Leonardo's caption, "tanburo a consonanza," although one cannot help wondering why the cones meant to produce different tones are of approximately the same size. Different tones, to be sure, for example, the tones forming a triad, could be produced by different tightening of the membranes, assuming they were so equipped.

At any rate there cannot be any doubt that we have here a drum intended to produce a chord. It is a pity, however, that the drawing does not give the faintest idea about the connection between the body of the drum and the cones, or whether the cones are open or closed at their wide end or perhaps at their small end, or how deep they reach into the drum itself. There are several possibilities. (1) They may be open at both ends. This possibility can be discarded: a model that I built does not succeed in producing different tones. (2) They may be equipped with membranes at either or both ends and therefore, in fact, be drums themselves.

Sketch 9.8H is another "consonance" instrument. The text says: "Una tabella a consonanza cioè 3 tabelle insieme." The body consists of three shallow boxes. To the upper left edge a ratchet mechanism is attached. A spindle turned by a crank is furnished with three sets of spokes that simultaneously operate springy tongues beating on the top of the three boxes. Thus this instrument was intended to produce a chord of three tones. We do not see from the drawing whether this instrument has

9.8H. Arundel 263 (BM) 175 r. Detail.

membranes. If not, it would, like that in sketch 9.8E, not be a drum in the technical sense of the word but an idiophone.

Still simpler in construction is the drum sketched at the lower right side of the page (see illus. 7.9). At first glance there may seem to be six compartments on the right side as opposed to five on the left. Actually, there are five skins at the left which bend around the edge of the whole box and are tied with cords around it. The text says: "Si come un medesimo tanburo fa voce gravi e acute secondo le carte più men tirate, così queste carte variamente tirate sopra un medesimo corpo di tanburo faran varie voce [Since one and the same drum produces high or low tones according to the tighter or looser stretching of the skin, so the present skins stretched at various degrees over the same body of a drum produce different tones]." The instrument clearly permits playing a scale.

The last two drawings of drums, sketches 9.8J and 9.8K, present greater difficulties to interpretation than all the others. Both are evidently pot drums with detachable drumheads and a mechanism inside to make them sound. No separate beater is visible.

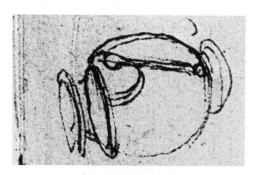

9.8J. Arundel 263 (BM) 175 r. Detail.

In the upper drum 9.8J, what appears to be a lid or cover at the left (or upper end of the pot) is detached. Whether this left end of the pot is simply open, or covered by skin, cannot easily be decided. Since Leonardo uses shading for open holes such as in sketches 9.8E and 9.8F, we are inclined to interpret the round shape at this end as a head affixed to the drum, in addition to the one which is removed. In the lower drum, the corresponding section is dark and thus, probably, an open hole.

Also difficult to explain are the curved lines at the right of the upper drum. They are likely to indicate a base or handle for holding the pot, or perhaps a device for activating the inner machinery. Since no outside beater or drum stick is illustrated we must assume that it is the inner mechanism that beats the drum from inside.

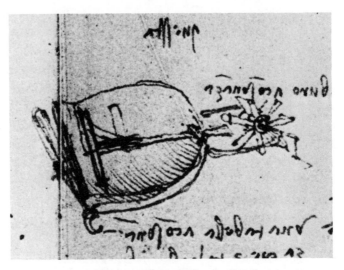

9.8K. Arundel 263 (BM) 175 r. Detail.

The lower drum 9.8K, of a different and longer shape, also has a detachable cover and an inner mechanism. The latter, in this case, is activated by a spoked wheel outside, which is turned by a crank. The ends of the wheel spokes beat against two nearly parallel sticks or wires protruding from the pot. This dual number makes one think that it is a device employed to turn the object inside the pot, which may be a friction wheel. Problematic also is the line curving on the lower side of the drum, clearly outside it, extending from the frame of the spoked wheel toward a hook on the rim of the pot.

9.9. From Virdung, *Musica getutscht.*

Although this attempt at interpreting the drawings themselves remains guesswork, we may find relevant information in contemporary instruments of Leonardo's time and recall certain folk instruments that show similarities to Leonardo's pot drum. One is a scrap pot as we find it illustrated occasionally after 1500 in German literature. It is shown in Virdung (illus. 9.9), evidently copied from there in Praetorius, where neither name nor explanation is given except that in chapter xiii of the "De Organographia" he refers to it by calling it a "Pritschen auf dem Hafen" (beater in the pot). It is also illustrated in a facetious set of "Musicians" by Tobias Stimmer, where the last picture is that of an old woman playing the pot with a spoon ending in a hook (illus. 9.10). No treatise gives the name or an explanation of how it is played, but from Stimmer we can safely conclude that the playing technique was that of scraping. The first two rhymes of the funny poem which accompanies the drawing say:

Nimmer zergaht ein Spil ohn Narren.
Drum muss ich auf dem Hafen scharren.

Never a play occurs without a fool, therefore *I* must scrape [scharren] the pot [Hafen].

There was also another folk instrument which combined pot and membrane and is so widely disseminated that it must have a very long history. Its most famous illustration is found in a painting by Frans Hals (illus. 9.11); it also plays a prominent role among the noisemakers in P. Breughel the Elder, *The Combat between Carnival and Lent* (illus. 9.12). It is the Rommelpot, to use its Dutch name mentioned already in Mersenne's *Harmonie Universelle* (Paris 1636). In Provence it was known as the *pignato*, in Naples as the *caccarella*, and in Apulia as the *cupacupa*.

Leonardo himself designed a version of the Rommelpot in MS 2037 Bib. Nat. C r (illus. 9.13). His version shows not actually a pot but a cylinder possibly fashioned out of bark or covered with fabric. It is closed on one side by a membrane that may be of animal skin or an equivalent flexible material. This instrument occurs in many versions in Europe and in the Orient. Some specimens have a stick or hollow reed attached to the center of the membrane. The stick is used either to set the membrane into vibration or is itself vibrated by the wetted palm of the hand. Various substances such as wax or tar are used to create friction. A similar effect can be produced by an attached bunch of hair or rope, as shown in illustration 7.14. The tone produced is a shrieking and, to most people, funny noise. In chapter 7 I drew attention to Leonardo's distinction among different kinds of noise such as *tono, strepido*, and *romore*, and that romore (rumor), meaning an inarticulate tone, is represented by the vulgar noise of the friction drum such as our Rommelpot. When Leonardo organized the Feste del Paradiso at the Castello Sforzesco in Milan in 1490 he showed the caccarella as the appropriate noisemaker for the twelve devils at the gate of hell.[7]

Immediately to the left of this Rommelpot Leonardo drew another instrument that is supposedly similar but with a very different function. A cylinder covered with fabric and tied at one end shows at the other end a cogwheel operated by a crank.

7. See p. 75.

9.10. Old woman with pot drum; wood-cut by Tobias Stimmer, sixteenth century.

9.11. Frans Hals the Elder, *The Rommel-pot Player.* Richmond, Collection Sir Herbert Cook.

9.12. Detail from P. Breughel the Elder, *The Combat between Carnival and Lent.* Kunsthistorisches Museum, Vienna.

The cogs of the wheel produce a rattle-like noise; a loop of rope forms a carrying handle.

9.13. MS 2037 Bib. Nat. C r.

Sketches such as the ones in Arundel 263 (BM) 175 r are interesting because of the originality of Leonardo's inventions and the superb economy of his drawing technique; they permit a glimpse at his forma mentis. He begins his series of drums with what was probably a passing idea: an unusual tone color or rather noise color for a drum and a mechanical contraption for playing it. But then a whole flood of novel ideas is let loose, all going beyond existing devices. Leonardo endeavors to enrich the traditional function of drums by making them capable of producing chords and scales. For this, he tries two different methods. One is the combination of several drums or skins of different pitch into one single instrument. The other consists of devices to make one skin produce tones of different pitch in rapid succession. This aim is realized by various methods: through the introduction of side holes; through the use of scissor levers or screw devices to change the tension of the skin while it is beaten: through slides that open and close a large hole in the resonating body; or, finally, by mechanisms that detach the skin cover from the body of a pot drum. Hardly an opportunity offered by nature is overlooked in this series of quick though methodical sketches, jotted down on a page which began with quite a different subject—theoretical mechanics—and is going to wind up with new ideas for wind instruments.

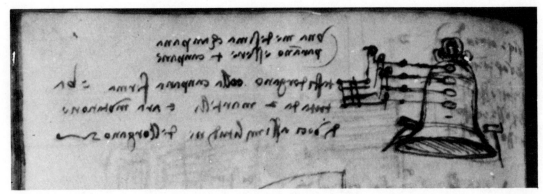

9.14. Madrid MS II, folio 75 v. Detail: bell with 2 hammers and a mechanism of 4 dampers.

TUNABLE BELLS

Madrid MS II folio 75 v shows in the upper right corner (illus. 9.14) a bell with a wide rim and no clapper inside. Two hammers strike the rim from opposite sides. To the left of the bell there is a mechanism including what seems to be a set of four keys operating on a tracker action that in its turn controls four levers that end in oval heads. In my opinion these heads must be dampers. The accompanying text says: "Una medesima campana parranno essere quattro campane. Tasti d'organo, con la campana ferma e battuta da due martelli. Ed avrà mutazione di voci, a similitudine dell' organo."[8]

Acoustically important in this explanation are the statements that the bell is firm, neither swinging nor equipped with a clapper in the manner of a church bell, and that it produces "a change of tones," which is in all probability one of pitch, not of timbre.[9] Thus, Leonardo must have believed that the upper section of the bell has ring-shaped areas that produce tones of different pitch if they are slightly muted when the rim is set into vibration by the hammers. I must, however, sadly add that my own experiments with smaller and medium-sized bells in the Metropolitan Museum's collection brought no conclusive results.

Hermann von Helmholtz, in his famous book *Die Lehre von den Tonempfindungen* . . ., did not rule out at least the possibility of areas of a bell producing tones of different pitch.[10] Anyhow, it is interesting that Leonardo, here, as in many other of his musical inventions, tried to obtain from one instrument what could normally only be produced by several or a whole set of instruments.

8. "One and the same bell will appear to be four bells. Organ keys, with the bell stationary and beaten by two hammers. It will have a change of tones comparable to that of an organ."

9. Theoretically the change of tones could also mean change of timbre; but this is not likely, since a difference among these four kinds of timbre would be small, and also because Leonardo insists that his invention enables the bell to do the job of four bells, implying probably that effect of a carillon.

10. "Der stärkste Ton ist nicht der tiefste; der Kessel der Glocken, angeschlagen, giebt tiefere Töne als der Schallring, letzterer dagegen die lautesten. Uebrigens sind auch wohl noch andere Schwingungsformen der Glocke möglich, wobei sich Knotenkreise bilden, die dem Rande parallel sind, diese scheinen aber schwer zu entstehen, und sind noch nicht untersucht" (*Die Lehre von den Tonempfindungen als Physiologische Grundlage für die Theorie der Musik*, 4th ed. [Braunschweig, 1877], p. 125).

CHAPTER TEN

Toys and Folk Instruments

In MS 2037 Bib. Nat. D r we find two adjacent leaves with curious drawings: some folk instruments, some fantastic instruments. The bizarre goat-jaw instrument has already been discussed in chapter 5 (illus. 5.1) as one example related to the craniomania of the time. Related to it also seem to be the three strange bone daggers or knives (illus. 10.1). The two upper curved ones have handles in the shape of

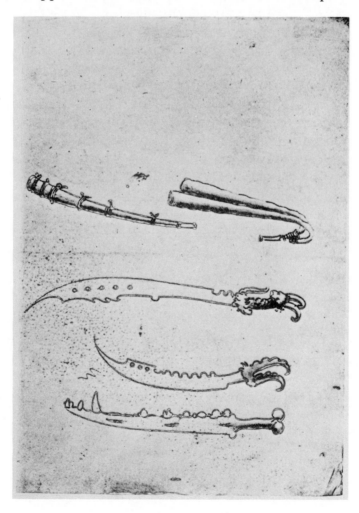

10.1. MS 2037 Bib. Nat. D r. Two realistic pipes, one single and one double, and three bizarre bone daggers.

187

animal horns, and one, even the whole neck of a goat; the lowest one is nearly straight and is furnished with teeth of different shapes, from pointed canine teeth to rounded molars, [1] but one hesitates to identify the whole dagger as a jaw because its handle with its two round bulbous projections resembles rather the upper end of the femur. In short, here, as in the drawing of the goat skull with musical strings and frets, Leonardo seems to have given free rein to his fantasy at its most playful.

The two wind instruments above the daggers are utterly mysterious. The upper double pipes seem vaguely to resemble an aulos (*tibia* in Latin), that famous double oboe of the ancients, which certainly must have been familiar to Leonardo from many ancient sarcophagi and other Roman art depictions. But the aulos consisted of two tubes, each with an independent mouthpiece, whereas the present pipes seem to converge toward one common mouthpiece. No finger holes are marked.

The other slightly curved instrument has a single pipe with the mouthpiece indistinctly drawn. Also problematic are the six loops of string, each neatly tied. Distances between the loops are unequal and, at first glance, one may be reminded of frets in a stringed instrument; but we have here a wind instrument and, at any rate, the distances do not correspond to the proportional arrangement one would expect of frets. Moreover, there is no trace of finger holes, as, for instance, in a cornetto.

With so many questions open, one may perhaps best return to the assumption that the pipes as well as the fancy bore daggers were children of a momentary fancy, and perhaps were meant to be used in some bizarre pageant, possibly for allegorical purposes, carried by satyrs or silens or other mythical creatures.

Quite different are the drawings in Arundel 263 (BM) 136 r (illus. 10.2). The most detailed drawing on this page is in the lower right corner. One distinguishes clearly a wheel or circle with a crank attached. The wheel, or rather the innermost circle, has at its periphery four teeth or cogs, and behind them, four sets each of seven rods, probably of wood or cane. The circular lines behind these rods seem to indicate their rotary motion through the air.

Leonardo's text at the left of the drawing is as follows:

Qui si fa una rota di m canne a uso di tabelle con un circulo musicale detto canone che si canta a quattro che ciascun cantore canta tutta la rota e poi faccio io qui una rota con 4 denti che ogni dente fa l'uffizio d'uno cantore.

It may be rewarding to compare this drawing in the lower right corner with another one near the center of the page, where the middle wheel is marked *tabella*. We recognize in a sketchier way the four sets of rods in graduated lengths. Their widths are surprisingly uneven; we also recognize the short teeth or cogs projecting from the middle wheel. There are, however, many more than the four clearly drawn in the lower drawing.

1. See Leonardo's drawing of various human teeth in F B 4k v, Windsor AN. B 19058v (B41v); Charles D. O'Malley and J. B. Saunders, *Leonardo da Vinci on the Human Body* (New York: Henry Schuman, 1952), 3, p. 44.

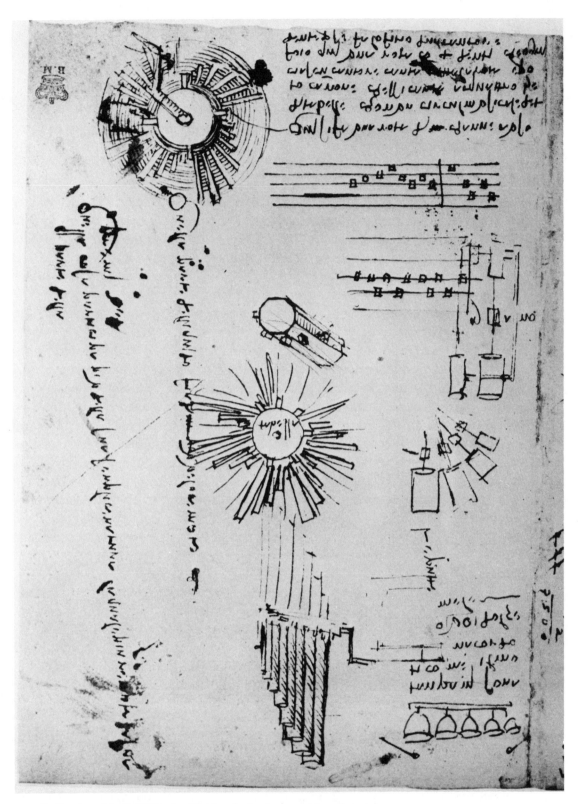

10.2. Codice Arundel 263 (BM) 136 r. Sketches for toy instruments and scores.

Beneath this drawing we see an octagonal barrel-shaped body, which must be the steering mechanism. At least four teeth do project from it, but from adjacent planes and at different distances from the end. One wonders whether the two pieces of score beneath represent the theme of the canon. It is interesting that the lowest score includes eight notes but in fact only four different pitches.

On top of the page we find a very different instrument related only in some regard to the former two wheels. Like the wheels, it has a crank and, very sketchily drawn, the middle barrel with a number of teeth projecting in different directions. But this drawing does not show rods of different shapes and irregular widths but clearly large cylindrical pipes like organ pipes, which show that if Leonardo wanted to draw hollow rods or pipes or tubes, he could do this admirably with a minimum of lines. Although there is a crank, one should not assume that the pipes were to be shifted by rotary motion to the lower side of the barrel, since the smallest pipe of the lower set is beneath the longest of the upper set.

Returning now to Leonardo's text at the bottom of the page, we are now prepared to examine the word *channe*. Whether we interpret Leonardo's channe as a solid or hollow object is central to our explanation because hollow objects would function as pipes or tubes or, at any rate, as wind instruments, whereas solid things would function only by vibrating when struck and, thus, as percussion instruments. If we have pipes, the difficulty arises as to how wind is made to fill them—rotation of the wheel may not be sufficient, and no bellows are shown. The word *channe* means, and meant at Leonardo's time, many different things, some hollow, some solid, and some hollow but not throughout their whole cavity. Among hollow things we find pipes, such as organ pipes, the pastoral flute, a glassblower's tube, a gun barrel, the human windpipe, and many others; on the other hand, *channe* often means solid things such as a fishing rod, a measuring rod, or a walking cane; finally, *channe* also designates slender stems such as shafts of grass or bamboo sticks, which are hollow but with the cavity separated into several compartments closed by strong diaphragms. One could not make a flute out of bamboo without removing these diaphragms.

The two large, nearly complete English translations of Leonardo's notebooks,[2] Jean Paul Richter's *The Literary Works of Leonardo da Vinci*, published in 1883 and in a second edition in 1939 (London: Oxford University Press), and Edward MacCurdy's *The Notebooks of Leonardo da Vinci*, first published in 1904 and then in expanded form in 1938 (London: Jonathan Cape), give remarkably different translations of this text.

In his translation Richter avoids committing himself to wind or percussion instruments and translates *channe* by the phonetically similar English word, *cane*. The English *cane*, like the Italian *channa*, can mean both a pipe or a solid rod. But Richter is not consistent, for his translation of *tabelle* as "clappers" suggests percussion. Here is his translation of the entire text: "Here there is to be a cylinder of cane after the manner of clappers with a musical round called a canon, which is sung in four parts; each singer singing the whole round. Therefore I here make a wheel with 4 teeth so that each tooth takes by itself the part of a singer."

---

2. Both published long before the recovery of the Madrid Codices in 1967.

MacCurdy takes sides uncompromisingly for the wind instrument by translating channe as "pipes." Yet, rather inconsistently, he suggests, like Richter, that they serve as clappers. Is it possible that the central issue, wind or percussion, has not been clearly seen by both translators? This is MacCurdy's translation: "Here you make a wheel with pipes that serve as clappers for a musical round called a canon, which is sung in four parts, each singer singing the whole round. And therefore I make here a wheel with four cogs so that each cog may take a part of a singer" (one-volume edition, p. 1052).

My own translation is based on the unequivocal position of facing the issue of wind or percussion, and Leonardo's clear distinction between the rods with irregular shapes and widths in the two middle drawings compared to the precisely drawn pipes in the top drawing. My translation follows: "Here one makes a wheel of so many rods to be used as sounding elements for a musical round called a canon, which is sung in four-part polyphony, each singer singing the whole round, and for this I make a wheel with four cogs so that each cog assumes the task of one singer."

By translating the word channe as "rods," the problem is greatly simplified. There would no longer be the question as to how the hollow channe could be filled with wind. The rods would simply be set into vibration by being hit in turn by the cogs. In short, the whole mechanism would be a version of what today is called a Swiss music box and could be classified as a merry toy for carnival or popular festivities.[3]

10.3. Madrid MS I folio 91 v.
Cylindrical snare drum operated by
pinbarrel cylinder.

Madrid MS I folio 91 v shows a sketch of three drums operated by a pin barrel cylinder (illus. 10.3). The drums are cylindrical, each one equipped with a snare. They differ in size: the diameter of the largest drum is three times that of the smallest drum and twice that of the middle-sized one. The revolving cylinder, whose support is not indicated, is equipped with projecting teeth that lift the beaters. One beater for the large drum and two for the middle-sized one are clearly indicated. The smallest drum also seems to have two beaters but this is not obvious from the drawing. The pin barrel itself is set into motion by a large, vertical master wheel with projections geared to the cylinder. The result which Leonardo must have had in mind was a three-part polyphony in elaborate rhythm, with the higher tones produced by the two smaller drums sounding more rapidly than the low tones of the large drum.

3. Carlo Pedretti kindly reminded me of the *tabella di Marzocco* mentioned by him in his *Commentary on the Literary Works of Leonardo da Vinci,* p. 333, and, in his belief, related to the yearly Florentine festival of St. Giovanni Battista, using the traditional *carro di Marzocco,* the wagon with the heraldic lion, the emblem of Florence. If Pedretti's idea is correct, it would greatly support my hypothesis that the *tabella con channe* is a children's toy.

CHAPTER ELEVEN

Wind Instruments:
The Glissando Flute,
Key Mechanisms for Wind Instruments,
and New Bellows

In CA 397 rb (illus. 11.1) we find, among numerous small sketches for various machinery, drawings of two pipes, evidently one of those countless passing ideas which were crying to Leonardo to be recorded just here and now, so as not to be forgotten in the perpetual flow of images, whims, and new ideas.

Every connoisseur of musical instruments will recognize immediately two recorders (*flauti dolci*) by their characteristic heads and mouth holes. Their basic structure has not changed substantially since Leonardo's time. Beneath the upper end held by the player's lips is a hole with a sharp edge which is struck by the air stream emanating from his mouth. Ordinarily recorders have on their sides six finger holes which are closed and opened by the finger tips of the player to produce the distinct tones of the scale. But Leonardo's recorders look strange. The one on the left has two broad slits on the side of the tube, and the other one long, thin slit. What can be the purpose of these slits? Fortunately we have an explanatory text in Leonardo's most beautiful calligraphy, running from right to left: "Questi due fiuti non fanno le mutazione delle loro voci a salti, anzi nel modo proprio della voce umana; e fassi col movere la mano su a giu, come alla tromba torta, e massime nel zufola a; e possi fare 1/8 e 1/16 di voce, e tanto quanto a te piace [These two flutes do not change their tone by leaps,[1] but in the manner of the human voice; and one does it by moving the hand up and down just as with the coiled trumpet and more so in the pipe a; and you can obtain one eighth or sixteenth of the tone and just as much as you want]." Obtaining an eighth and one sixteenth obviously means (in acoustical language) to reach the upper octaves; and "moving the hand up and down" evidently means not to stop prearranged finger holes but to move along the slits to change pitch gradually or, as we say today, to produce glissandos (gliding tones).

Such a glissando instrument would not have fitted into the orchestra of Leonardo's day. Could he have foreseen in one dreamy corner of his incredible brain glissando instruments such as the one invented in 1924 by the Russian scientist Lev Theremin and called by the inventor's name and later also by the name

1. As most wind instruments do.

aetherophone? But, come to think of it, did Benjamin Franklin foresee all the implications when he, a late-born Prometheus, stole lightning from heaven? Did Leonardo perhaps want to imitate birdcalls? Or did he just think of inventing another of his tricky toys to baffle or amuse the cavaliers and ladies at the court of Lodovico Sforza, an occupation to which he devoted much time, too much time, instead of pushing forward his many projects in the natural sciences, his many planned books, mentioned so often in his notes but never completed; not to speak of his work as a painter, sculptor, and architect! We see that Leonardo was forced, on occasion, to promote *non*-useful knowledge.

Whatever the purpose of this invention was, what was its origin? Where could he have found the idea or a model for his glissando pipes? The clue or key for this problem lies in the words *voce umana*, although I must confess that I found the solution by chance and *then* had it confirmed by Leonardo's own words. The model for our glissando pipes is found in the larynx, and it is significant that Leonardo calls the larynx "voce humana," thus applying this term to the human voice as well as to the machinery that produces it.

Illustrations 11.2 and 11.3 show some of the designs of the larynx and the trachea that Leonardo made in the Quaderni d'Anatomia V 17 r (illus. 11.2) and Quaderni d'Anatomia V 16 r (illus. 11.3). We recognize immediately that the upper opening resembles that of a recorder. Furthermore in the accompanying texts in the Fogli d'anatomia (now in Windsor Castle) the trachea is called *fistola*, which is also the name of a vertical flute, for instance, the recorder.

There is, however, one flaw, in our analogy: Leonardo wrongly attributed the change of pitch of the human voice to the narrowing or widening of what he called *anuli della trachea* (the cartilage rings of the trachea) and failed to observe the function of the vocal cords in the larynx. This failure was probably caused by the technical difficulty of dissecting the small and fragile larynx. By the way, Leonardo's drawings of it have been believed to have been based on the anatomy of an ox, a dog, or a pig. Leonardo was not everywhere permitted to perform dissections of the human body. He could do so in Florence at the Ospedale di Santa Maria Nuova because he had good friends there, as we may infer from the fact that he sent his savings there for safekeeping from war-threatened Milan. It was, so to speak, his Swiss bank account.

At any rate, we have here in Leonardo's glissando recorder a new musical instrument which actually opened, or could have opened, a new musical horizon; which works well (some reconstructions that I have made function); and which was patterned after an anatomical analogy, the larynx, whose actual function was misunderstood by Leonardo. Hence we have here a positive result built upon wrong premises.

The transference of a correctly observed structure in the human body into an eminently practical mechanism is found in Arundel 263 (BM) 175 r (illus. 11.4), which we have discussed before because of its many sketches of drums. In its lower section it contains several extremely interesting sketches for the mechanism of wind instruments. On the upper left, we find two straight tubes, the lower with the mouthcup

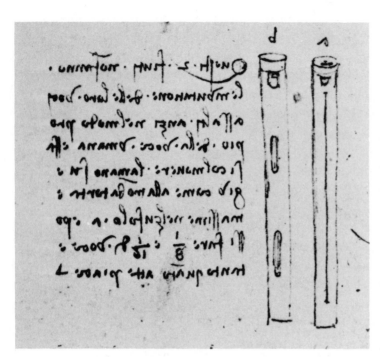

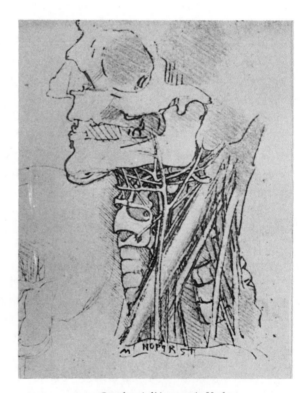

11.1. CA 397 rb. Detail: recorders with side slits instead of finger holes for glissando effect.

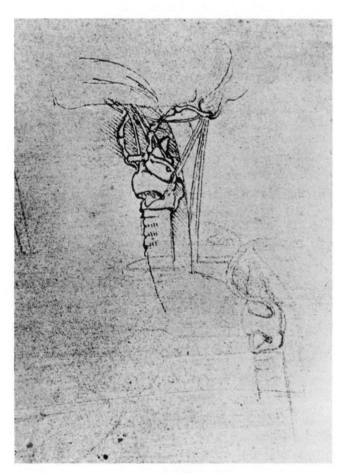

11.2. Quaderni d'Anatomia V 17 r: Sketch of larynx.

11.3. Quaderni d'Anatomia V 16 r: Sketch of neck with larynx.

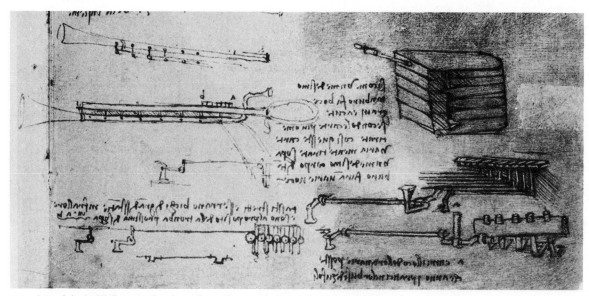

11.4. Arundel 263 (BM) 175 r, sketches of new key mechanisms for wind instruments.

of a trumpet. Both instruments have a second, auxiliary tube. What is its purpose? Here we must recall that the wind instruments of Leonardo's time did not possess the many keys which we find in our modern orchestral instruments. It was the fingertips of the players that closed and opened the six or seven finger holes which were spaced along the tube not at random but according to acoustical ratios. Now, when *lower*, and therefore *longer*, instruments were needed, a problem arose. The stern laws of acoustics demanded finger holes spaced at certain mathematically determined intervals, but these holes would have been too far from one another to be controlled by the short ten fingers of the player. Leonardo found a solution, actually several, although we will deal here with only one.

Leonardo draws the main tube, perforated by seven holes for the seven tones; seven little double lines, evidently levers for closing pads, reach over to the main tube from the auxiliary tube, which also possesses a compact keyboard of seven keys comfortably close to one another. But where is the connection between this central keyboard and the distant closing pads where motion is required? My suggestion is that Leonardo thought of wires; he indicated them at the right of the open end of the auxiliary tube. Leonardo knew that the mechanism of the human hand and fingers contained a solution for a problem of this kind. In Windsor AN. A 19009 r (A10r) (illus. 11.5), he draws the tendons of the hand as they transfer motion from a central point to the point where motion is needed, the fingertips. A similar situation exists in the fingers: see, for example, Windsor AN. A. 19009v (A10v) (illus. 11.6). There remains only to say that Leonardo's idea stayed buried in his notebooks: we do not even know whether he himself ever built an actual instrument embodying his invention. Still, the significance and novelty of his invention are indisputable. Four-hundred and fifty years later the wind instrument with a complete keyboard (illus. 11.7) was invented in Munich by Theobald Böhm. Böhm (not without significance for

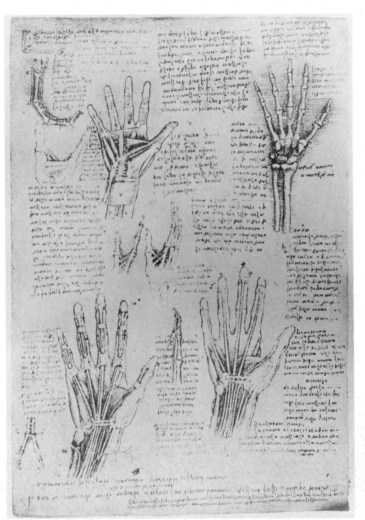

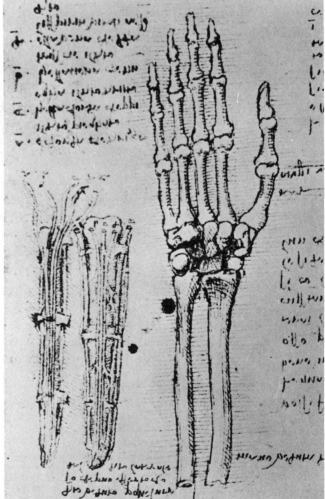

11.5. Windsor AN. A 19009r (A10r), drawings of the tendons of the hand.

11.6. Windsor AN. A 19009v (A10v), drawings of the finger with the cords for straightening and bending.

11.7. Transverse flute by Theobald Böhm with complete key system. Metropolitan Museum of Art, 23.273.

our theme) was a flutist, a connoisseur of theoretical acoustics, and a silversmith.

In Madrid MS II folio 76 r (illus. 11.8), the sketch in the upper right corner represents a wind instrument: two pipes point into the air, a third one points down. They all emerge from a contraption that is, beyond doubt, a bellows. The three pipes give the instrument a superficial similarity to a bagpipe in that they resemble its chanter (the melody pipe) and its drones. And indeed, Leonardo begins his verbal description with the explanation that the new bellows used here are made "per piva."[2] The word *piva* means, or at least can mean, "bagpipe."

The bellows is indeed ingenious—it consists of two sections arranged to the left and right of an immovable dividing wall. If the right section is pushed against the wall, the air enclosed is compressed and pushed toward the pipes; at the same time, the left section is automatically expanded, inhaling air. This kind of automatically synchronized, alternating breathing is an improvement—or at least a simplification—of the conventional two alternating bellows, which were ordinarily used in Leonardo's time and long thereafter for organs and, of course, for many extramusical purposes, such as the blacksmith's forge and metal-smelting furnaces, and which had to be pumped by two people or two motor impulses.

Leonardo's accompanying explanation reads as if this contraption had occurred to him as a new invention. In fact I do not know of earlier examples of this type of bellows in texts or illustrations. Perhaps it worked best in small sizes, while for smelting and other industrial purposes the arrangement of two alternating large, separate bellows proved more practical.

At the end of his explanatory text Leonardo claims that his new bellows produces "continuous wind." This claim, of course, has to be taken with a certain reserve. There is, first, the inevitable dead point, when, one of the bellows sections having reached its maximum volume and the other its minimum expansion, the

2. The page is headed "De strumenti armonici." Then follows the text: "Per piva, sia fatto il tramezzo del mantice .a., fermo alla cintura. Ed il .b. sia fermo con il braccio, il quale braccio poi, muovendosi in dentro ed in fuori, aprirà e serrerà il mantice, al bisogno, cioè quando il mantice .n. aprirà, il mantice .m. serrerà. E quando .m. aprirà, .n. serrerà. E così il vento sarà continuo."

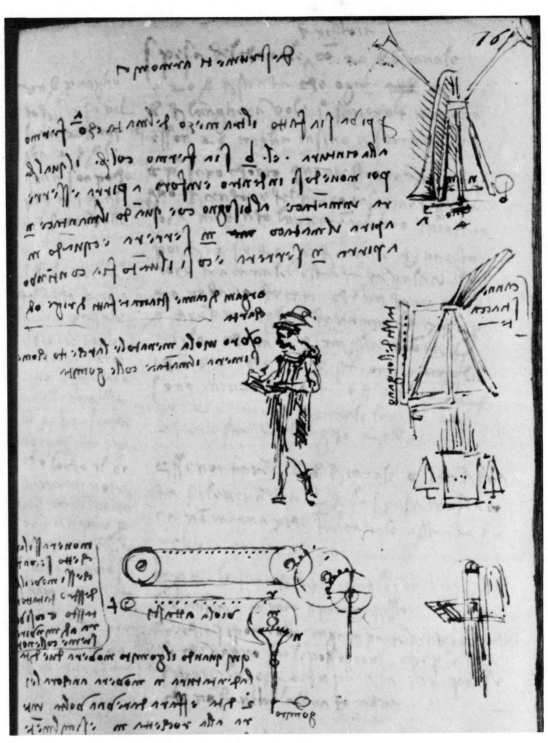

11.8. Madrid MS II folio 76 r.

pumping action goes into reverse. This imparts to the pipes a moment of silence, which, however short, is just as noticeable as the pauses between the upstroke and the downstroke of a fiddle bow, or when the player of a concertina turns from the expanding phase to the compressing phase, or vice versa.[3]

Quite apart from this dead moment of silence we have to bear in mind the fact that the wind stops immediately when the bellows action stops. This is not the case with the bagpipe. The sounding pipes of a bagpipe are supplied with wind by a bag, made of the skin of an animal. This flexible wind reservoir is filled with air either from the player's mouth by means of a blowpipe or, in later specimens, such as the musette of the eighteenth century, from a pair of bellows.[4] A bag of this type supplies wind for some time, even after the player has ceased to breathe into the blowpipe or to pump the bellows with his arm. In this way a real continuity of sound is achieved.[5] Such a bag is missing in Leonardo's contraption.

Furthermore, another essential feature of the bagpipe is missing: the chanter, or melody pipe, which is a reed pipe equipped with finger holes. These are stopped by the fingers of the player to produce the melody, while the larger drone pipes supply the continuous humming bass. Normally, the chanter has a shape different from that of the drones. In Leonardo's sketch, only the pipe on the left pointing down is approximately in the position of a bagpipe chanter, but it has the same shape as the other two pipes and, more importantly, does not show the faintest trace of finger holes. Therefore, Leonardo's contraption is certainly not a bagpipe, and if he calls it *piva*, he uses this word not as an equivalent for *cornemusa* or *zampogna*, both common names for bagpipes, but in its original meaning, that is, *pipa*, "pipe" or "pipe instrument."

What then is our instrument? Because there are only three tubes—not enough for a scale or melody—and because there is not even machinery for selecting or alternating single tones, we can only assume that three simultaneous tones of different pitch formed a chord, in all probability a triad. The tubes would then be trumpets rather than reed pipes, and the whole machine would be not an instrument designed to play actual music but possibly a gadget created to sound a three-voice signal as a kind of fanfare. One recalls the manifold activities of Leonardo as an organizer of fêtes, processions, and stage entertainments. Perhaps our musical gadget served as a hidden machine that produced fanfares easily to accompany the

3. How much Leonardo was aware of the mechanical limitations of bellows is clear from an observation he made in quite a different realm: "If flies produced with their mouths the sound that can be heard when they fly, they would need a great pair of bellows for lungs in order to produce a wind so strong and long, and then there would be a long silence in order to draw into themselves an equal volume of air; therefore, where there was a long duration there would be a long intermission" (Arundel 263 (BM) 257 r).

4. The blowpipe, unbecoming to a lady's cheeks, was replaced by a dainty little bellows attached to her wrists. This was the case in the elegant and lavishly decorated musette, the fashionable bagpipe of the perfumed pseudo-shepherdesses in the *fêtes champêtres* of Versailles and Fontainebleau.

5. For the evolution and mechanism of bagpipes, including those of Leonardo's time, see E. Winternitz, "Bagpipes and Hurdy-gurdies in their Social Setting," *The Metropolitan Museum of Art Bulletin* 2 (1943): 56–83.

appearance of allegorical figures, such as Fama or Gloria, who, by long iconological tradition, had trumpets or even multiple trumpets. Just as one example, I might mention the beautiful quadruple trumpet in the hands of Fama (illus. 11.9) in one of the early sixteenth-century tapestries at the Metropolitan Museum, representing the Triumph of the Fame over Death, one of the numerous illustrations of Petrarch's *trionfi* in Leonardo's time.[6]

Leonardo must have been more impressed with his new bellows than with the whole triple trumpet machine, for in the next two drawings he applied it to a small set of organ pipes and even to a large chamber organ.

The sketch of the portable organ (illus. 11.8, second drawing from top right) bears two inscriptions: on the left, *tasti dell'organo* ("keys of the organ"), and on the upper right, *canne stiacciate* ("flat pipes"). As the text on the left reveals, they are made of wood (*righe*) or cardboard (*carta*).[7] Six pipes can be distinguished—a strange number, too many for a chord and too few for a scale, although the sketch may, of course, be only a hasty suggestion.

An indispensable element of an organ, the one by which the single keys open up and shut off the access of the wind to the single pipes, is not indicated at all. Here again Leonardo may not have taken the trouble, as so often happened in his quick embodiments of passing ideas, to include technical details that he took for granted.

The combination of organ pipes and bellows recalls immediately the construction of an *organetto,* an immensely popular and practical instrument used in Leonardo's time and for centuries before. We may, therefore, cast a quick glance at various types of *organetti,* concentrating on the question of bellows. If we disregard the larger instruments, which were played on a table and which required the use of both hands on the keyboard and therefore an extra person to operate the alternating bellows at the back (illus. 11.10), we find the following arrangements used in organetti: one small bellows beneath the wind chest, operated by the player's left hand (illus. 11.11); a single large bellows at the back of the wind chest, operated by the player's left hand while his right hand pressed the keys with the fingers in a position that would strike a later musician as very awkward (illus. 11.12); and two small alternating bellows at the back of the wind chest, operated by the player's left hand (illus. 11.13).

In all these small instruments, where the single or alternating bellows had to be worked by one hand, there was an inevitable pause in the wind supply, and therefore in the music, between the movements of the bellows. Nevertheless, as the fingers on the keys could play only melodic lines without substantial chords, the pause caused by the bellows mechanism was not more noticeable than that of an experienced singer breathing in the middle of a phrase. Still the wind chest, essential to every organetto, must have helped somewhat to bridge these pauses although it did not have the flexibility of the bag in the bagpipe as a wind reservoir.

---

6. See James J. Rorimer, "The Triumphs of Fame and Time," *The Metropolitan Museum of Art Bulletin* 35 (1940): 242–44.

7. "Organi di canne schiacciate fatti di righe o di carta."

11.9. Fama with quadruple trumpet, in a tapestry depicting the *Triumph of Fame,* North French or Flemish, sixteenth century. Metropolitan Museum of Art.

11.10. Positive organ with alternating bellows, from the *Unicorn Tapestries,* about 1500. Cluny Museum, Paris.

11.11. Angel musician playing an organetto. Museo dell'Opera del Duomo, Florence.

11.12. Angel playing an organetto with a large single bellows on the back of the instrument. Detail of the organ panels from Nájera by Hans Memling, ca. 1465. Art Museum, Antwerp.

11.13. Angels, one of whom plays an organetto with two alternating bellows. Relief by Agostino di Duc-
cio, ca. 1460. Rimini Cathedral.

At any rate, our sketch does not include any visible wind chest. Thus the wind
supply depended exclusively on the action of Leonardo's special bellows, which,
however, as we have already pointed out, immediately stops providing air when
pumping ceases. One possibility that would justify the new bellows remains. The
sketch shows a little curve at the lower left corner of the bellows. If this indicates a
handle, it was perhaps worked with the elbow (*con gomito*), thus leaving both hands
free for the keyboard, an achievement that would indeed have meant notable progress if we assume that this instrument was supposed to have many more pipes than
the six delineated.

Even more problematic is the small sketch of a chamber organ (illus. 11.8, third
drawing from top right) flanked by two bellows evidently of the same construction
as those in the two upper sketches. The big box from which the pipes arise contains,
of course, the inevitable wind chest that, in every pipe organ, guarantees an even
wind pressure and a continuous sound just as the bag does in the bagpipe. Therefore, the application of Leonardo's special bellows to this organ makes little sense.
Any simple conventional bellows would do just as well.

CHAPTER TWELVE

The Paragone:
The Role of Music in
the Comparison of the Arts

Leonardo's most interesting ideas about the nature of Music and her noble status as an art are included in his *Paragone* (comparison of the arts), a treatise animated by the intention to exalt the noblest of all arts, Painting, "the grandchild of Nature and relative of God." Yet for the reader between the lines it is a fascinating spectacle to see how Music, the inferior sister of Painting, and "ill of many defects," appears at closer study and at second thought to be an art equally as noble as Painting and a discipline in her own right, the *figuratione dell' invisible*. The *Paragone*, or Comparison of the Arts, is part of the *Trattato della Pittura*, a book arranged after Leonardo's death from his writings on the arts scattered throughout many of his manuscripts, including some now lost, by his pupil Francesco Melzi. Melzi's manuscript is now in the Vatican library, known as Codex Vaticanus (Urbinas) 1270. We can only guess why Leonardo did not himself arrange and edit these ideas in book form—most probably he did not have the time.[1] Often in his manuscripts he reminds himself to write "a book" on this or another matter, but none of these has come to us.

The first printed editions of the *Trattato* appeared in 1651, in French as well as Italian. The *Paragone* forms the first part of the *Trattato* and is comprised of 45 small sections, which we will call chapters, retaining the numbers given to them in the edition by Heinrich Ludwig.[2]

If we seek to clarify the role and rank assigned to music by Leonardo, we find that the existing translations do not suffice, because the translators were not familiar enough with all the evidence of Leonardo's theoretical and practical concern with the art of music; also they were not sufficiently acquainted with the structure of music as an aesthetic phenomenon and with the musical thought and terminology of

---

1. The most recent accounts of the *Trattato* are: Anna Maria Brizio, *Il Trattato della Pittura di Leonardo*, in Scritti di Storia dell'Arte in onore di Lionello Venturi, Rome 1956; A. Philip McMahon, *Treatise on Painting by Leonardo da Vinci* (Princeton University Press, 1956); Kate Trauman Steinitz, *Leonardo da Vinci's Trattato della Pittura, a bibliography* (Copenhagen, 1958); Carlo Pedretti, *Leonardo da Vinci, On Painting, A Lost Book* (Berkeley 1964).

2. Heinrich Ludwig, *Leonardo da Vinci: Das Buch von der Malerei*; vol. 15 of the *Quellenschriften für Kunstgeschichte* (Vienna, 1882).

Leonardo's day. Thus, I had to make my own translations of the chapters, or parts thereof, relevant to music.

Whenever my translation of certain passages did not seem to me to be the only possible one, or when no exact equivalent existed in English, I inserted an alternative in square brackets.

TEXTS AND COMMENTS

Trattato 21

❖ CHE DIFFERENTIA È DALLA PITTURA ALLA POESIA. La pittura è una poesia muta, et la poesia è una pittura ciecha, e l'una e l'altra va imitando la natura, quanto è possibile alle loro potentie, e per l'una e per l'altra si pò dimostrare molti morali costumi, come fece Apelle con la sua calunnia. ma della pittura, perchè serue al' occhio, senso più nobile, che l'orecchio, obbietto della poesia, ne risulta una proportione armonicha, cioè, che si come di molte uarie uoci insieme aggionte ad un medesimo tempo, ne risulta una proportione armonicha, la quale contenta tanto il senso dello audito, che li auditori restano con stupente ammiratione, quasi semiuiui. ma molto più farà le proportionali bellezze d'un angelico uiso, posto in pittura, della quale proportionalità ne risulta un' armonico concento, il quale serue al' occhio in uno medesimo tempo, che si faccia dalla musica all' orecchio, e se tale armonia delle bellezze sarà mostrata allo amante di quella, da chi tale bellezze sono imitate, sanza dubbio esso resterà con istupenda ammiratione e gaudio incomparabile e superiore a tutti l'altri sensi. Ma della poesia, la qual s'abbia à stendere alla figuratione d'una perfetta bellezza con la figuratione particulare di ciaschuna parte, della quale si compone in pittura la predetta armonia, non ne risulta altra gratia, che si facessi à far sentire nella musicha ciaschuna uoce per se sola in uarj tempi, delle quali non si comporrebbe alcun concento, come se uolessimo mostrare un' uolto à parte à parte, sempre ricoprendo quelle, che prima si mostrano, delle quali dimostrationi l'obliuione non lascia comporre alcuna proportionalità d'armonia, perchè l'occhio non le abbraccia co' la sua uirtù uissiua a' un medesimo tempo. il simile accade nelle bellezze di qualonque cosa finta dal poeta, le quali, per essere le sue parti dette separatamente in separati tempi, la memoria nō ne riceue alcuna armonia.

❖ WHAT THE DIFFERENCE IS BETWEEN PAINTING AND POETRY. Painting is mute Poetry, and Poetry is blind Painting, and both aim at imitating nature as closely as their power permits, and both lend themselves to the demonstration [interpretation] of divers morals and customs, as Apelles did with his "Calumny." But since Painting serves the eye—the noblest sense and nobler than the ear to which Poetry is addressed—there arises from it [from Painting] harmony of proportions, just as many different voices [tones of different pitch] joined together in the same instant [simultaneously] create a harmony of proportions which gives so much pleasure to the sense of hearing that the listeners remain struck with admiration as if half alive. But still much greater is the effect of the beautiful proportions of an angelic face represented in Painting, for from these proportions rises a harmonic concent [chord[3]]

3. The terms *chord* and, for that matter, *polyphony* were not yet idiomatic in the musical treatises of Leonardo's time, although polyphonic musical practice used chords. In fact, full triads had become fashionable about one generation before Leonardo.

which hits the eye in one and the same instant just as it does with the ear in Music; and if such beautiful harmony be shown to the lover of her whose beauties are portrayed, he will no doubt remain struck by admiration and by a joy without comparison, superior to all the other senses. But if Poetry would attempt a representation of perfect beauty by representing separately all particular parts [features] that in Painting are joined together by the harmony described above, the same graceful impact would result as that which one would hear in music, if each tone were to be heard at separate times [in different instruments] without combining themselves into a concert [chord], or if [in Painting] a face would be shown bit by bit, always covering up the parts shown before, so that forgetfulness would prevent us from composing [building up] any harmony of proportions because the eye with its range of vision could not take them in all together in the same instant—the same happens with the beautiful features of any thing invented by the Poet because they are all disclosed separately at separate [successive] times [instants] so that memory does not receive from them any harmony.

Comments on *Trattato 21*

The precedence of the eye over the ear—or rather, of sight over hearing—is mentioned throughout almost all chapters of the *Paragone* that deal with the comparison between Painting and Poetry. But as soon as Leonardo sets out to demonstrate this preeminence of the eye, he seems to fall immediately into contradictions, for the distinction of Painting is based on a fundamental feature of music—harmonious proportions; and Painting is accorded precedence over the arts of the ear because it shows harmony, just as does an art for the ear—music. Very clearly, Leonardo describes the phenomenon of the chord (the simultaneous occurrence of several tones) although the term *chord* is not yet in his vocabulary; he rather speaks of the *armonico concento* created simultaneously by proportions—evidently the proportions among tones of different pitch.[4]

Although Music is a temporal art like Poetry, it has proportions, of which Poetry is deprived. This is demonstrated by comparing a poem with a piece of music performed, not by all voices simultaneously, but one voice after another (*in vari separati tempi*), an absurd procedure that would prevent the formation of vertical harmony.

Memory is briefly mentioned in the last sentence, but its basic function in the temporal arts of retaining the past sections of the work is not described.[5] Otherwise, Leonardo would have been forced to acknowledge, besides pitch, proportions of simultaneous musical tones, proportions between successive portions of works of music or poetry.

4. Leonardo was, of course, well versed in the tradition of Pythagorean proportions and entirely at home in the theory of harmony, especially the musical treatises of his friend, Franchino Gaffuri. He also was familiar with Leon Battista Alberti's theory of proportions in *De Re Aedificatoria,* completed 1452, published 1485. There, Alberti recommends borrowing the laws of visual shapes (*figure*) from the musicians since "the same numbers that please the ears also fill the eyes and the soul with pleasure."

5. About Leonardo's notion of memory as victor over time, see the "Epilogue" (pp. 219-23).

Trattato 23

❖ DELLA DIFFERENTIA ET ANCHORA SIMILITUDINE, CHE HA LA PITTURA CO' LA POESIA. La pittura ti rapresenta in un' subito la sua essentia nella uirtù uisiua e per il proprio mezzo donde la impressiua riceue li obbietti naturali, et anchora nel medesimo tempo, nel quale si compone l'armonicha proportionalità delle parti, che compongono il tutto, che contenta il senso; e la poesia rifferisce il medesimo, ma con mezzo meno degno che l'occhio, il quale porta nella impressiua più confusamente e con più tardità le figurationi delle cose nominate, che non fa l'occhio, uero mezzo infra l'obbietto e la impressiua, il quale immediate conferisce con somma verità le vere superfitie et figure di quel, che dinnanzi se gli appresenta. delle quali ne nasce la proportionalità detta armonia, che con dolce concento contenta il senso, non altrimente, che si facciano le proportionalità di diverse uoci al senso dello audito, il quale anchora è men degno, che quello dell' occhio, perchè tanto, quanto ne nasce, tanto ne more, et è si veloce nel morire, come nel nascere. il che intervenire non pò nel senso del vedere, perche, se tu rappresenterai all' occhio una bellezza humana composta di proportionalità di belle membra, esse beliezze non sono si mortali nè si presto si struggono, come fa la musica, anzi, ha lunga permanentia e ti si lascia vedere e considerare, e non rinasce, come fa la musica nel molto sonare, né t'induce fastidio, anzi, t'innamora ed è causa, che tutti li sensi insieme con l'occhio la uorrebbon possedere, e pare, che a garra uogliono combatter con l'occhio. pare, che la bocca se la uorebbe per se in corpo; l'orecchio piglia piacere d'udire le sue bellezze; il senso del tatto la uorebbe penetrare per tutti gli suoi meati; il naso anchora vorebbe ricevere l'aria, ch'al continuo di lei spira. . . .

. . . un medesimo tempo, nel quale s'include la speculatione d'una bellezza dipinta, non può dare una bellezza descritta, e fa peccato contro natura quel, che si de'e mettere per l'occhio, a uolerlo mettere per l'orecchio. lasciaui entrare l'uffitio della musica, e non ui mettere la scientia della pittura, uera imitatrice delle naturali figure di tutte le cose.

❖ OF THE DIFFERENCE AND AGAIN THE SIMILARITY BETWEEN PAINTING AND POETRY. Painting presents its content all at once to the sense of sight [and it does so] through the same means [organ] by which the perceptive sense receives natural objects, and it does so in [at, within] the same span of time, in which there are established the harmonic proportions of those parts which together make up the whole that pleases the sense; and Poetry presents the same thing, but through a means [organ] less noble than the eye, and brings to our perception with more confusion and more delay the shapes [forms, delineations] of the designated [verbalized] things [the things presented]. The eye [on the other hand], that true link between the object and the sense of perception, presents [supplies] directly and with greatest precision the actual surfaces and shapes of the things appearing before it. From these [surfaces and shapes] arise those proportions called harmony which in their sweet combination [unity, concord] please the sense, in the same manner in which the proportions of diverse voices please the sense of hearing which again [as I said before] is less noble than the eye, because there [in the sense of hearing] as soon as it is born, it dies, and dies as fast as it was born. This cannot happen with the sense of sight; for if you [as a painter] represent to the eye a human beauty [the beauty of the human body] composed by the proportions of its beautiful limbs, all this beauty is not as mortal and swiftly destructible as music; on the contrary, it [beauty] has permanence [long duration] and permits you to see and study it [at leisure]. It is not reborn [does not need to reappear, come back] like music is when played over and over again up to the point of boring [annoying] you; on the contrary, it enthralls you [makes you love it] and is the reason that all the senses, together with the eye, want to possess it, so that it seems as if they wanted to compete with the eye. [In fact] it seems as if the mouth wants to swallow it bodily, as if the ear took pleasure to hear about its attractions [the beauties of it], as if the sense of touch wanted to penetrate it through all its pores, and as if even the nose wanted to inhale the air exhaled continually by it [by beauty]. . . . The same instant within which the comprehension of something beautiful rendered in Painting is confined cannot offer [give] something beautiful rendered by [verbal] description, and he who wants to consign to the ear what belongs [must be consigned] to the eye, commits a sin against nature. Here, let Music with its specific function enter, and do not place here [into this role] the science of Painting, the true imitator of the natural shapes of all things. . . .

Comments on Trattato 23

Although here only painting and poetry are compared, music comes into the argument. The argument focuses on the simultaneity of all elements of a painting ("in un subito," "nel medesimo tempo"). The main argument contrasts the eye, as the more noble instrument of perception, with the ear. The eye as the real ("vero") mediator between the world of objects and human receptivity presents shapes at once and simultaneously. Only in this way harmony based on proportions can materialize. The ear, or rather the sense of hearing upon which poetry depends, furnishes the shapes of things less clearly and with delays. "Delay" ("tardità") evidently means "not in medesimo tempo." "L'armonica proportionalità delle parti" is evidently synonymous with expressions used frequently later such as "proportionalità detta armonia." The discussion of this *armonia* gives occasion to throw a side glance upon music, which, paradoxically enough, is considered to lack this harmony that is made possible only by a simultaneously composed object such as the limbs of a beautiful harmonious body and their proportions. Music suffers from the defect of repetitiousness or rather its need to be performed over and over again ("molto sonare"), which creates nausea, boredom ("fastidio").[6] This implies, of course, another flaw of music, its main defect, namely, its quick passing or fading away; in TP 29, 30, and 31b Leonardo again refers to this flaw.

After this brief side glance at music, Leonardo returns to poetry and painting, and arrives at a sharper formulation of their basic difference by introducing the concept of, as we would call it today, art in space versus art in time. In poetry, time separates one word from the next; oblivion interferes and prevents any harmony of proportions.

This is a rather naive and unfair criticism of poetry. Oblivion does not prevent the listener and even less the reader of Poetry from retaining past parts of the work of art; there is *memory,* for the function of which Leonardo finds beautiful formulations, for instance, in CA 76a and CA 9a, and a poem can be envisaged in retrospect as a harmony of its successive parts. More important for our purpose, Leonardo himself seems, later in the *Paragone,* to suggest proportions between successive parts. But he does so only for Music, not for Poetry (see TP 30 and 32 and also

6. Leonardo does not explain whether Poetry is not affected by this same disadvantage.

perhaps 29). Here, however, Leonardo does not elaborate any further on successive parts and their proportions. Yet he makes an important statement that seems to take Music out of its position as sister of that other temporal art, poetry, and seems to suggest that if the flow in time prevents harmonious *proportionalità* in Poetry, this is not necessarily so in Music, if only Music is considered by its own rights and merits. Poetry, as we must read between the lines, cannot legitimately do for the ear what Painting can do for the eye, and he insists it is a sin against nature to blur this borderline. But where does this leave music? "Here let music with its specific function take its own place [assume its specific role] and do not confuse it with the science of painting, "that true imitator of true shapes of all things."

Two words deserve comment here: *l'uffitio della musica* and *imitatrice.* The first emphasizes music's characteristic role and realm; it does not aim at imitation but is *hors de concours,* in a class of its own and not inferior to either painting or poetry. This term of the argument anticipates the more explicit definition of music in TP 32 as *figuratione delle cose invisibili.* In his writings on anatomy Leonardo gives a long and careful outline of a planned book on anatomy. Immediately after this outline he says: "Then describe perspective through the office of the sight or the hearing. You should make mention of music and describe the other senses."

Imitatrice and *imitare* in general must not be understood as literal, or rather passive copying but as the act of re-creation of shapes and figures; only this interpretation of the function of painting supports its claim to being the noblest and most scientific of the arts.

Trattato 27

❖ RISPOSTA DEL RE MATTIA AD UN POETA, CHE GAREGGIAUA CON UN PITTORE. Non sai tu, che la nostra anima è composta d'armonia, et armonia non s'ingenera, se non in istanti, ne quali le proportionalità delli obietti si fan uedere, o' udire? Non uedi, che nella tua scientia non è proportionalità creata in istante, anzi, l'una parte nasce dall' altra successiuamente, e non nasce la succedente, se l'antecedente non more? Per questo giudico la tua inuentione esser assai inferiore à quella del pittore, solo perchè da quella non componesi proportionalità armonica. Essa non contenta la mente del' auditore, o' ueditore, come fa la proportionalità delle bellissime membra, componitrici delle diuine bellezze di questo uiso, che m'è dinanzi, le quali, in un medesimo tempo tutte insieme gionte, mi danno tanto piacere con la loro diuina proportione, che null' altra cosa giudico essere sopra la terra fatta dal homo, che dar la possa maggiore.

Con debita lamentatione si dole la pittura per esser lei scacciata del numero delle arti liberali, conciosiachè essa sia uera figliuola della natura et operata da più degno senso. Onde attorto, o scrittori, l'hauete lasciata fori del numero delle dett' arti liberali; conciosiachè questa, non ch'alle opere dit natura, ma ad infinite attende, che la natura mai le creò.

❖ REPLY OF KING MATHIAS TO A POET WHO COMPETED WITH A PAINTER. Do you not know that our soul is composed [made up] of harmony, and that harmony is generated only in those instants in which the proportionality of things can be seen or heard? Do you not see that in your art [Poetry] proportionality is not created in an instant, but that on the contrary, one part is born from the other, succeeding it, and that this succeeding one is not born if the preceding one does not die? Therefore I regard your invention [art] much inferior to the painter's for the sole reason that in your art no harmonious proportionality is formed. Your invention [art] does not satisfy the mind of the listener or beholder like the proportionality of the beautiful parts that together form the divine beauties of this face here before me, which joined together in the same instant give me so much pleasure with their divine proportion, that I believe there is no man-made thing on earth that can give greater pleasure. . . . It is a justified lamentation if Painting complains of being expelled from the number of the Liberal Arts, [justified] because she [Painting] is a true daughter of nature and serves the noblest of all senses. Therefore, it was wrong, oh writers, to have left her out from the number of the mentioned Liberal Arts; because she devotes herself not only to the creations of nature but to countless others that have never been created by nature.

Comments on Trattato 27

TP 27, which introduces King Mathias Corvinus, does not contain a direct reference to Music; still it is important in our context because of its reference to *armonia*, *proportionalità,* and *divina proportione* in relation to the minds of the listener and the onlooker. Harmony is denied to Poetry because in Poetry one part is born from its predecessor "successively." Here, if a reference to Music would have been made at all, it would have become clear that Music knows at least one form of harmony, namely, harmony in simultaneity ("nel medesimo momento"), i.e., as a combination of tones of different pitch into chords; and this alone would have established the superiority of Music over Poetry. As it is, this is suggested only later in TP 29. By the way, Leonardo does not recognize explicitly harmony or proportionality between successive portions of a poem or any work of Poetry, for instance, the formal balance between the strophes or the lines of a sonnet, although he seems to recognize this kind of proportionality in Music (see TP 29).

The last two phrases of TP 27 are of interest because here Leonardo proffers openly his complaint that Painting is unjustly omitted from the ranks of the liberal arts, which is especially unfair if one considers that Painting is not only dedicated to the works of nature but can create infinite works never created by nature.

Trattato 29

❖ COME LA MUSICA SI DE' CHIAMARE SORELLA ET MINORE DELLA PITTURA. La Musica non è da essere chiamata altro, che sorella della pittura, conciosiach' essa è subietto dell' audito, secondo senso al occhio, e compone armonia con le congiontioni delle sue parti proportionali operate nel medesimo tempo, costrette à nascere e morire in uno o più tempi armonici, li quali tempi circondano la proportionalità de' membri, di che tale armonia si compone non altrimenti, che si faccia la linea circonferentiale le membra, di che si genera la bellezza umana. ma la pittura eccelle e signoreggia la musica, perch' essa non more imediate dopo, la sua creatione, come fa la sventurata musica, anzi resta in essere e ti si dimostra in vita quel, che in fatto è una sola superfitie. . . .

❖ HOW MUSIC SHOULD BE CALLED THE YOUNGER SISTER OF PAINTING. Music cannot be better defined than as the sister of Painting, for she depends on hearing, a sense inferior to that of the eye, and establishes harmony by uniting her proportional parts [elements] that are performed simultaneously [i.e., the voices or melodic strands that run at the same time, that is, in juxtaposition within the polyphonic web], elements that are destined [forced] to be born and to die in one or more harmonic sections which confine [include] the proportionality of the elements [members], a harmony composed [produced, established] the same way as is that outline of the members [of the human body] which creates human beauty. But Painting surpasses and outranks Music since it does not die instantly after its creation as happens to unfortunate Music; on the contrary, it stays on [remains in existence] and so shows itself to you as something alive while in fact it is confined to a surface. . . .[7]

Comments on Trattato 29

Trattato 29 begins with a meditation on Music itself and is fraught with seeming contradictions. Clear is the statement that Painting excels and lords over Music because Music dying immediately after birth lacks permanence. Leonardo has stressed this aspect before (TP 23). Yet Music, in spite of its flow, is credited with harmony of proportions, which poses the question of whether Leonardo means proportions between successive portions of the work of Music. It is here that the text seems obscure or at least inconsistent. For first harmony is described as a conjunction of proportionate parts performed simultaneously ("nel medesimo tempo"); but right afterward the text introduces the plural: "in uno o più tempi armonici," and this seems ambiguous. It could mean that chords occur one after another and that each is equipped with harmony in the sense defined. But it could also refer to successive portions of Music and in favor of this interpretation is the formulation that the "tempi armonici circondano la proportionalità de membri," which could be translated as instants in the flow that include between them sections of Music proportionate to one another. If this interpretation is correct, then Leonardo, in a remarkably independent approach to the phenomenon of Music, would have applied the concept of proportion to the relation between successive portions of Music and thus established the notion of a quasi-spatial structure of portions balanced against one another.

There are two facts that would invite such an interpretation of TP 29: first, it falls in with Leonardo's definition of Music as the *figuratione del invisible* (figuration evidently meaning shape or form [see TP 32]); second, the text of TP 29 goes on to compare the proportional sections ("membri") of Music with spatial portions or members that by their proportions produce the beauty of the human body. The limbs of the body could, of course, hardly be compared with musical chords but only with sections of the musical flow.

It is thus the painter Leonardo, who, starting from his most beloved art, Painting, finds similarities with Music, an approach basically different from that of the musical theories of his time. As far as I can see, no treatise on Music of Leonardo's day developed this notion of musical form as a balance between the parts of a composition, although contemporary treatises abound, of course, with the notion of

7. The remainder of TP 29 is of no interest for Music.

numerical ratios between tones of different pitch. Leonardo must have been familiar with this traditional element in musical theory, at least through the treatises of his friend Gaffurius.

Trattato 30

❖ PARLA IL MUSICO COL PITTORE. Dice il musico, che la sua scientia è da essere equiparata a quella del pittore, perchè essa compone un corpo di molte membra, del quale lo speculatore contempla tutta la sua gratia in tanti tempi armonici, quanti sono li tempi, nelli quali essa nasce e muore, e con quelli tempi trastulla con gratia l'anima, che risiede nel corpo del suo contemplante. ma il pittore risponde e dice, che il corpo composto delle humane membra non da si se piacere a' tempi armonici, nelli quali essa bellezza abbia a variarsi, dando figuratione ad un altro, ne che in essi tempi abbia a nascere e morire, ma lo fa permanente per moltissimi anni, et è di tanta eccellentia, che la riserva in vita quella armonia delle proportionate membra, le quali natura con tutte sue forze conservare non potrebbe. quante pitture hanno conservato il simulacro d'una divina bellezza, ch'el tempo o' morte in breve ha distrutto il suo naturale esempio, et è restata più degna l'opera del pittore, che della natura sua maestra!

❖ THE MUSICIAN SPEAKS WITH THE PAINTER. The Musician claims that his science is [of a rank] equal to that of the Painter because it [music] produces a body of many members whose whole beauty is contemplated by the listener [observer, contemplator] in as many sections of musical time[8] as are contained between birth and death [of these sections]; and it is these [successive] sections with which Music entertains the soul residing in the body of the contemplator.

But the Painter replies and says that the human body, composed of many members, does not give pleasure at [successive] time sections in which beauty is transforming itself by giving shape (form) to something else, nor that it [beauty] needs, in these time sections, to be born and to die, but rather that he [the Painter] renders it [the body] permanent for very many years and the painting is of such excellence that it keeps alive that harmony of well-proportioned members which nature with all its force would not be able to preserve—how many Paintings have preserved the image of divine beauty whose real model has soon been destroyed by time or death, so that the Painter's work has survived more nobly than that of nature, his mistress.

Comments on Trattato 30

TP 30 actually does not expound any new arguments in favor of the Musician, but repeats his claim that his science equals that of painting because it operates by combining one "corpo" out of many members. Whether these members are successive sections of the musical flow is not entirely clear but seems to be suggested by the term *tanti-tempi armonici* confronting the contemplation of the listener—if *speculatore* could be at all translated by "listener."

When the Painter, however, tries to defend his claim of superiority, he adds to

8. Mistranslated with "rhythms" by J. P. Richter and Irma Richter, *Paragone* (London, 1949), p. 75.

his old arguments one new angle: he credits painting with the capacity of "figuratione," implying that this capacity is lacking in music. We must emphasize this here because later in TP 32 that "figuratione" is regarded also as a characteristic of music, although, unlike the "figuratione" used by painting, it is the figuration of the invisible.

The end of chapter 30, emphasizing the power of painting to preserve the image of a person beyond his death, echoes Ovid, *Metamorphoses*, book xv, with the famous lamentation of the aging Helen of Troy observing in the mirror the wrinkles of her face and weeping about Time, the great destroyer of things, and Leonardo's own paraphrase in CA 71 ra:

O tempo, consumatore delle cose, e, o invidiosa antichità, tu distruggi tutte le cose e consumi tutte le cose da duri denti della vecchiezza a poco a poco con lenta morte!

Elena quando si specchiava, vedendo le vizze grinze del suo viso, fatte per la vecchiezza, piagnie e pensa seco, perchè fu rapita due volte.

O tempo, consumatore delle cose, e o invidiosa antichità, per la quale tutte le sono consumate.

O Time, thou that consumest all things! O envious age, thou destroyest all things and devourest all things with the hard teeth of the years, little by little, in slow death! Helen, when she looked in her mirror and saw the withered wrinkles which old age had made in her face, wept, and wondered to herself why ever she had twice been carried away.

O Time, thou that consumest all things! O envious age, whereby all things are consumed.

Trattato 31

❖ IL PITTORE DÀ I GRADI DELLE COSE OPPOSTE ALL' OCCHIO, COME 'L MUSICO DÀ DELLE VOCI OPPOSTE ALL' ORECCHIO. Benchè le cose opposte all' occhio si tocchino l'un e l'altra di mano in mano, nondimeno farò la mia regola di XX. in. XX. braccia, come ha fatto el musico infra le voci, che benchè la sia unita et appiccha insieme, nondimeno a pochi gradi di voce in voce, domandando quella prima, seconda, terza, quarta e quinta, et così di grado in grado ha posto nomi alla varietà d'alzare et bassare la voce.

Se tu o musico dirai, che la pittura è meccanica per essere operata con l'esercitio delle mani, e la musica è operata con la bocca, ch'è organo humano, ma non pel conto del senso del gusto, come la mano senso del tatto. meno degne sono anchora le parolle ch'e' fatti; ma tu scittore delle scientie, non copij tu con mano, scrivendo ciò, che sta nella mente, come fa il pittore? e se tu dicessi la musica essere composta di proporzione, o io con questa medesima seguito la pittura, come mi vedrai.

❖ THE PAINTER USES DEGREES FOR THE OBJECTS APPEARING TO THE EYE, JUST AS THE MUSICIAN DOES FOR THE VOICES RECEIVED BY THE EAR. Although the objects confronting the eye touch one another, hand in hand [one behind the other], I will nevertheless base my rule on [distances of] XX to XX braccia, just as the Musician has done, dealing with [the intervals between] the tones [voices]: they are united and connected with one another, yet can be differentiated by a few degrees tone by tone, establishing a prime, second, third, fourth, and fifth, so that names could be given by him to the varieties [of pitch] of the voice when it moves up or down.

If you, oh Musician, will say that Painting is mechanical because it is performed by using the hands, [you should consider that] music is performed with the mouth, which is also a human organ though not [in this case] serving the sense of taste, just as the hands [of the Painter] do not serve the sense of touch—[and as for word-arts] words are even more inferior than actions [such as those just described]—and you, oh Writer on the sciences, doest thou not copy by hand, like the Painter, that which is in the mind? And if you say that Music is composed of proportion, then I have used the same [method] in Painting, as you will see.

Comments on Trattato 31

TP 31 touches on another comparison between music and painting which is far-fetched but reveals how eager Leonardo is to do justice to music within the *Paragone*. He compares the objects as they confront the eye in a continuous receding row or chain ("opposte all' occhio si tocchino l'un altra di mano in mano") with the grada-tion of tones, that is, with the musical tones that by their numerical ratios ("gradi di voce in voce") form a scale. The mathematical rationalization of pitch values of tones is, of course, old Pythagorean and Boethian tradition and was commonplace in Leonardo's time; it is this mathematical quality of music that gave it a place among the liberal arts, but to credit painting with a similar rational basis was a relatively novel idea. Leonardo's argument is expressly, although only in passing, stated in TP 31b: "Since you accorded to music a place among the liberal arts, either place there painting also, or remove music from there."

It is, of course, the science of perspective which Leonardo has in mind when he speaks of "la mia regola di XX in XX Braccia" (receding of objects from the eye by a standard distance of 220 yards). It is easy to see how forced the whole comparison is—a much more substantial comparison between linear perspective and acoustical phenomena is found in MS L 79 v, where Leonardo tries to find the ratios of fading sound or, more precisely, the proportions between the volume of sound and the distance between the ear and the source of sound; there he establishes a "regola," which in his own language could be termed a perspective of sound.

TP 31a deals with the art of sculpture.

Trattato 31b

Quella cosa è più degna, che satisfa a miglior senso. Adonque la pittura, satisfatrice al senso del vedere, è più nobile che la musica, che solo satisfa all' udito.

Quella cosa è più nobile, che ha più eternità. Adonque la musica, che si va consumando mentre ch'ella nasce, è men degna che la pittura, che con uetri si fa eterna.

Quella cosa, che contiene in se più universalità e varietà di cose, quella fia detta di più eccellentia. adonque la pittura è da essere preposta a tutte le operationi, perchè è contenitrice di tutte le forme, che sono, e di quelle, che non sono in natura; è più da essere magnificata et esaltata, che la musica, che solo attende alla voce.

Con questa si fa i simulacri alli dij, dintorno a questa si fa il culto divino, il quale è ornato con la musica a questa seruente; con questa si dà copia alli amanti della causa de' loro amori, con questa si riserua le bellezze, le quali il tempo e la natura fa fugitive, con questa noi riserviamo le similitudini degli huomini famosi, e se tu dicessi la musica s'eterna con lo scriverla, el medesimo facciamo noi qui cō le lettere. Adonque, poi chè tu hai messo la musica infra le arti liberali, o tu vi metti questa, o tu ne levi quella, e se tu dicessi li huomini vidi la d'operano, e così è guasta la musica da chi non la sa.

That thing is worthier which satisfies the higher sense. Thus, Painting, since it satisfies the sense of seeing is nobler than Music, which satisfies only the ear.

That thing is nobler which has longer duration. Thus Music, which withers [fades] while it is born, is less worthy than Painting, which with the help of varnish renders itself eternal.

That thing which contains within itself the greatest universality and variety of objects may be called the most excellent. Thus Painting is to be preferred to all other activities because it is concerned [occupies itself] with all the forms which do exist and also with those which do not exist in nature; it is to be more praised and exalted than Music, which is concerned only with sound [voice].

With Painting one makes the images of gods, around which divine rites are held which Music helps to adorn; with the help of Painting, one gives lovers likenesses [portraits] of those who aroused their ardor; through Painting one preserves the beauty which time and nature cause to fade away; through Painting we preserve the likenesses of famous men, and if you should say that Music becomes eternal when it is written down, we are doing the same here with letters. Thus, because you have given a place to Music among the Liberal Arts, you must place Painting there too, or eject Music; and if you point at vile men who practice Painting, Music also can be spoiled by those who do not understand it.

Comments on Trattato 31b

TP 31b, combining earlier and new arguments, expounds various reasons for the preeminence of painting over music. (1) Painting satisfies the highest sense, sight, music only the sense of hearing—but why sight should be nobler than hearing is not elaborated. (2) Painting is permanent, music evanescent. (3) Painting occupies itself with objects of more universality and variety than music, which is based only on sound (an argument so questionable that one is not surprised to find it nowhere else in Leonardo's writings).

The passage on the place of painting and of music among the liberal arts has been commented on in my explanation of TP 31.

Other arguments proffered here, such as the comparison between musical scores and letters, are rhetorical rather than serious.

Trattato 31c

Se tu dirai le scientie non mecaniche sono le mentali, io ti dirò che la pittura è mentale, e ch'ella, sicome la musica e geometria considera le proportioni delle quantità continue, e l'aritmetica delle discontinue, questa considera tutte le quantità continue e le qualità delle proportioni d'ombre e lumi e distantie nella sua prospettiva.

If you [the Musician] say that only the nonmechanical [physical, bodily, material] sciences [liberal arts] are concerned with the mind[9] and that, just as Music and Geometry

9. Mistranslated by Irma Richter, *Paragone*, p. 77: "If you say that the sciences are not 'mechanical' but purely of the mind," which implies that *all* sciences are not mechanical, while Leonardo evidently wants to distinguish between *scientie meccaniche* and *scientie mentali*.

deal with the proportions of the continuous quantities, and Arithmetic with the proportions of the discontinuous quantities, [so] Painting deals with all the continuous quantities and also with the qualities of the proportions [degrees] of[10] shades and lights and distances in their [its?] perspective.

Comments on Trattato 31c

TP 31c introduces a new basis of comparison, the question of whether Painting and Music are concerned with proportions of "continuous quantities," as is geometry, or with "discontinuous quantities," as is arithmetic. The answer given is that both arts concern themselves with continuous quantities. This statement must be understood in the light of the former explanation that Painting is based on perspective ("le cose si toccano l'un l'altra di mano in mano") (TP 31) and of the awareness that Music exists as continuous flow. Heretofore its flow, by a poetic rather than scientific argumentation, was proffered as evidence of its transience and mortality, flaws not inherent in the nobler art of Painting. Now the flow—that is, the smooth gliding from one tone to the next—elevates Music to a "scientia mentale" dealing with continuous quantities, like Geometry and Painting. Thus, under scientific scrutiny, a sort of equality of rank is established between Painting and Music.

Leonardo's distinction between continuous and discontinuous quantities comes, of course, from Aristotelian tradition (see especially *Metaphysics*, 6. 1, 2). Its application to the arts of Painting and Music is Leonardo's own. According to Aristotle (*Logic* 5a), line, space, and time belong to the class of continuous quantities, "for it is possible to find a common boundary at which their parts join." Leonardo's judgment of Poetry (or "speech" in Aristotelian terminology) as inferior to Music and Painting is probably also based on Aristotle: "Speech is a discontinuous quantity, for its parts have no common boundary" (Aristotle, *Logic* 4b32).

As for the distinction between *scientie meccaniche* and *mentali,* one should look at TP 33, not reprinted here, because it does not deal with Music. There, the problem is approached through the consideration of "esperientia," that is, empirical research. The classification of arts into *artes mechanicae* and *artes liberales* is medieval.

Trattato 32

❖CONCLUSIONE DEL POETA, PITTORE E MUSICO. Tal diferentia è inquanto alla figuratione delle cose corporee dal pittore e poeta, quanto dalli corpi smembrati a li uniti, perchè il poeta nel descrivere la bellezza o' brutezza di qualonche corpo te lo dimostra a membro a membro et in diversi tempi, et il pittore tel fa vedere tutto in un tempo. el poeta non può porre con le parole la vera figura delle membra di che si compone un tutto, com el pittore, il quale tel pone innanti con quella verità, ch'è possibile in natura; et al poeta accade il medesimo, come al musico, che canta sol' un canto composto di quattro cantori, e canta prima il canto, poi il tenore, e così seguita il contr' alto e poi il basso; e di costui non risulta la gratia della

10. I. Richter mistranslates as follows: "... with the qualities of proportions, shadows and light...."

proportionalità armonica, la quale si rinchiude in tempi armonici, e fa esso poeta a similitudine d'un bel volto, il quale ti si mostra a membro a membro, che cosi facendo, non remarresti mai satisfatto dalla sua bellezza, la quale solo consiste nella divina proportionalità delle predette membra insieme composte, le quali solo in un tempo compongono essa divina armonia d'esso congionto di membre, che spesso tolgono la libertà posseduta a chi le vede. e la musica ancora fa nel suo tempo armonico le soavi melodie composte delle sue varie voci, delle quali il poeta è privato della loro discretione armonica, e ben che la poesia entri pel senso dell' audito alla sedia del giuditio, sicome la musica, esso poeta non può descrivere l'armonia della musica, perchè non ha potestà in un medesimo tempo di dire diverse cose, come la proportionalità armonica della pittura composta di diverse membra in un medesimo tempo, la dolcezza delle quali sono giudicate in un medesimo tempo, cosi in comune, come in particolare; in comune, inquanto allo intento del composto, in particolare, inquanto allo intento de' componenti, di che si compone esso tutto; e per questo il poeta resta, inquanto alla figuratione delle cose corporee, molto indietro al pittore, e delle cose invisibili rimane indietro al musico. ma s'esso poeta toglie in prestito l'aiuto dell' altre scientie, potrà comparire alle fere come li altri mercanti portatori di diverse cose fatte da più inventori, e fa questo il poeta, quando s'impresta l'altrui scientia, come del oratore, e del filosofo, astrologho, cosmografo e simili, le quali scienze sonno in tutto separate dal poeta.

❖ CONCLUSION OF [THE DISCUSSION BETWEEN] THE POET, THE PAINTER, AND THE MUSICIAN. As for the representation of bodily [corporeal] things, there is the same difference between the Painter and the Poet as between dismembered and united things, because when the Poet describes the beauty or ugliness of a body, he shows it to you part by part and at different [successive] times, while the Painter lets you see it in one and the same moment [simultaneously]. The Poet cannot create [establish] with words the real shape of the parts which make up a whole, as does the Painter, who can put them before you with the same truth that is possible in nature [in the concrete appearance of nature], and the same thing happens to the Poet [the Poet encounters the same difficulty] as would to the Musician, if the latter would sing by himself some music composed for four singers, by singing first the soprano part, then the tenor part, and then following it by the contralto and finally the bass; from such a performance does not result [ensue] the grace [beauty] of harmony by proportions [musical harmony as produced by the consonance of several voices of different pitch as established by the acoustical proportions], which is confined to moments of harmony (endowed with harmony, i.e., chords)—this is precisely what the Poet does to the likeness of a beautiful face when he describes it feature by feature. You would never be satisfied by such a representation of beauty [of the beauty of the face], because that can only be the result of the divine proportionality of these features taken all together since it is only at the very same moment [simultaneously] that they create this divine harmony of the union of all features which so enslaves the beholder that he loses his liberty.

Music, on the other hand, within its harmonious flow [time], produces the sweet melodies generated by its various voices, while the Poet is deprived of their specific harmonic action, and although Poetry reaches the seat of judgment through the sense of hearing, it cannot describe [render, create] musical harmony because he is not able to say different things at the same time as is achieved in Painting by the harmonious proportionality created by the various [component] parts at the same time, so that their sweetness can be perceived at the same time, as a whole and in its parts, as a whole with regard to the composition, in particular with regard to the [single] component parts.

For these reasons the Poet remains, in the representation of bodily things, far behind the Painter and, in the representation of invisible things, far behind the Musician. But if the Poet borrows from the other arts he can compete at fairs with merchants who carry goods made by various inventors [makers]—in this way he acts when he borrows from other sciences such as those of the orator, philosopher, astronomer, cosmographer, and others which are totally separate from his own art.

Comments on Trattato 32

First, a difference is stated between Painting and Poetry as far as they occupy themselves with the representation of bodily things ("figuratione delle cose corporee")—disjointed features are found to be the subject of Poetry, and united features the subject of Painting. In fact this distinction is only another version of the distinction between arts which present their objects in succession, in the flow, and those arts which present their objects in simultaneity (see TP 30). It must, however, be pointed out that Leonardo does not mean to restrict altogether the field of Poetry to *figurazione delle cose corporee,* because later in this chapter 32, he has it compete also with music in the field of the *figuratione delle cose invisibili.*

A very important point is touched upon when Leonardo exalts Painting for being able to put before us features with the truth of nature ("con quella verità, che'è possible in natura") because here a basic aesthetic phenomenon is accounted for—the concreteness of visual appearance—or to say it more precisely, the simultaneous impact of an infinite number of features integrated in their concrete, immediate appearance. This observation of Leonardo's goes beyond the famous paragone of the eighteenth century, Lessing's "Laokoon," which strangely enough, does not analyze this phenomenon of the visual arts. Goethe, we recall, was deeply aware of it, for instance, when he admired Delacroix's illustrations for Faust, which, as he remarked (Gespräche mit Eckermann, Nov. 29, 1826) added, or rather, were forced to add by their very medium, details to the scene which were beyond his, the Poet's, medium.

Very striking and almost humorous is Leonardo's argument to prove the inferiority of Poetry to Painting by the absurd picture of the performance of a polyphonic four-voice composition by one single singer, who could sing the four parts of the polyphonic web one after another, thus losing harmony and thereby the whole musical purpose altogether. At the same time, this caricature of Music reveals that Leonardo credits Music, if correctly performed, with *proportionalità armonica,* one of the important advantages inherent, according to him, also in Painting.

The remainder of TP 32 returns to the argument about proportions which was taken up before in TP 21, 23, 27, 29, and 30. We will briefly examine later in the epilogue whether proportions can really mean the same thing in Painting and in Music.

In a peremptory summary Leonardo states that in the figuratione delle cose corporee the Poet ranks behind the Painter, and in the figuratione delle cose invisibili, behind the Musician. What then, we ask, is the comparative rank between Leonardo's most beloved and exalted art, Painting, and Music? He has accorded proportionality and harmony to both of them; he seems also to ignore here the cliché disparagement of music—its evanescence—*la malattia mortale* (see TP 29: "la pittura eccelle e signoreggia la musica, perche essa non more immediate dopo la sua creatione"). Nothing then hinders him from regarding Music as equally noble in its own right, in consideration of the peculiarities of this discipline. But this ultimate verdict had already been pronounced in chapter 23 [of *Paragone*], which warns against the confusion of arts for the eye and arts for the ear, concluding:"*Lasciavi entrare l'uffitio della musica* (the peculiar business of music): Let music enter by its own merits and do not confuse it with painting, the true imitative science."[11]

EPILOGUE

These chapters of Leonardo's *Paragone* seem to amount to a mixture of naive, often contradictory statements, commonplaces of his time, rhetorical attempts to bolster the social status of the Painter, and profound original ideas about the nature of the arts, including that of Music.

To be fair, we have to recall that the *Trattato* was not a book compiled by himself but composed by Francesco Melzi out of relevant passages—but by no means all the relevant passages—in Leonardo's notebooks and manuscripts.

Furthermore, Leonardo himself was never a consistent organizer of his thoughts, although he frequently reminds himself in his notebooks to write a treatise on this or that—treatises never found and most probably never written in the continuous onslaught of tasks and problems upon him, the artist, scientist, engineer, and provider of entertainment for the court.

Leonardo states clearly in TP 34 (not included in our selection) that it is only through ignorance that Painting was classed below the "sciences," by which he means the liberal arts. This ignorance is the lack of familiarity with the most recent achievement of Painting, linear perspective: an exact rationalization of sight based on mathematical proportions. This made Painting a quasi-mathematical science of the same nobility as Music, for centuries one of the members of the quadrivium together with geometry, arithmetic, and astronomy. Leonardo was not the only one to fight for the inclusion of Painting among the liberal arts. Half a century earlier Leon Battista Alberti had taken the same stand. And when Pollaiuolo in 1493 designed the tomb of Sixtus IV, he added the allegorical figure of *Prospettiva* to the figures of the quadrivium and trivium (illus. 12.1).

For a summary it seems practical to list the criteria and arguments proffered by Leonardo in his *Paragone* for judging the comparative nobility of Music among the arts. Many notions were in the air, so to speak; some echo arguments indispensable in the fashionable, intellectual pastime of Leonardo's day, the disputation of the arts

11. André Chastel, *The Genius of Leonardo da Vinci* (New York: Orion Press, 1961), p. 33, seems to underrate this assessment of music when he says: "Ultimately these [the spatial] arts take a higher position than the temporal arts," perhaps because he does not reprint the critical chapters 23 and 32 of the Trattato.

12.1. Detail from Pollaiuolo's tomb for Sixtus IV, 1489. Significantly, Pollaiuolo added to the traditional seven *artes liberalis* three more, among them, for the first time, Prospettiva. Prospettiva, for its mathematical background, was used by Leonardo to claim for painters, heretofore regarded only as artisans, the status of scholars.

and their merits among courtiers and humanists; some are contradicted by deeper thoughts in the Codice Atlantico and other notebooks of Leonardo, where they are mostly just hinted at and jotted down in Leonardo's typical "self-reminder" fashion. A few, finally, contain new and ingenious ideas.

Cliché Arguments (the numbers indicate the chapters in which they occur):

a. The eye (Painting) more noble than the ear (Poetry and Music): 16, 20, 21, 24, 27, 28, 29, 31b.
b. The evanescence of Music; her mortal disease: fading: 23, 29, 30, 31b. Strangely enough, the same blame is not laid on Poetry.
c. Boredom and disgust caused by repetitiousness:23.[12]
d. Poverty of the musical realm; Music concerned only with sound, while Painting is universal, concerning itself with all things that enter the mind: 31b.

12. On evanescence and disgusting repetitiousness, see also CA 332 va: "La musica ha due malattie, delle quali l'una è mortale, l'altra e decrepitudinale: la mortale e sempre congiunta allo instante sequente a quel della sua creazione; la decrepitudinale la fa odiosa e vile nella sua replicazione." (Music has two ills: one is mortal, the other is related to its decrepitude [feebleness]; the mortal one is always linked to the moment that follows its incipience [each tone of it]; its feebleness causing repetitiousness makes it hateful and vile.)

e. Mechanical arts: Music performed with the mouth: 31; see also, 19, 31c; and, deviating from the clichés, 33, not included in our selection.

Serious Criteria

1. *Spatial Arts vs Temporal Arts*
   Arts for the Eye vs Arts for the Ear

The distinction is retained in various versions throughout nearly all the chapters of the Trattato included in the present essay: 16, 20, 21, 24, 27, 28, 29, 31b. Curiously enough, the exaltation of Painting as the foremost visual art is often based on harmony, which is an integral feature of a temporal art: Music. In these contexts Leonardo stresses harmony as a phenomenon restricted to one single instant, namely, the combination of several tones of different pitch in one chord (or as he terms it, "concento"); he never fails to emphasize *in medesimo tempo*. It is perhaps a pity that the compiler of the Trattato did not include also some of the most salient statements of Leonardo on the nature of time as a continuous quantity, for instance, Arundel (BM) 263, 173v, 190v, and 132r.

2. *The Role of Proportions and the Continuous Quantities: 23, 27, 29, 30, 31, 32*

A discussion of the various meanings of "*proportions*" in Leonardo's writings would go far beyond the limits of this little chapter. In the *Paragone* two kinds of "harmonious proportions" are ascribed to Painting: first, the proportions of the single features of a face or any other object of representation that create the harmony of the whole; second, the numerical proportions that are implied in mathematical perspective, that as a new method used by the Painter made Painting a mathematical art worthy of admission into the quadrivium. The first kind of proportions is [seen] paralleled in musical harmony, that is, in the numerical relations between the pitch of the tones united in one chord. This would restrict proportions to the "vertical" aspect of the flow of music. However, Music admits also the concept of "lengthwise" or "horizontal" proportions—that is, the relation between successive sections of a piece of music. There is no direct acknowledgment of such proportions in the *Paragone* (see my comment to TP 30), but Leonardo's awareness of the problem appears clearly from statements in British Museum Arundel 263, 173b. There he discusses, in the Aristotelian vein, the concept of continuous quantities in geometry (already touched upon in TP 31c), compares point and line with their counterparts in time, and, on this basis, affirms the proportionality of time sections. The passage is too interesting for its bearing on musical time not to quote it here:

> Benchè il tenpo—sia annumerato infra le continue quātità, per essere inuisibile e sanza corpo, non cade integralmēte sotto la geometrica potentia, la quale lo diuide per figure e corpi d'infinita varietà, come continuo nelle cose uisibili e corporee far si uede; Ma sol co' sua primi principi si cōuiene—, cioè col punto e colla linia—; il punto nel tempo è da essere equiparato al suo instante, e la linia à similitudine colla lūghezza d'una quantità d'un tempo, e siccome i pūti sō principio e fine della predetta linia—, così li instanti sō termine e principio di qualūche dato spatio di tempo; E se la linia è diuisibile in īfinito, lo spatio d'ū tê(n)po di tal diuisione non è alieno, e se le parti diuise della linia sono proportionabili infra sé, ancora le parti de tenpo saraño proportionabili infra loro.

Although time is included among the continuous quantities, it does—since it is invisible and incorporeal—fall into the realm of geometry, whose divisions consist of figures and bodies of infinite variety, as a continuum of visible and corporeal things. But only in their principles do they [geometry and time] agree, that is, with regard to the point and the line; the point is comparable to an instant in time; and just as a line is similar to the length of a section of time, so the instants are ends and beginnings of each given section of time. And if the line is infinitely divisible, so is the section of time resulting from such division; and if the sections of a line are proportionable to one another, so are the [successive] sections of time proportionable to one another.[13]

Similar statements based on Aristotle's book 6 of *Physics*, esp. 231b, 7; 232a; 233a; and 233b, 15, are found in Leonardo, Arundel 263 (BM) 176r and 190v; but the reference to proportions between successive sections of time is Leonardo's own, and so is the application of Aristotle's concept of continuous quantities to the field of aesthetics, particularly to music.

If Leonardo thus admits proportions between successive sections of time and therefore also of successive sections of a work of music, it remains strange that he does not explicitly recognize the role of memory in creating forms in the flux. Memory is hardly ever investigated or analyzed by Leonardo as a psychological or philosophical problem, except in connection with Painting, the art that stems the flight of time by eternalizing the presence of a visual image. One of his rare general references to memory is found outside the *Paragone,* in CA 76 a:

A torto si lamētā li omini della fuga del tenpo, incolpando quello di troppa velocità, nō s'accorgiēdo quello essere di bastevole trāsito, ma (la) bona memoria—, di che la natura ci à dotati, ci fa che ogni coas lungamēte passata ci pare essere presente.

Wrongly do men lament the flight of time; they accuse it of being too swift and do not recognize that it is sufficient [sufficiently moderate] in its passage; good memory, with which nature has endowed us, makes everything long past seem present to us.

FIGURATIONE DELLE COSE CORPOREE VS FIGURATIONE DELLE COSE INVISIBILI. This distinction may seem at first glance similar to that between arts for the eye and arts for the ear; yet it goes deeper. In chapter 12 Leonardo speaks of the divinity of the science of Painting and, paraphrasing Dante,[14] calls the Painter the lord and creator (*padrone, signore, creatore*) of all the things which occur in human thought. This concept seems to go far beyond the qualification of Painting as an art copying nature.[15] Should not then the idea have occurred to him that Music is still more free and god-like, since it creates "out of nothing"? This seems to be implied in his concept of the figuratione dell invisibile.

Music in the last analysis is not anymore the "younger and inferior sister of

13. See n. 4, above.
14. "Arte, nipote di Dio."
15. When Leonardo speaks of Painting as an art or a science "imitating" nature, he means, in line with current theory, by "imitare," recreating nature, and not "ritrarre," i.e., redrawing, as for instance in a camera obscura. See on this point also the forcible statements at the end of chap. 27, that Painting can concern itself with creations that have never been created by nature.

Painting" (TP 29) but in every sense "equiparata" (equivalent) to Painting (TP 30). If Leonardo had never said anything else about Music beyond defining her as a figuratione dell invisibile, this definition alone would suffice to convince us of his profound understanding of the nature of Music as a discipline that is not bound to copy nature but with an unparalleled degree of freedom creates forms ("figure") out of a material neither tangible nor visible.

Conclusion

O tēpo, consumatore delle cose, e o invidiosa antichità, tu distruggi tutte le cose, e consumi tutte le cose da duri dēti della vecchiezza a poco cō lēta morte!... (CA 71 ra)

O Time, consumer of all things! O envious age! Thou dost destroy all things and devour all things with the hard teeth of years, little by little in a slow death....[1]

A book attempting to add one facet to the oeuvre of a multifaceted genius should perhaps conclude with a sort of meditation on how a mind like Leonardo's, so diversified, so flexible, so torn and driven by unbounded curiosity into manifold directions of thinking and doing, was demonically obsessed by the strong conviction that creation is a cosmos, an organic structure, and that all the innumerable phenomena observed are guided by basic, simple, interdependent laws; that creation is a universe in the deeper meaning of the word, and that all seeming contradictions could be reconciled, if only he, Leonardo, had had the time to search longer and deeper. His incessant struggle to see order in disorder, cosmos in chaos, was his credo. References in his writings to the sacred books and to creation are not sufficiently frequent nor resolute enough to connect his thoughts with religion in a dogmatic sense.

The contradictions in the infinite realm of phenomena seem paralleled by and related to apparent contradictions within the structure of Leonardo's personality. One could easily choose a number of such violently opposed tendencies, which almost seem to tear asunder the unity of a complex character. To single out two pairs, each consisting of two antithetical, divergent tendencies: one, the contradiction between extreme slowness in artistic creation versus extreme, even explosive rapidity; the other, the infatuation with rational, ornamental patterns versus the fantastic in its wildest extremes.

In the first antithetical pair the slowness of creation can be exemplified by nearly all of Leonardo's large works. One is also reminded of the words of Pope Leo X about Leonardo. In Vasari's report, Leo X, who knew Leonardo from their days in

---

1. Jean Paul Richter, *The Literary Works of Leonardo da Vinci* (London: Oxford University Press, 1939), vol. 2, no. 1163. See Ovid, *Metamorphoses* 15: "Tempus edax rerum, tuque, invidiosa vetustas."

13.1. Sketch of profiles. Windsor 12276 v.

Florence, refused to give him a commission in Rome because, as the pope said, "This man will never finish because he always thinks of the end of the work before beginning it."

The extreme rapidity is manifested throughout the notebooks in the sketches, studies, and versions swiftly replacing each other through alternatives until the pen or stylus finds the solution.

In the second antithetical pair, the clean, cool, unemotional preference for rational, geometric, decorative patterns is expressed in his many designs for intricate knots which we find, for example, delicately woven into the twigs of the trees in the ceiling fresco of the Sala delle Asse in the Castello Sforzesco, and also expressed in his infatuation for *lunulae*, those little moons or, rather, curved sections of circles drawn in enormous quantities to indulge in the traditional *Ludus Geometricus*. In architecture there is a proclivity for polygonal church designs.

In strong contrast to these dispassionate entertainments for the eye and the mathematical mind is Leonardo's passion for the fantastic, the unrestrained, wild or eerie, and spectral. We mention here as examples only the large drawings in Windsor Castle of volcanic eruptions, explosions, floods, apocalyptic visions, and other cataclysms destroying the civilized earth.

These are, of course, only two imperfect examples of contradictory character traits. But we are here at the end of the book, not at the beginning; and of a book concentrating on one interest of Leonardo—music. Therefore, we have to restrict ourselves to the relation within Leonardo's mind between the temporal realm and the spatial one, or, if you please, the musical and the visual.

The reader may rightly ask whether relations exist between Leonardo the painter and Leonardo the musician. There are relations, and at the end of my book, it may be appropriate to illustrate this by at least one example, a famous sheet (that is, two pages) with drawings, Windsor 12276 r and 12276 v. Both these pages deal profoundly, I believe, with the flow of time, showing Time "questo consumatore delle cose," as the great variation master who modifies incessantly the shape of living beings.

On one of our two pages, the largest drawing shows the profile of a pretty young boy who carries the conviction of an actual physical presence (illus. 13.1).

Next to it, at the right, a little smaller, we find the same profile—but not quite the same: it is harder, the arch of the nose a little more pronounced, the chin more projecting, the sweet mouth more resolute, with a fuller lower lip. A similar profile is in the lower left corner of the page, and immediately above it is an old man's profile with the same features transformed by old age—with flabby throat, the lower lip strongly protruding, the bridge of the nose sharply set in, yet with still some remnants of the silky locks.

Three other sketches on the lower part of the page translate the boy's profile into the feminine. The profile in the upper left corner leaves the question of sex undecided.

It has almost become a cliché to see, in the simultaneous appearance of an old and a young head such as these in the Windsor drawings, the deliberate antithesis of

13.2. Study for *Madonna and Child with St. John*. Windsor 12276 r.

the lyric and heroic types, the contrast between the classical warrior and the epicene pretty boy: "the two hieroglyphs of Leonardo's unconscious mind, the two images his hand created when his attention was wandering... virile and effeminate... symbolizing the two sides of Leonardo's nature."[2]

Without denying that such contrasts exist in Leonardo's art, I do not believe that this explains all that there is to see in drawings like the present ones. If this were the only explanation, why then the transition faces? Why the use of the same substance for modification? Why, in other words, the use of the same theme for variations?

Our problem becomes even clearer if we turn the page and look at the reverse side: the famous study of *The Madonna and Child with St. John* (illus. 13.2). Let us here disregard the sketch of the Madonna and the two sketches of the infant St. John, and instead concentrate on some of the many doodles that fill the page. The profile of the boy dominates—no fewer than twelve versions of it. In the lower right corner we recognize again the sweet profile contrasted to two others which are a little more robust and older. In the upper left corner, again the metamorphosis of sex is represented. And in the lower left corner, again the sex is undecided. The most touching and, from our point of view, certainly the most telling three profiles are in the center: (1) the boy with the flowing locks, similar to the center drawing of the other page; (2) then the same face after seventy or eighty years of life have left their mark; (3) and, finally, turning the wheel of time in the opposite direction, the profile of the child, jotted down in only one or two lines of admirably sure physiognomical calligraphy.

What we witness here is nothing less than a meditation, a graphic meditation, in the form of doodles, on time. Leonardo creates a number of different versions of the same human profile, something that a musician may compare to a set or cycle of variations. But actually they do not constitute a strict musical form, with elements following in predetermined sequence. Creating the single sketches, Leonardo, by virtue of his subtle connoisseurship of anatomy and physiognomy and of the impact of aging on one and the same subject, records what Time has done or could do to it at different phases of life, and thus evokes Father Time, not as the great destroyer, but as generating visual variations complementing the capacity of music as the "figurazione dell invisibile."

2. Kenneth Clark, *Leonardo da Vinci* (Cambridge: Penguin, 1958), p. 71.

APPENDIX

Italian Texts

A 61 r: The Eddies at the Bottom of Water Move in an Opposite Direction to Those Above

Io dico: se tu gitterai 'n un medesimo tempo 2 picciole pietre, alquanto distanti l'una dall' altra, sopra un pelago d'acqua sanza moto, tu vederai causare, intorno alle due dette percussioni, 2 separate quantità di circuli, le quali quantità acresciendo, vengano a scontrarsi insieme, e poi a 'ncorporarsi, intersegandosi l'un circulo coll' altro, sempre mantenendosi per cientro i lochi percossi dalle pietre. E la ragion si è che benchè li apparisca qualche dimostrazion di movimento, l'acqua non si parte dal suo sito, perchè l'apertura fattale dalle pietre subito si richiuse, e quel moto fatto dal subito aprire e serrare dell' acqua fa in lei un cierto riscotimento, che si pò più tosto dimandare tremore, che movimento. E quel ch'io dico ti si facci più manifesto: poni mente a quelle festuche, che per lor leggerezza stanno sopra l'acqua, che per l'onda fatta sotto loro dall' avenimento de' circuli, non si partano però dal loro primo sito. Essendo adunque questo tal risentimento d'acqua piuttosto tremore che movimento, non possan per riscontrarsi, rompere l'un l'altro, perchè avendo l'acqua tutte le sue parti d'una medesima qualità, é necessario che le parti appichino esso tremor l'una all' altra, sanza mutarsi di lor loco: perchè stando l'acqua nel suo sito, facilmente pò pigliare esso tremore dalle parti vicine, e porgerle all' altre vicine, sempre diminuendo sua potentia insino al fine.

Triv 36 r (Tavola 64 a): The Duration of a Blow

che chosa e sono . fatto dal cholpo

Il cholpo . ella
Il tenpo . nel quale . *sigie* sigienera . il colpo ella più breve chosa che per lomo . si possa fare . e non e si gran corpo che essendo sospeso . cho chon breve cholpo non facci subito movimento il quale movimento . riperchote nellaria ellaria . sona . chettocha la cosa mossa

Sel remore e nel martello o nellanchudine dicho . perche lanchudine non e . sospesa . non po resonare resona il martello . /// nel balzo cheffa dopo il cholpo esse

lan chudine . sonassi . il sono fatto . inessa daogni picholo martello sichome la chanpana . per ogni varia chosa chella batte . a vna medesima basseza di boce chosi fare
lanchu dine battuta da ogni vario martello . e v//dendo tu varie voci per varie
grandeze di martelli . adunque la uoce e nel martello e non nelanchudine

    perche la chosa non sospesa non sona

    essendo sospesa ogni picholo chontatto

    le toglie il sono

la chanpana battuta fa subito . triemito . el subito triemito subito batte la cir-
chunscrivente aria . la quale subito resona essendo inpedito . chonogni picholo .
chontatto . non triema e non batte e non risona laria

CA 77 vb: The Sound of the Echo

Voce d'eco.

    Li lochi d'equali intervalli la diminuiscano nelli sua intervalli in ogni grado di
tempo, e li spazi inequali, crescendo in verso il fine, fan li spazi delle risposte equali.

    La boce d'eco è continua e discontinua, sola e accompagnata, di brieve e lunga
continuazione, di finito e infinito (*ali*) sono, subita o distante.

    Continua è quando la volta dell'eco, dove si genera, è di uniforme concavità.
Discontinua è la voce d'eco quando il loco che la genera è discontinuato e interrotto.
Sola è quando in un sol loco si genera. Accompagnata è quando in più lochi si
genera. Brieve, lunga è quando s'aggirarà nella campana percossa, o in cisterna, o
altra concavità, o nuvoli, nelli quali la voce s'astende a gradi di spazio, con gradi di
tempo, e sempre diminuendo, essendo il mezzo uniforme, e fa come l'onda circulare
nel pelago *m*.

    La voce spesse volte si sente nel simulacro, e non nel sito della voce reale; e
questo accadde in Ghiera d'Adda, che 'l foco ch'essa prese, nell'aria dette 12 simu-
la(*cri*)cri di tono in 12 nugoli, e non si senti la causa.

C 24 r: Analogy between Sensations Received by the Eye and by the Ear

—Infra icorpi. dipari. qualita. Chessien dallocchio. equal mente. distanti
Quello. apparira. diminor figura chedappiv. lumi noso. canpo. circhundato fia—
n s f jlcolpo dato in. n. para. allorechio. f. chesia. in. s
—Omni corpo evidente fia dallume conbra circhundato
—Quelchorpo dequale retondita *par* chedallume
c onbra circhundatofia para avere tanto piv
grande luna parte chellaltra quanto fia piv
aluminata luna chellaltra—

CA 270 vc: Qualities of the Sun

qua lita de l sole

I lsole a corpo . figura . moto . sprēdore . chalore . e virtu gie nerativa . le quali chose (*l*) parte tutte dasse | sāza . sua ꝑ mj (*njvtio*) nvitione

ꝑco . laujrtv visiuale astēdersi . ꝑ li razi visuali î sino alla supfitie . de chorpi nōtrāsparētj | ella virtu . dessi . chorpi . asstendersi . insino . alla . virtu . visiuale . e ognj . simjle chorpo | ēpiere . tutta . la antjposta aria . della sua simjlitudne Ognj . chor po ꝑ se . e ttuttj îsie me fano | il simjle . e nō sola mēte lēpiano . della . (*loro*) . simjlitudne della forma . Ma etiādo della (*uirtu sprituali*) simjlitudne | de l la . potētja (*tu ve*)

esēplo

T u ve ꝑ . il sole . quādo . (*givgnj*) sitrova . nel mezo . del nostro . emjsperio . e essere le spetie | de lla sua . forma . ꝑ tute le parte doue si dmostra . ved essere le spetie del suo splēdore | in tuttj quellj . medesimj lochi . e a ncora vi sagivgnje la si mj li tudne della potēza | del cha lore . e ttutte que ste potētie dsciēdano dalla sua cavsa . ꝑ linje radose nate nel suo | corpo e fi nj ti ne ii o bietti oppachi sāza ꝑ mjnvitjone ꝑ se

latra mōtana . sta . chōtinva mēta chola . si mj litudne . de lla sua potētia . a ste sa (*ic*) e incorporata | no che ne chorpi . ra ri Ma ne dēsi . trāsparētj e oppachi . e nō ꝑ mj nuisse ꝑo ꝑ sua figura

cōfutare

adūque . questj . mate maticj . che dcha no lochio (*c*) nō navere virtu spiritua le che | sastēda . fori ꝑ luj . ī ꝑro . che se chosi . fussi . nō sarebe sāza grā sua . ꝑ mjnvitione ne lu sare | la ujrtu visiva . e che se lochio fussi grāde quāto . (*questo mo do*) e lcor po dela terra . chō ue re be ne risguardare | alle stele . che ssi chōsvm̄assi . e ꝑ que sta (*maghera*) ragione . a segnjano lochio ricievere | e nō mādare niēte ꝑ se

Index of Codex References

General Index